Hopkins in the Age of Darwin

Hopkins

in the Age of Darwin

By Tom Zaniello

University of Iowa Press
Iowa City

University of Iowa Press, Iowa City 52242

Printed in the United States of America
First edition, 1988

Book design by Sandra Strother Hudson
Typesetting by G&S Typesetters, Inc., Austin, Texas
Printing and binding by BookCrafters, Chelsea, Michigan

Library of Congress Cataloging-in-Publication Data

Zaniello, Tom, 1943–
Hopkins in the age of Darwin.

Bibliography: p.
Includes index.
1. Hopkins, Gerard Manley, 1844–1889—Knowledge—Science. 2. Darwin, Charles, 1809–1882—Influence. 3. Literature and science—Great Britain. 4. Science in literature. I. Title.
PR4803.H44Z96 1988 821'.8 87-19243
ISBN 0-87745-178-8

To Fran, Sarah, and Benjamin, who took turns saying,
"Does this place have anything to do with Hopkins?!"

Contents

Acknowledgments

I am especially grateful for all the courtesies shown me by numerous libraries and archives in the United States and England. Although in some instances I have not been able to name the principal source of aid, I am nevertheless in debt to the librarians, archivists, and staff of the following:

Archives of the English Province of the Society of Jesus, Farm Street, London (especially Father Francis Edwards, S. J.)
Atmospheric Sciences Library, Rockville, Maryland
Balliol College Library
The Bodleian Library
The British Library
Campion Hall, Oxford (especially Father Joseph Gill, S. J., and Michael Suarez, S. J.)
The Catholic Truth Society
The Cincinnati Public Library
The Library of Congress
The Norman Lockyer Archives at the Observatory, Sidmouth (University of Exeter)
Northern Kentucky University Library
Rochester Museum and Science Center
The Royal Institution
The Royal Society
The Science Museum, South Kensington (especially Judy Turner)
Stonyhurst College Library (especially Frederick Turner, S. J.)

For permission to quote from Hopkins' unpublished manuscripts I am grateful to the Father Provincial of the English Province of the Society of

Jesus, holders of the copyright, and to Peter Hackett, S. J., executive trustee, and Michael Suarez, curator, both of Campion Hall, Oxford, where the majority of the manuscripts are located. I would also like to thank the following for granting permission to quote from manuscripts in their care:

Balliol College, for passages from their holdings of Hopkins' "Oxford Essays"

The Bodleian Library, for passages in letters to and from members of Hopkins' family

The English Province of the Society of Jesus, for passages from the diaries and notes of Joseph Rickaby, S. J.

The Royal Institution, for passages from John Tyndall's diaries

The Royal Society, for passages from the letters of William Ascroft and John Sanford Dyason and from an essay by Stephen J. Perry in their Krakatoa Committee files

I would especially like to thank Mary Ellen Rutledge, now director, Debbie Tucker and Mary Kelm, both formerly in charge of interlibrary loans, and Sharon Taylor, currently in charge of interlibrary loans, all of Northern Kentucky University, for their pleasant and very substantial support.

Father Anthony Bischoff, S. J., of the Regis Community also deserves a special word of thanks for his encouragement of my Hopkins studies, for his kindness in supplying materials and answering questions, and for his extremely helpful catalogue of Hopkins' Oxford Essays.

The following individuals kindly read various sections of this book in manuscript and are now responsible for a number of near-invisible improvements, but they bear no fault for anything untoward that remains: Judy Bechtel, Terry McNally, and L. Mackenzie Osborne, all of the Literature and Language Department of Northern Kentucky University.

The Faculty Benefits Committee of the Faculty Senate, the Provost's Office, and the Literature and Language Department, all of Northern Kentucky University, have provided both material and spiritual aid for this study. Over the years Lyle Gray, Darryl Poole, Frank Stallings, Bill McKim, and Paul Reichardt have cheerfully supplied much necessary administrative support.

Sections of this book have appeared in different form in the *Hopkins Research Bulletin, Victorian Newsletter, Hopkins Quarterly, American Notes and Queries,* and the *Annals of the New York Academy of Sciences.*

My study could not have been written, at least in its present form, without the fine work of five scholars: Humphrey House, Graham Storey, and Christopher Devlin, editors of the five volumes of Hopkins' prose works; Alfred Thomas, author of *Hopkins the Jesuit;* and Edmund F. Sutcliffe, editor of the *Bibliography of the English Province of the Society of Jesus, 1773–1953.*

I would like to thank Beth Merten and the Educational Media Staff of Northern Kentucky University for preparing the figures. A special note of appreciation goes to the editorial and design staff of the University of Iowa Press for their help in preparing this book.

Finally, I would like to thank Martin Friedman, who supervised my first study of Hopkins at Tufts University, and Bob Wallace, who was only a few steps away at Northern Kentucky University when I needed his advice.

Preface

In 1865 Hopkins wrote in his Oxford University notebook that "the stars themselves are sensuous and therefore their observation for any but abstract problems is the very opposite of the use for which the sciences are prescribed." He was translating loosely one of Plato's guidelines in the *Republic* for the ideal philosopher-king. Such a person should understand the science of the stars but not be unduly, that is, emotionally or aesthetically, moved by their beauty and power; otherwise he or she might be distracted from important tasks of state. After his undergraduate years at Oxford studying philosophy, Hopkins himself became a Jesuit priest, a very unworldly philosopher-king. He was also a poet, a naturalist, and an amateur scientist. My intention here is to show how a Victorian poet, trained as a philosopher and priest but with a keen interest in science, confronted the revolutionary problems generated by the discoveries known collectively as the Age of Darwin.

In 1877, a little more than ten years later, Hopkins ignored Plato's advice and began his poem "The Starlight Night" with these lines:

> Look at the stars! look, look up at the skies!
>   O look at all the fire-folk sitting in the air!
>   The bright boroughs, the circle-citadels there!
> Down in dim woods the diamond delves! the elves'-eyes!

Plato, who would banish star-gazing poets from an ideal state, would probably have been even more critical of Hopkins' use of these stars as metaphors, for the poet is describing here his discovery of imaginary communities of tiny "fire-folk" in the patterns of the stars. Hopkins concluded in his poem that all such perceptions of beauty are like "purchases" or "prizes" at an auction. In order to properly appreciate them, we must go beyond their beauty and place our "bids" (prayers) for them with God.

The combination of precise nature imagery and religious conclusion is characteristic of so many of Hopkins' poems that not a few readers, especially in our century, have wondered if he really understood how many complications the Age of Darwin introduced into the traditional nineteenth-century admiration of nature.

In this study I offer Hopkins as an extraordinary witness to the Age of Darwin, a Victorian intellectual who did understand many of the momentous changes in the science, philosophy, and theology of his time. Much of what I present here may be new to many readers, for Hopkins' relationship to his age with respect to these important scientific and philosophical matters has been obscured, partly by time and partly by accident. I trace his career chronologically, taking up decade by decade the key issues that confronted Victorian intellectuals like Hopkins during this period. Chapters 1 and 2 portray the situation in Oxford education and Victorian philosophy as atomist and Darwinist trends began to alter the received wisdom of the mid-Victorian period. Chapters 3 and 4 bring Hopkins through the 1870s, as his interest in language and perception developed in the context of the major challenges to theology put forward by the supporters of Darwin. Chapter 5 discusses Hopkins' most significant achievements as an amateur scientist. The Conclusion then offers an overview of his career, from Oxford undergraduate to Jesuit philosopher and from amateur scientist to accomplished poet who discovers in science a complement to art.

Although I have used a number of standard published sources—the five volumes of Hopkins' letters, journals, essays, and sermons published by Oxford University Press—the chapters that follow are also based on extensive and original research of my own in the unpublished writings of Hopkins and other Victorian Jesuits (located at Campion Hall and other Oxford University libraries as well as the Archives of the English Province of the Society of Jesus in London), in archival materials (drawings, letters, and journals located at the Royal Institution, the Royal Society, and the Science Museum in South Kensington), and in other published documents (Oxford Examination Questions, for example) that Hopkins and his contemporaries knew firsthand but no biographer has yet explored. The narrative itself does not always distinguish unpublished from published sources, but this information is available in the Notes and Sources at the end of the book.

Selective Chronology of Hopkins' Life with His Contacts in Science and Philosophy [and Some Principal Public Events in Brackets]

CHRONOLOGY

April 1863	Matriculates at Balliol College, Oxford
June 1863	Passes Responsions or Little Go
November 1864	First-Class Honors in Mods
December 1865	In confession with Pusey of Christ Church
May 1866	Coaches with Pater for exams
June 1866	Visits Benedictine monastery with Addis
October 1866	Received by Newman into Catholic Church
June–July 1867	First-Class Honors in Greats
September 1867	Begins teaching at Newman's Oratory School
July 1868	To Switzerland with Bond; meets Tyndall at the Matterhorn
September 1868	Begins Jesuit novitiate at Roehampton
[1869–1870	Vatican Council at Rome:
April 1870	—condemnation of materialism and evolution;
July 1870	—infallibility of the pope declared]
[September 1870	Huxley's Liverpool Address on biogenesis: life creates life]
September 1870	Begins philosophate at St. Mary's Hall, Stonyhurst
[October 1870	Spectacular northern lights all over England]

SUPERIORS

Benjamin Jowett, Regius Professor of Greek (Oxford)
William Newman, Balliol (Oxford); lecturer, modern and Greek history
Canon H. P. Liddon of Christ Church, main supporter of Pusey
E. B. Pusey, professor of Hebrew; original Tractarian
Walter Pater, fellow of Brasenose (Oxford)
T. H. Green, fellow and tutor of Balliol

John Henry (later Cardinal) Newman

Robert Williams

Henry Coleridge: leads retreat at Oratory School (first Jesuit Hopkins meets)

Christopher Fitzsimon, novice-master at Roehampton (1867–69)
Peter Gallwey, novice-master at Roehampton (1869)

Edward Purbrick, rector of Stonyhurst
Thomas Harper, professor of philosophy, Stonyhurst
S. J. Perry, professor of mathematics and director of the observatory, Stonyhurst (1868–87)

PEERS

Robert Bridges, Corpus Christi student (Oxford)
William Addis, Balliol student (1861–66)
Francis de Paravicini, Balliol student (1862–66); later married to Robert Williams' sister, Frances

Alexander Baillie, Balliol student (1862–67)
Edmund Martin Geldart, Balliol student (1863–67)
R. L. Nettleship, Balliol student (1864–68) and fellow (1868–92)
H. S. Holland, Balliol student (1866–70); later canon, St. Paul's
William Wallace, Balliol student (1865–67); succeeds Green as Whyte's Professor of Moral Philosophy (1882)
W. H. Mallock, Balliol student (1870–73)

Henry Marchant, later science master, Mount St. Mary's and Stonyhurst College
John Rickaby (1847–1927)
Joseph Rickaby (1845–1932)
Herbert Lucas (1852–1933)
Richard F. Clarke (1839–1900),

CHRONOLOGY

[1870	Jowett becomes master of Balliol]
August 1873	Begins teaching classics at Roehampton
[August 1874	Tyndall's Belfast Address on Lucretius]
August 1874	Begins theologate at St. Beuno's (Wales)
October 1874	Bathes at St. Winefride's Well
September 1877	Ordained as priest with Joseph Rickaby and others
October 1877	Bursar at Mount St. Mary's (Chesterfield)
[March 1878	Wreck of the *Eurydice*, south of the Isle of Wight]
August 1878	Preaches at London's Church of the Immaculate Conception (Farm Street home of the Jesuits)
November 1878	Parish priest at St. Aloysius, Oxford
1879	Supply priest at Bedford-Leigh (Manchester) and St. Francis Xavier (Liverpool)
September 1881	Begins tertianship at Roehampton
August 1882	Professor of classics, Stonyhurst
1883–84	Observes Krakatoa sunsets: letters to *Nature*
February 1884	Professor of Greek, University College, Dublin (and fellow of the Royal University of Ireland)
[May 1886	S. J. Perry exhibits solar drawings and William Ascroft exhibits Krakatoa drawings at Royal Society of London]
1888	Royal Society report, *The Eruption of Krakatoa*, quotes Hopkins' letter to *Nature*
April 1889	Perry's assistant, Cortie, quotes Hopkins' letter to *Nature* in Jesuit magazine, *The Month*
June 1889	Dies of typhoid fever in Dublin

SUPERIORS	PEERS
Harper, professor of theology, St. Beuno's Ignatius Gartlan, master, Stonyhurst (1873–80) Gallwey, Father Provincial for England (1873–76) Gallwey, rector and professor of moral theology, St. Beuno's	fellow, St. John's College at Oxford (1860–69); editor of *The Month* (1882–93); head of Pope's Hall, Oxford (1896–1900)
Hopkins meets with Pater and Green (1878–79)	
	Thomas Arnold, professor of modern literature, University College, Dublin John Casey and Morgan Crofton, professors of mathematics, University College, Dublin
Perry receives honorary degree at Royal University in Dublin	

Hopkins in the Age of Darwin

Introduction: The Portraits of Hopkins

> Surely one vocation cannot destroy another: and such a Society as yours will not remain ignorant that you have such gifts as have seldom been given by God to man.
>
> —Letter from Richard Watson Dixon to Hopkins

When Gerard Manley Hopkins was in training for the Jesuit priesthood at Stonyhurst College in Lancashire in the winter of 1870, it was his habit to examine closely ice crystals in the college pathway, noticing on one occasion some potsherds, each one with "long icicles . . . most of them bended or curled like so many tusks or horns." André Bremond, one of his fellow "philosophers" (as the seminary students were nicknamed), recalled a conversation between a Stonyhurst priest and the college gardener about Hopkins. Having been told that Hopkins was "a very fine student," the gardener replied: "Impossible. I watched him the other day. He was staring at a bit of glass in the path, walking round about it. I thought he was simple-minded."

Such was one of the legends among the English Jesuits of the man whose poetry still conveys to modern readers the thrilling language of landscape and prayer. During his lifetime, however, and before he became posthumously famous, his contemporaries celebrated that intense gaze on the icicle, that absorption in both the regularities and oddities of natural phenomena—behavior that to some seemed "simple-minded." A mixture of admiration, tolerance, and condescension runs through other reminiscences. Clement Barraud, a fellow "theologian" (as the advanced seminary students of St. Beuno's in Wales were called), agreed that his was a singular personality: "Everything bizarre had a charm for this whimsical genius." With the publication of his poetry and prose thirty years after his death, modern readers discovered what his colleagues, friends, and family already knew. Hopkins, in the words of another Stonyhurst "philosopher," Henry Marchant, "was naturally somewhat eccentric in his views and ways: but these ways were pleasing and many of them original."

My study places these "views and ways" in the context of the Age of Darwin, during which Hopkins came to maturity, lived as a Catholic priest, and died, leaving many of his projects, eccentric or not, unfinished. Frances de Paravicini, a close Oxford friend for many years, summed up Hopkins' career for his mother in June 1889, the month of Hopkins' death: "Father Gerard's work in the world, so to speak—his literary work—was always, for him, mixed with a certain sense of failure and incompleteness, yet he had the life he chose for himself."

Today most readers are willing to acknowledge the genius of Hopkins' poetry. His other work in the world, his science and philosophy, is the subject of this study. Hopkins was a priest and a poet, but he was also a naturalist, an amateur scientist, and a philosopher by education and religious profession. He was a key witness to the Age of Darwin, during which radical changes dominated not only biology but also the physical sciences, philosophy, and theology.

Charles Darwin's *Origin of Species* was published in 1859. Hopkins entered Oxford University in 1863 as an Anglican, poet, naturalist, and classicist; by the end of the decade he was also a Catholic priest and amateur scientist. This was a crucial decade in Oxford's history as well, for the 1860s saw the opening of the Oxford University Museum devoted to science, a building based on a number of John Ruskin's ideas in design; the great Huxley-Wilberforce debate on evolution; and the establishment of a sceptical atmosphere and scientific curriculum that together altered Oxford's traditional role as a preserve for classicism and orthodox thought. By the end of the decade the Vatican Council of all the bishops of the Catholic Church, strongly supported by Hopkins' Jesuits, condemned evolution and sceptical thought and argued for the importance of miracles.

The position of a Catholic priest like Hopkins in the Victorian world was a curious one, and not simply because Catholics were isolated as a tiny minority in a Protestant country. Like his Anglican colleagues, Hopkins knew that evolutionary theory would upset many religious and philosophical beliefs about the origin and purpose of life. But his situation was further complicated by his being an inveterate speculator on things both scientific and miraculous, on imaginary numbers and remarkable cures. What smoothed his intellectual transition from Oxford University to the English Province of the Jesuits was that in many ways his Jesuit training, in terms of science and philosophy, was essentially a continuation of his Oxford years.

What Hopkins wrote in his journals fits our image of the sensitive nature poet perceiving form and beauty in the quotidian: "All the world is full of inscape and chance left free to act falls into an order as well as purpose: looking out of my window I caught it in the random clods and broken heaps of snow made by the cast of a broom." Although "inscape," a form perceived in nature, is the neologism most readily identified with Hopkins, four other words in this brief entry are also highly charged terms of scientific and philosophical debate in the 1860s that sum up Darwinism in biology, scepticism in religious studies, and materialism in philosophy. They fall into pairs: "chance" and "random" are Darwinian shorthand for natural selection, "order" and "purpose" the watchwords of the religiously orthodox. Hopkins would eventually join with other Jesuits in attempting to reconcile these pairs of conflicting concepts.

Thus when a friend, William Addis, from his Oxford days asked Hopkins, "What philosophy good *or* bad—what *system* did we ever learn at Oxford?" Hopkins' reply was simple: none. But Hopkins also realized that even if "system" was too strong a word, nonetheless a philosophical ethos dominated Oxford in the 1860s, influencing both curricular and extracurricular affairs. That ethos was sceptical materialism, typified by the chance clashing of atoms in the scientific and materialist worldview based on Lucretius' ancient definition of the universe as a "fortuitous concourse of atoms." "A form of atomism," Hopkins wrote in 1867, "like a stiffness or sprain seems to hang upon and hamper our speculation." Inscape eventually countered this atomism: "All the world is full of inscape and chance left free to act falls into an order as well as purpose." This was not Darwin's theory of natural selection, that is, random selection, even if it was sound Romantic theology and even Catholic teleology. "I do not think I have ever seen anything more beautiful than the bluebell I have been looking at," wrote Hopkins; "I know the beauty of our Lord by it."

The most familiar portrait of Hopkins is that of the poet of inscape. It is not the portrait I shall offer here, although inscape is necessarily a part of his story. Instead I shall describe a Hopkins who had a reputation, both inside and outside his Society, for scientific and philosophical skill, who was part of a small but significant group of Jesuits known as the Stonyhurst Philosophers. Why has this Hopkins remained obscure? His posthumous fame began shakily in 1918 with the publication of the *Poems of Gerard Manley Hopkins,* edited by Robert Bridges, poet laureate and Hopkins' old friend. Within two years a selection of his prose, published in the *Dublin Review,* revealed a Hopkins who was also a discerning naturalist, a keen observer of bluebells, sunsets, thunderstorms, the northern lights, and comets—in brief, the man his Jesuit contemporaries knew him to be. His early reputation, such as it was in the 1920s, was established by writers as diverse as the linguist Edward Sapir, who reviewed the *Poems* in *Poetry* magazine; the poet Yvor Winters, who circulated Hopkins' poetry among his friends, including Hart Crane; and the critic I. A. Richards, who used Hopkins' poems as an experiment in practical criticism among Cambridge undergraduates. Although the poetry and prose were complementary, most commentators presented the prose simply as a remarkable storehouse for the brilliant images of the poetry.

With the publication in the 1930s of four volumes of his journals, undergraduate essays, lectures, religious notes, and letters, there emerged other portraits, which attempted to take the measure of this substantial body of prose. But these were often contradictory: Hopkins was a Victorian poet but also a forerunner of modernist poetics; he was a repressed priest but also a chastened aesthete. These portraits provoked many questions, most of them still unanswered. Did the Jesuits encourage or suppress his art? Why were the poems published so long after his death? Was he a saint?

In this study I ask a different question, based on information and opinions from those contemporaries who knew him and his work firsthand. Although many were Jesuits, their assessment of Hopkins was unfailingly frank; moreover, I have sought corroboration for my views from non-Jesuits when it is available. My question is essentially this: How did a Catholic intellectual, who was also a priest and poet, bear witness to the Age of Darwin, an age of rapid scientific, philosophical, and theological change?

Hopkins received a somewhat routine and short obituary in the private English Jesuit journal *Letters and Notices* in March 1890. But as it was also traditional in the English Province of the Society of Jesus to commemorate outstanding members in its public journal, *The Month*, Hopkins eventually received his due, albeit after quite a delay, in Father Joseph Keating's tribute there in 1909. Keating's series of three essays stressed Hopkins' friendship and critical exchanges with the poets Coventry Patmore and Canon (Richard Watson) Dixon. Of Bridges Keating said little. Keating's notice in *The Month* was not necessarily overdue, but it reflected his desire to rescue Hopkins, especially his poetry, from Bridges, who, if we put the matter in the most charitable light, had his own mental timetable for Hopkins' public arrival in the world of twentieth-century poetry. Approval for Bridges' first edition of 1918 grew slowly but steadily throughout the 1920s; and the decided success of a second edition in 1931 indicates that Bridges, regardless of motive, may indeed have had a good sense of the right moment for his friend's poetic return. As a young man Keating had known and admired Hopkins, and had begun collecting his poems when he became assistant editor of *The Month*. He wrote the tribute to Hopkins as part of an unsuccessful campaign to publish an edition of the poems himself. Bridges retained control of the poems and published them, in the end, when he saw fit.

In 1920, over thirty years after Hopkins' death, the *Dublin Review* published a full and quite revealing collection of reminiscences, poetry, and prose. It began as a rebuttal, written by Frederick Page, to Bridges' anti-Jesuit introduction to the first edition of the *Poems* (1918). The *Dublin Review* published an expanded version (that is, not Bridges') of Hopkins' poem "Dorothea and Theophilus," a gentle portrait of the martyred Dorothea, followed by a collection of prose extracts from Hopkins' then-unpublished journals and from his letters published in 1883–84 in *Nature*, the leading scientific journal of the English-speaking world. This collection included his now-well-known piece on the inscape of bluebells as well as a handful of notes on cathedrals and natural scenery. Hopkins' meteorological notes and letters predominated, however, with passages on dramatic sunsets, unusual solar phenomena, thunderstorms, the northern lights, and Coggia's Comet of 1874. (All of these will be discussed in chapters 3 and 5.) A general reader might have concluded from this first batch of prose that the writer, a priest and poet, had also been a naturalist with at least some success as a published contributor to an important scientific journal.

The final section of the *Dublin Review* collection was titled "His Character"; its author was identified only as "Plures," that is, "by several hands." Since the details of this section indicate close personal and intellectual contact, I believe that "Plures" represents the Stonyhurst Philosophers, Jesuits such as Herbert Lucas and the brothers Rickaby (Joseph and John) who had had long-standing friendships with Hopkins and knew his Oxford experiences, characteristic habits of mind, and talents firsthand. All of these men were alive in 1920 and would have assented, I believe, to the dramatic and melancholy opening sentence of Plure's essay: "Thirty years have passed over his grave and Gerard Hopkins remains the elusive Jesuit, the obscure melodist, the lost Victorian."

The judgment of Plures amounts to this: Hopkins was "an English mystic compounded of Benjamin Jowett and Duns Scotus," with an extraordinary talent for "freakish" mirth and for searching out "the odd and the whimsical." He had nonetheless chosen a hard and unrewarding life as a Jesuit, fit neither by character nor discipline to be one. Although Plures did not quote Hopkins' "St. Alphonsus Rodriguez" (1888), a poem that had appeared two years earlier in Bridges' edition and that celebrated a Jesuit saint, the character sketch implied that Hopkins' life resembled that of the poem's namesake, a hall porter for forty years: "Those years and years by of world without event / That in Majorca Alfonso watched the door."

Plures argued that Hopkins' sensitive nature had been built upon Walter Pater's and John Ruskin's aestheticism, his philosophical views upon Jowett's Platonism, and his Catholicism upon Cardinal Newman's doggedness. Hopkins had had extensive personal and intellectual contact with everyone in this group except Ruskin. The influence of Oxford had been crucial. Plures' gently ironic description of Hopkins as a "scholar gypsy, pitching his tent in all the arts" was a fair one. Plures also dwelt in detail upon Hopkins' Dublin days, the last five years of his life, which had been filled with an Irish nationalist politics he couldn't respect and a demanding academic regimen made even more difficult by what Plures called his "neurasthenia." One incident, legendary among the Jesuits, reveals how he had been affected by fervent Dublin nationalism. Hopkins' old scientific colleague from Stonyhurst, Stephen Perry, an internationally famous Jesuit astronomer, came to University College in Dublin, where Hopkins was then teaching. Perry was to be awarded an honorary degree, surely a moment of pride and pleasure for Hopkins. Yet Hopkins left the room abruptly when "God Save Ireland" was sung. "I would not have done that," Hopkins said, "if it [the song] hadn't been so wicked."

Plures' assessment of Hopkins' contradictions and the evidence in the *Dublin Review* of his poetry and naturalist's prose create a convincing portrait. It needs substantial touching up, however, in terms of the Age of Darwin. My interpretation of Hopkins' place in that age is based on the working assumption that he was confronted by a number of cultural imperatives to which he reacted, sometimes systematically, sometimes not. His most organized response to the pressures of religious crisis was to convert to Roman Catholicism at Oxford and to join the Jesuits, who were among the most rigorous of orders. The study of his conversion and his subsequent career as a priest, both fascinating topics, lies generally outside the bounds of this book, although it is important to remember that the record of Jesuit participation in the mainstream of European science was long and distinguished. The major imperative of Hopkins' art and science derives from the legacy of Romantic nature description, whether in prose (Gilbert White and Philip Gosse) or poetry (John Clare among others). Although Hopkins knew only a fraction of Clare's work, the same drive for precision, obsession with detail, and love of the unusual were typical of both men, and both actively sought out the dialect words that would render an experience distinctly.

Henry Marchant summed up this imperative for Hopkins when he told Humphrey House, the editor of Hopkins' *Journals,* that Hopkins "had a keen eye for peculiarities in nature, and hunted for the right word to express them, and invented one if he could not find one." Thus Marchant long ago recognized Hopkins' obsession with both dialects and neologisms. Hopkins once described an unfinished project, a book on rhythm, as "full of new words without which there can be no new science." We may not give credence to the somewhat cavalier attitude towards his own poems in the following excerpt from a letter to Canon Dixon in 1887, but the fastidious drive for precision in philosophical work rings true:

> What becomes of my verses I care little, but about matters like this, what I write or could write on philosophical matters, I do; and the reason of the difference is that the verses stand or fall by their simple selves and, though by being read they might do good, by being unread they do no harm; but if the other things are unsaid right they will be said by somebody else wrong, and that is what will not let me rest.

This search for "new words" was characteristic of Hopkins' response to still another Victorian imperative, that of the English tradition of empiricism together with some of its epistemological shortcomings, as Hopkins interpreted them. That his words *inscape* and *instress* as well as *scape*—his to a lesser extent—have all been canonized in the recent *Oxford English Dictionary* (*OED*) *Supplement* indicates some degree of success, however belated, in developing new ways of understanding how we know things. Hopkins developed such words to solve both the task of rendering nature with fidelity and the problems posed by atomistic trends in philosophy and science.

Hopkins may have used such "new words" less freely than he wished. His first major long poem, "The Wreck of the Deutschland," which was never published in his lifetime, stated that Christ's beauty must be "instressed, stressed." Had that poem appeared in *The Month*, as Hopkins at first hoped it would, "instressed" would have been totally unfamiliar to Victorian readers. Nevertheless, in public or in private, his verbal palette rarely failed him. His description of the atmospheric afterglow of the Krakatoa volcanic eruption of 1883, published in *Nature*, rendered a green sky as "between an apple-green or pea-green (which are pure greens) and an olive (which is tertiary color): it is vivid and beautiful, but not pure." Twenty years before, in his undergraduate diary, he described the shade of green on Oxford fields:

> Note on green wheat. The difference between this green and that of long grass is that first suggests silver, later azure. Former more opacity, body, smoothness. It is the exact complement of carnation. Nearest to emerald of any green I know, the real emerald *stone* [his emphasis]. It is lucent. Perhaps it has a chrysoprase bloom. Both blue greens.

And in 1874, midway between these two passages, he wrote the following note to himself on an ordinary, pre-Krakatoa sunset seen from Richmond Park:

> This has been a very beautiful day—fields about us deep green lighted underneath with white daisies, yellower fresh green of leaves above which bathes the skirts of the elms, and their tops are touched and worded with leaf too. . . . Blue shadows fell all up the meadow at sunset and then standing at the far Park corner my eye was struck by such a sense of green in the tufts and pashes of grass, with purple shadow thrown back on the dry black mold behind them, as I do not remember ever to have been exceeded in looking at green grass. I marked this down on a slip of paper at the time, because the eye for color, rather the zest in the mind, seems to weaken with years, but now the paper is mislaid.

Fortunately not all such papers were mislaid; the record both published and unpublished shows that this poet and naturalist always retained a keen "eye for color" as well as "the zest in the mind." This talent and enthusiasm made him an invaluable witness to the Age of Darwin. Chapters 1–5, then, follow Hopkins from his Oxford days in the 1860s to his death in Dublin in 1889, tracing the development of the key issues of the age and Hopkins' engagement with them.

1 Oxford and the Cockatrice's Den

From the mere analysis of the idea of an infinite, self-existent God, His other attributes are deduced by a process as strictly logical as that by which from geometrical axioms and postulates Euclid deduces the several propositions of his system.

—John Rickaby

Turrets of "Chemical Stinks"

Oxford labored for a number of years under the illusion that it could be blown to atoms. Before Hopkins arrived at Balliol College, its garden quad, in particular its chapel, had been remodeled by a leading architect of the Gothic Revival, William Butterfield. The alternating bands of pink and cream stone on the exterior were controversial, and the chapel soon became known as Butterfield's "pink obscenity." In one of his Oxford poems Hopkins called attention to these "vigorous horizontals." The interior of the construction turned out to be no less controversial, for the cellars of the new quad were converted for use by Oxford's chemical laboratory, one of the early presences of universitywide organized science at Oxford. When Benjamin Brodie gained the Chair of Chemistry in 1855, he moved into the Balliol laboratory, which proved too confining despite its recent construction. Brodie's influence in the university and his chemical experimentation had become legendary. In just a few years his laboratory moved again. His insistence on proper facilities for science at Oxford allowed him to give his lectures in the still-unfinished university museum as early as 1858. When in 1860 an unrelated incident, the accidental leakage of gas in St. Mary's Church, caused an explosion, a tutor lecturing at Brasenose College assumed that the explosion had destroyed the new museum: "There, gentlemen," he told his students, "Brodie has done it at last!"

Oxford, like Stonyhurst, was at midcentury a volatile mixture of fact and legend. The entrance of organized science helped create that mixture. Slow in coming, it arrived dramatically enough in the end. Oxford feared not only Brodie's explosions but theological repercussions as well. As a preserve of religious and philosophical orthodoxy, it had weathered its Newman years—the Oxford Movement of the 1840s with its Roman Catholic conversions—and had attempted to settle in the 1850s into a new Anglican complacency. Cambridge University was the nation's center of science, and Oxford's aristocratic patrons were no doubt content to let it remain so. There was more pathos than heroism in Henry Acland's role as a science teacher when he assumed the Lee's Readership in 1847. Beginning as a reformer of the study of medicine, he persisted and eventually established the scientific curriculum at Oxford. But at midcentury, Acland's laboratory at Christ Church College was equipped with a miniature railway, which passed through the class delivering microscopic specimens. Although the official reason for the shutdown of Acland's lab work together with his railway was a strict interpretation of the rules of the readership—a readership meant lectures only—it seems there were other reasons. After examining one of Acland's laboratory preparations, Dr. Kidd, professor of medicine, reportedly said that he did not "believe in it" and, secondly, that if it were true he did not "think that God meant us to know it."

The new university museum was ultimately considered Acland's triumph, although its success may in fact have depended upon the annual conventions of the British Association for the Advancement of Science (BAAS), which held three meetings at Oxford, in 1832, 1847, and 1860 (see p. 13). In 1832 Ruskin's master teacher, William Buckland, delivered a dramatic lecture on the fossil of Megatherium, the giant sloth, which seemed to contradict the received paradigm of the Great Chain of Being and led an expedition of delegates to do geology at nearby Shotover Hill, east of Oxford. Fifteen years later, at the culmination of the BAAS meeting in 1847, the leading scientists at Oxford, including Acland, Buckland, and C. J. B. Daubeny (a featured Darwinian speaker in the years to come), petitioned the university for the "erection of an edifice . . . for the better display of materials illustrative of the facts and laws of the Natural world." The time perhaps was right, if not the atmosphere. One nonscientific don evoked the ancient monster who kills by

The British Association for the Advancement of Science

The development of a professional body of scientists in the Victorian period reflects the rise of British theoretical science in the eighteenth century as well as the imperial climb to industrial and technological leadership in the nineteenth century. But there is also a direct intellectual source for the British Association for the Advancement of Science or BAAS, as it was usually called: Coleridge's notion of the "clerisy," an elite of intellectual leaders, mainly clerical, which he proposed in 1830 in his book *On the Constitution of the Church and State, According to the Idea of Each.* Coleridge believed that "science, and especially moral science, will lead to religion and remain blended with it."

The first meeting of the BAAS was held at York in 1831. At the 1834 meeting at Cambridge, Coleridge himself was the attending celebrity; but as a somewhat ungracious guest he told the members not to call themselves philosophers. One of the founders, William Whewell, soon responded by coining the word *scientist.*

In the thirty years that followed, actual clergymen were as prominent in the BAAS as those whom we would regard today as professional scientists, but the Huxley-Wilberforce debate certainly marked the beginning of the end of a major religious presence. Still, at the Oxford meeting in 1860, the Reverend Dingle spoke on "the mechanical causes of the formation of the earth's crust" and the Reverend Dennis analyzed "the mode of flight of the Pterodactyles . . . near Cambridge." Both of these were "purely" scientific topics, of course; and perhaps the Huxley-Wilberforce debate would have convinced most clergymen that while it might be dangerous to cross swords with a Huxley, it was perhaps a moral imperative for them to do so. Certainly both Protestants and Catholics, regardless of intramural differences, carried on their struggle with Darwinism for many decades to come—but usually not at BAAS meetings.

looking when he referred to the new building as a "cockatrice's den," while others attacked the proposal that the profits from the sale of the Clarendon Bible be used by the museum committee for its building. The struggle of science versus religion had thus begun in earnest at Oxford, for the final vote in Convocation, the university assembly, was very close, the old liberal religious reformers (Tractarians) having allied themselves with the scientifically minded; Edward Pusey, the powerful Oxford Movement leader, was, after all, a friend of Acland. In 1854, then, the vote of seventy to sixty-four approving the proposal established the first building at Oxford devoted exclusively to modern science.

The collections of the older, crowded science museums at Oxford were to be transferred to the new building. The differences in organizing principles are instructive. The Ashmolean collections of natural history, for example, were based on the argument in William Paley's *Natural Theology* (1802) that natural phenomena are divinely inspired and designed. According to the Ashmolean catalogue of 1836, these natural objects would "induce a mental habit of associating natural phenomena with the conviction that they are the *media* of Divine manifestation; and by such association to give proper dignity to every branch of natural science." A different kind of dignity was proposed for the new museum by George Rolleston, Acland's successor in the Lee's Readership and chief instructor in the early days of the museum. Rolleston, noted a contemporary, viewed Man as "the crown" of "biological conceptions": "But Man in his material origin and descent; Man in his evolution, social, moral, and intellectual; Man of every time, character, aspiration; Man in his highest relations to his fellow men and to his God." Within three years, by 1860, Rolleston's accommodation of both evolution and God was to be put to the test.

With approval for the erection of the university museum, the scientists' demand for proper labs was satisfied; but an era of academic and architectural strife began. Acland encouraged his friend Ruskin to apply to the new building at least two features of his personal approach to aesthetics and social questions. The design of the new chemistry laboratory followed closely that of the abbot's kitchen in the thirteenth-century Glastonbury Abbey, from a period of Gothic architecture Ruskin was willing to bless, and the carved columns of the "Rhenish" or Gothic exterior were the more or less freehand work of master carvers using natural forms as their models. Thus the stones of Oxford were to rival those of Venice. Pusey, at least, was not worried about Italy. His support for the museum was based in part on his conviction that its interior should resemble the open network of iron and glass in the new London rail stations (it does). The building signaled a new force on the Oxford skyline.

Science was undergoing change at Oxford on a curricular level as well, but only among the orthodox theologians was there fear that scientific study was growing at an alarming rate. The university reforms of the 1850s had established a natural science option for undergraduates, but the change did not in the short run have the effect the scientists desired. The number of students sitting for exams in science did not increase as dramatically as they had hoped and the theologians had feared.

Natural science was actually one of two new schools or divisions of study; the other was law and modern history. They joined the established pair in the liberal arts, classics and mathematics. Successful exams in any one of the four would lead a student to a B.A. The range of debate before and after the midcentury reforms anticipated the Huxley-Arnold controversy over science and culture by almost two decades. Even the very terms used by Huxley and Arnold were present. The rector of one Oxford college, Mark Pattison, characterized the controversy as a "dispute between science *versus* classics in education"; an Oxford historian, Edward A. Freeman, said the struggle was between the "really liberal" education "leading to the highest culture" and the "specialism" of scientific studies.

Pattison was rector of Lincoln College. He had moved from a close association with Newman and a great interest in miracles in the 1840s to become an authoritative and well-known sceptic. Pattison designated 1865, Hopkins' third year at Oxford, as the year that the new schools shifted the primary emphasis of Oxford away from the classics. He believed, however, that the new emphases were not necessarily misguided. Since the "philosophical element," traditionally a part of classical studies, had "outgrown" the Greeks, it should instead be "transferred to the basis of real science" in the contemporary world.

Freeman felt outmaneuvered by the reforms and took delight in bringing such academic problems out in the open—for public censure, if necessary. These reforms, he argued, actually interfered with some of the aspects of science that the reformers wanted to introduce into the curriculum. In the first place, classical studies were crippled; Greek texts were "taken up for the language only, and not for the matter." In the second place, by establishing a separate school for natural science, the students of the arts studied even less geology, paleontology, and natural history than in previous years.

Much of the disagreement as to what Oxford students should study may ultimately be traced to larger, usually philosophical differences among members of the university. Religious leaders thought Oxford students read too many sceptical books, both inside and outside the curriculum. One favorite among Hopkins' classmates was a translation of Ernest Renan's *Life of Jesus,* a book typical of what was then regarded as the scientific approach to Christian history. Renan routinely describes Christ as a magician and exorcist, for example, because he worked miracles and cures, and reminds his readers that Christ knew no "rational medical science." For their part the scientists believed that Oxford students had too little exposure to practical laboratory science. While science in fact played a major role in the curriculum, it did so in ways virtually invisible to us now. The history of science was often a category of philosophy, while the methods of science were treated as categories of logic.

Key terms like *logic* have shifted in meaning over the last century, obscuring even more the actual content of the liberal arts curriculum that confronted Hopkins. A. C. Bradley, the great Shakespearean scholar, was a Balliol student of R. L. Nettleship, Hopkins' undergraduate friend. Logic at Oxford, Bradley noted, covered in a broad sweep scientific method, psychology, and metaphysical questions. On one of their exams (Greats) Hopkins and his classmates had to handle this question: "Is it possible to deduce the laws of motion . . . from the principle of the 'ratio sufficiens'?" Any one of a number of standard guides to logic in circulation at Oxford in the 1860s would have prepared Hopkins for Leibniz's Principle of Sufficient Reason ("Nothing happens without a reason why it should be so rather than otherwise"); but unless he took care to distinguish centripetal from centrifugal force, his essay might still have been insufficiently rigorous.

At least logic, even in its most scientific moments, was done on paper. But the physical proof as well as the symbol of a changing Oxford was the university museum building. A gallery of glamorous minerals, fossils, and laboratories supported by the curriculum reforms of the 1850s certainly augmented the threat of scientific materialism. But an entire building infused with the spirit of modern science was the last straw.

Even before the building was officially dedicated, Oxford felt its impact. Within its unfinished walls Brodie had already been at work attacking the atomist orthodoxy in the physical sciences. Ruskin's spiritual handymen, the O'Shea brothers, who were hired to sculpt the building's exterior, had been denied the chance to carve monkeys as decorative elements on windows. They began instead to use the heads of members of the University Convocation as models for the gargoyles (these were eventually lopped off).

When the BAAS returned in June 1860, the Oxford scientists may have expected their building to have been completed in time for the meetings. *The Origin of Species* had only recently (November 1859) been published. Although the Huxley-Wilberforce debate has memorialized this Oxford meeting of the BAAS as the occasion upon which science defeated religion, members at various meetings tilted at many things, including Darwinism and atomism. That this was to be not just "science at Oxford" but a celebration of "Oxford science" was apparent as soon as Lord Wrottlesbury, the outgoing BAAS president, gave the opening address on June 27 in the newly remodeled Sheldonian Theatre, Sir Christopher Wren's neoclassical amphitheater. Lord Wrottlesbury emphasized the progress of science at Oxford, calling particular attention to the new museum; he boasted of its appropriation of £100,000, tactfully omitting the actual source (sale of the Clarendon Bible) of most of the money. He added—did he realize the implication?—that a "beneficent and enlightened lady" had endowed two scholarships with "the view of extending among the clergy educated at the University a knowledge of geology." By 1860 a little "knowledge of geology" had already become code for a little dangerous sceptical learning about the actual, as opposed to the biblical, age of the earth.

The day after Wrottlesbury's speech, June 28, should have brought the Darwinian confrontation many scientists expected, since that Thursday's meeting of Section D, Zoology and Botany, featured C. J. B. Daubeny's paper "Remarks on the Final Causes of Sexuality of Plants, with Particular Reference to Mr. Darwin's Work, *On the Origin of Species by Natural Selection*," a somewhat lukewarm endorsement of Darwin's conclusions.

J. S. Henslow, the section's chair, then invited Thomas Huxley to comment on "the truth of Mr. Darwin's theory," but Huxley somewhat peremptorily declined. Richard Owen, England's leading comparative anatomist and a not-so-secret anti-Darwinist, ignored the general content of Daubeny's talk in his eagerness to speak. He announced that the brain of the gorilla "presented more differences, as compared with the brain of man, than it did when compared with the brains of the very lowest and most problematical form of the Quadrumana" (the four-handed primates, as they were then known, to distinguish them from "two-handed" humans). He added—although it seems almost everyone knew what was coming—that what he specifically meant was that the gorilla did not have what was considered a distinctly human feature, the hippocampus minor, a mysterious ridge of the cerebral ventricle that we now know plays a key role in memory. At this juncture Huxley was moved to make a very sharp rebuttal to Owen's remarks, even administering the ultimate scientific insult, that Owen had not consulted the most obvious scientific papers on the dissection of gorillas. Huxley concluded that "the gift of speech" was what really distinguished "man from monkey." It was a prophetic remark.

Perhaps it was the notoriously obscure hippocampus minor, perhaps it was Huxley's coolness towards open debate, perhaps it was the rumor that Owen was coaching Samuel ("Soapy Sam") Wilberforce, the bishop of Oxford, on the errors of Dr. Draper, the featured pro-Darwin speaker for Saturday, June 30. For whatever reason, the next meeting of Section D saw unprecedented numbers of people from town, gown, and ecclesiastical robe, probably seven hundred to one thousand souls, crowding into Wren's theater of the intellect to hear the bishop attempt to burke Darwin. Henslow, and perhaps some other BAAS and Oxford officials, decided to move the meeting to a larger hall. Only the pure of heart, however, could have believed that their change of venue was dictated merely by the size of the hall, for the meeting was moved to the barely finished university museum. A procession from the eighteenth century to the nineteenth was underway.

If the bishop of Oxford led the procession out of the Sheldonian, down Park Road to the back side of Oxford where the new museum was located, it is only what we would have expected, for he was supposed to play the crucial role that day in establishing orthodoxy over scepticism.

If the bishop noticed that he had entered a natural-history trap, a Gothic temple to science, a building of fossils and reconstructed dinosaurs—with turrets to let off "chemical stinks," as a local newspaper had sneered—it is not recorded. And he probably failed to notice that the new room, the library gallery, was no more commodious than the room at the Sheldonian. We must assume he simply thought that here would be another large and familiar audience—clergymen, undergraduates, a few liberal and freethinking scientists, local women of good standing—for his speech. (The logical move from his point of view would have been to the divinity school adjoining the Sheldonian, whose main hall, used for generations of lectures in theology, would have provided just as much space for the crowd. Perhaps the scientists were sufficiently tempted not to want a traditionally theological setting for the bishop.) The Balliol contingent was obvious that day, with Benjamin Jowett and T. H. Green, two of Hopkins' most important tutors, in attendance, although keen observers, including Huxley himself, noted that the sceptical Green did not join in the undergraduates' applause for Huxley.

The section meeting, with both undergraduates and clergy conspicuous in their robes, reassembled in the library gallery. Dr. John Draper, an American scientist whose views we would today call social Darwinist, presented his paper "On the Intellectual Development of Europe, Considered with Reference to the Views of Mr. Darwin and Others, That the Progression of Organisms Is Determined by Law." Using the materialist assumptions of his atomist worldview, Draper set out to demonstrate that the advancement of human beings was not simply the result of a "fortuitous concourse of atoms" but rather under the "control of immutable law." He concluded that the "production, life, and death of an organic particle in the person, answers to the production, life, and death of a person in the nation." After Draper's neo-Hobbesian speech, most of the audience expected to hear either the bishop or "the Agnostic," as Huxley eventually came to be known, set off rhetorical fireworks. These they did eventually hear, but not before a number of revealing diversions.

The Reverend Cresswell of Worcester College denied Draper's essential premise. One should not equate human or intellectual progress with animal development, for Homer's works were produced in the infancy of the race. The unfortunate Mr. Dingle, a clergyman from Lancashire, attempted to use a blackboard illustration, marking point A for monkey, which he pronounced "mawnkey," and point B for human, no doubt imitating Darwin's own chart with similar designations in *The Origin of Species*. But the undergraduates, despite their pro-Darwinism, hooted whenever Dingle said "monkey," and he was unable to demonstrate why A could never lead to B. Benjamin Brodie, the leading critic of the atomic theory of matter, made a few brief, sober remarks. He stated that Darwin's "primordial germ" (gemmule) "had not been demonstrated" to exist and that human self-consciousness, conspicuously lacking in the lower organisms, was "identical with the Divine Intelligence." Although the intellectual circus that ensued overshadows the symbolism of the meeting, Brodie's remarks, however incomplete the record, indicate the lines along which religious scientists were to discuss what they regarded as Darwin's errors.

Those in Darwin's camp believed that the bishop more than lived up to his slippery nickname that day, even if he was capable of some scientific understanding, as his review of *The Origin of Species* published not long before in the *Quarterly Journal* indicated. He may have been tempted by the audience to favor ridicule over argument, rhetoric over substance. "What have they [the evolutionists] to bring forward," the bishop asked, "some rumored statement about a long-legged sheep?!" (Darwin had referred to a sheep born with an additional vertebra as a confirmation of his ideas about variation.) The bishop's real energy went into his closing statements. Darwin's views were simply contrary to Genesis. And in a final gesture, still controversial to this day, he either turned or leaned towards Huxley and asked, if evolution were true, would he trace his descent from an ape through his grandfather's or his grandmother's side? Huxley was reported to have slapped Brodie's knee at this moment, saying, "The Lord hath delivered him into my hands!"

Huxley's reply touched on a number of scientific issues with religious and philosophical implications. He told the bishop that the moment of consciousness in the development of a human being was impossible to determine: "With regard to the psychological distinction between man and animals: man himself was once a monad—a mere atom, and nobody could say at what moment in the history of his development he became consciously intelligent." His atomist approach challenged the bishop directly: "You say that development [evolution] drives out the Creator; but you assert that God made you: and yet you know that you yourself were originally a little piece of matter no bigger than the end of this gold pencil case." A woman, Isabel Sidgwick of Rugby, who signed her account of the debate "A Grandmother," reported Huxley's rejoinder to the bishop's genealogical slur: "He was not ashamed to have a monkey for his ancestor, but he would be ashamed to be connected with a man who used great gifts to obscure the truth. No one doubted his meaning, and the effect was tremendous. One lady fainted and had to be carried out; I, for one, jumped out of my seat." Until that moment Huxley had certainly been encouraged by the undergraduates. With this last remark he also neutralized many of his clerical opponents by pointing out to them that the bishop, in the judgment of another witness, "had forgotten to behave like a perfect gentleman."

After the commotion in the hall had died down, the remaining speakers proved more or less perfunctory, despite a fearful symmetry in their order. Two spoke against Darwin. The captain of *The Beagle,* Robert Fitzroy, with whom Darwin had explored exotic lands, denied the logic of Huxley's remarks, regretted the publication of Darwin's book, and stood up for Genesis; some observers reported that Fitzroy held the Bible aloft at this moment. Professor Beale of the University of London offered some lukewarm criticism with regard to minor issues. The two final speakers felt that they, not Huxley, had saved the day for science. Sir John Lubbock reported hearing no arguments for the "fixity of species," the phrase used to denote God's creation as opposed to evolution. Someone had just sent Henslow wheat from an Egyptian mummy to show that it had not changed for thousands of years, but under analysis it proved to be a kernel of corn! The last word was had by the most prestigious botanist of the day, Dr. Joseph Hooker, director of Kew Gardens, who said that he had adopted the Darwinian hypothesis after careful study of its validity in the interpretation of the plant kingdom. He would be "ready to lay" Darwin's hypothesis down "should a better be forthcoming, or should the now abandoned doctrine of original creation regain all it had lost in his experience." And thus Section D closed; Genesis was now being spoken of, at least by a number of distinguished scientists, in the past tense only.

The Logic of Oxford

Hopkins arrived at Balliol in April 1863, three years after the BAAS meeting. His Oxford college had a mixed reputation. Balliol was known first and foremost as an intellectual center, all of whose students (after 1856) were required to strive for honors in exams, especially Greats. This final exam of the classics school leading to the B.A. was regarded at Oxford, according to a contemporary guidebook, as "the Examination 'par excellence.'" At other colleges, in contrast, the students called passmen could sit for a less rigorous set of questions on the exams. Balliol was also, however, the college that the orthodox fretted most about, even if science was not its main business. Although it shared with Oxford "a sort of cloudy rumor of infidelity about it," as Nettleship told a friend in 1870, their college was known especially for the "unorthodoxy of many of its fellows" or faculty. This waywardness was both religious and philosophical, for two of Hopkins' tutors, T. H. Green of Balliol and Walter Pater of Brasenose College, were not only sceptical about Christianity in most of its traditional forms but were also chipping away at the foundations of British empiricism (see pp. 24–25). Even though the magisterial Platonism of Benjamin Jowett dominated Hopkins' thinking in his early college years, constant association with Green, Pater, and other tutors ensured that Hopkins' college essays, now called the Oxford Essays, grappled with problems in Aristotelian and other "common sense" philosophy. Hopkins' attraction to the natural world and his interest in science were nicely complemented, then, by his tutors' interest in epistemological problems.

Jowett, however, was the most obvious symbol of Balliol:

> Here come I, my name is Jowett;
> There's no knowledge but I know it.
> I am the Master of this College.
> What I know not isn't knowledge.

This undergraduate epigram surfaced at Oxford soon after Jowett became master of Balliol in 1870. But his reputation and to a great extent his notoriety had already been established in the 1860s. W. H. Mallock, who came to Balliol three years after Hopkins left in 1867, portrayed Jowett unfavorably in *The New Republic* (1877), his satire on Victorian intellectuals, as well as in his *Memoirs* more than forty years later. Mallock wrote that Jowett was typical of the Balliol dons who tried to establish a "system of quasi-scientific ethics," since he always dismissed miracles as having no scientific basis. Mallock's animus against Jowett was very great; he went so far as to lay a Balliol man's suicide in 1870 to Jowett's "sceptical teachings," which had purportedly deprived the young man of his faith. Hopkins' friend Martin Geldart, whose suicide in 1885 was likewise attributed to a loss of faith, portrayed a similar Jowett in his thinly fictionalized autobiography, *A Son of Belial* (1882). The character "Jewell," professor of Greek at "Belial" College, dismisses an evangelical and fundamentalist minister from his presence because the clergyman accepts the cosmogony of Genesis: "It is a great pity," Professor Jewell remarks, "to mix up questions of science and questions of religion. They are totally distinct."

Yet Geldart was proud of his old university. *A Son of Belial* portrays a university of "plain living and high thinking," an environment where "no topic . . . was tabooed, whether religious or political" and "no one was thought the worse for any opinions he might profess." Balliol was the very "focus or center point" around which formed a theological "vortex" of "currents and counter currents." Geldart was not surprised when Hopkins, represented as his "ritualist" friend "Gerontius Manley," joined the "Rome-ward movement" as Newman and others had done two decades before. In this vortex of opinion Hopkins, like so many other ritualists or Anglo-Catholics, "gushed." But Hopkins at least "meant it," Geldart added, as the young convert flew from the "hollowness of Protestant orthodoxy" to the "authority" of the Roman church.

Jowett is the central figure in many of the memoirs of Oxford undergraduates. They remember him as walking with them, often silent, but occasionally offering valuable advice, or as senior tutor reading their weekly essays with an eye towards preparation for the exams. He fascinated his enemies as well, for the orthodox religious leaders of Oxford worried about his scepticism and went so far as to have him up for a heresy trial, forcing reductions in his salary. Insiders at Oxford, however, especially the dons and administrators interested in reform, did not take Jowett as their target. For them the tutor system, in particular the coaching of students for exams, fostered an atmosphere that encouraged sceptical thought, due in part to the nature of cramming and in part to the personalities and special interests of the tutors.

An Oxford Circle of Family and Friends

Both T. H. Green and Walter Pater, two of Hopkins' most prominent tutors, were part of a remarkable network of family and friends at Oxford in the 1860s, when Matthew Arnold's brother Thomas came to Oxford to become a private tutor of students and a free-lance professional scholar. He had no direct academic affiliation and in fact was often a hot topic of gossip. After a successful period at Oxford with his brother in the 1840s, Thomas Arnold had quixotically gone off to New Zealand to farm. He had then converted to Roman Catholicism, gone to Dublin to teach at Newman's newly established University College, and finally, a deconverted Catholic, had come back to Oxford. His daughter Mary Augusta, later known as Mrs. Humphrey Ward, the successful novelist of *Robert Elsmere* (1888), left in *A Writer's Recollections* (1918) an account of her circle of family and friends, a circle that did not actually include Hopkins but intersected his life in fascinating ways.

Mary Augusta's mentor was Mark Pattison, the rector of Lincoln College. She married a young scholar, T. Humphrey Ward, of Brasenose College. Their close friends and neighbors were Pater and Green. She also endured the unofficial tutoring of Benjamin Jowett, the master of Balliol. Perhaps it was inevitable that so intellectual a woman, by nurture a scholar but virtually forbidden by society to be one, would turn to novel writing to express her ideas.

In *Robert Elsmere,* the best-seller of 1888, she portrayed a number of her friends and colleagues. The effete Langham and the sober Gray of the novel loosely represent the alternative visions of Pater and Green; the sceptical and ultimately agnostic squire of the novel is based somewhat on Pattison. The novel's hero, Robert Elsmere, who leaves the Anglican church because of his loss of faith in miracles, establishes a settlement or mission in a poor district of London. Elsmere's character may be a composite of a number of actual defectors from the Anglican church, but his ideas closely follow those of both Green and Richard Lewis Nettleship, Hopkins' Balliol classmate and friend as well as Green's disciple. Although Nettleship had planned to become an independent scholar who labored among the poor in London, he became instead one of Green's spiritual successors at Balliol when Green died in 1869.

It is Hopkins who actually became a scholar who labored among the poor. Green felt that Hopkins' choice of the Jesuits, who represented a "monastic form of ascetic cooperation," was unwise. Instead, as he wrote to H. S. Holland, another Balliol student who expressed "a lurking admiration for Jesuitry," he believed that "new forms of religious society" were necessary. (More details concerning this interesting exchange of letters about Hopkins will be found in chapter 4.)

Hopkins touched this circle again at the end of his life. He was called to University College in Dublin in the 1880s to join another Newman disciple, now reconverted and teaching once more at his old post: Tom Arnold (see the Conclusion).

Mark Pattison, one of the leading reformers, was vehemently opposed to the tutor system. The "university of Duns Scotus and Occam," he wrote, at one time a leader in philosophy "animated by religious interests," had in the 1860s become an arena for students who followed star coaches rather than distinguished professors—in short, cramming prevailed over steady work. The examiners themselves rewarded students who "learned to write in the newest style of thought, and to manipulate the phrases of the last popular treatise." Jowett himself contributed somewhat to this pressure, it would seem. His introductions and notes to his translations of Plato's dialogues provided succinct analyses of contemporary issues. Was Socrates a utilitarian? (Yes.) Was Hegel a Sophist? (No.) Green, on the other hand, remained aloof. Students sought him as a tutor but did not want to attend his lectures. In the first place, they complained, his lectures "were too difficult to follow," and second, his enthusiasm for Hegel and Kant was misplaced, since they were tested on Plato and Aristotle.

In Pattison's view the tutor/exam system was the enemy within, while the "ecclesiastical platform" that denounced Oxford teaching as "sceptical, infidel, anti-Christian" was the enemy without. Plato and Aristotle, who made up much of the classical curriculum, had been more or less sanitized in the Christian Middle Ages, but John Stuart Mill's *Logic* was hardly safe. Richard F. Clarke, a Stonyhurst Philosopher and one of Hopkins' early friends in the Jesuits, was a fellow of St. John's at Oxford in the 1860s and had also converted. He agreed with much of Pattison's critique but went further. He saw the tutors as deliberately lying in wait for those students who took communion at St. Mary's, the ritualist or Anglo-Catholic stronghold where Newman had once preached. Once they read for Greats, the tutors believed, "modern philosophy" would "directly or indirectly" subvert their faith. Jowett's rise to the mastership of Balliol in 1870 involved some stormy sessions with the tutors, whom Jowett wanted to cease proselytizing among the students.

How did Hopkins manage to sail these sceptical seas and emerge on a Roman shore? And from an Oxford, as Clarke wrote, that had "lost its hold on the supernatural"? The answer is hardly simple. Oxford friends and, later, Catholic colleagues attributed it to Hopkins' saintly qualities; others mentioned his finicky conscience. In any case, an undergraduate like Hopkins would have encountered, Clarke argued, one "fashionable form of paganism" after another: "Agnosticism, Buddhism, Comtism, Hegelianism." It is true that Hopkins studied Buddhist texts, wrote about Comte, and argued Hegel, yet he came out a Catholic. Nevertheless, Clarke was not altogether sure that other potential converts would make it, and he asked some difficult questions. Should Catholics go to Oxford? Should there be a Catholic college there? These questions were finally answered with the establishment of a hall, nicknamed Pope's Hall, at Oxford in 1896, with Clarke at its head. (Named Clarke's Hall after his death in 1900, it was the forerunner of today's Jesuit residence, Campion Hall.) When Hopkins' friend Robert Bridges revealed that he was still interested in such fashionable pagans as Hegel, Hopkins replied with some heat that he himself read Duns Scotus: "I care for him more even than Aristotle and more *pace tua* than a dozen Hegels." His response was characteristically quaint; Oxford may at one time have been the "university of Duns Scotus," as Pattison pointed out, but Oxonians had long ago stopped studying him.

How could a Balliol student keep his head among the ritualists, the rationalists, and the materialists with their "scientific" approach to philosophy and religion? These competing factions, satirized by Geldart, all had to contend with an obsession shared by students throughout history: studying for exams. The Oxford exam system in the 1860s was three-tiered. Hopkins' first exam, the Responsions or Little Go, which he began in June 1863 during the Trinity term, was a pass/fail qualifying exam with five sections: Latin prose, grammar (Greek and Latin), arithmetic, Euclid, and algebra. Despite the formidable mathematical sections, an outstanding Highgate scholar like Hopkins with an "exhibition" or scholarship to Balliol apparently had no trouble. (In later years, however, as a professor in Dublin, Hopkins struggled with fractional grades.) Hopkins joked about being "a little gone" after taking his "Little Go," but he passed.

For the second and third sets of exams, students chose either pass or honors, with corresponding questions for their written responses. Both exams ended a few weeks later with a "viva voce" or oral exam, by which, according to Oxford tradition, a student's standing based on the written section could be raised or remain the same but could not be lowered. Vive voce sessions launched a number of extraordinary legends, such as the so-called test questions asked undergraduates during the Oxford Movement, when Newman and his supporters were accused of introducing Catholic ideas into the Anglican church. The master of Balliol at that time, Dr. Jenkyns, would ask the student: "Of all the religious sects and parties which exist among us, which would you say corresponds the most with the Pharisees of the Gospel?" When the student replied, "the Roman Catholics," he would then be asked, no doubt rhetorically, to name "any sect . . . which tends to introduce the errors of the Roman Catholics into the Protestant church." Oscar Wilde was asked during his vive voce to translate from the Greek the biblical account of Christ's trial. When he was stopped by the examiner, who found his progress satisfactory, Wilde supposedly replied: "Oh, do let me go on; I want to see how it ends."

Hopkins, like other Balliol students striving for excellence, elected to sit for honors in the two so-called public exams. His decision meant a more rigorous set of materials to study and, of course, two sets of difficult exam questions, which, like Responsions, were published after the exam by an Oxford firm. His second exam, the First Public Examination in Literis Graecis and Latinis, also known as Moderations or Mods, began in November 1864 during the Michaelmas term (see p. 28). This exam, especially for honors, was more substantial than Responsions. It required English translations (with appropriate annotations and expla-

A Typical Oxford Examination Question and a Possible Response

On November 21, 1864, during the Michaelmas term, Hopkins left his Balliol rooms, crossed to the other side of Broad Street, and entered the old Schools Quadrangle (now part of the Bodleian Library) to sit for Moderations or Mods, his First Public Examination in Literis Graecis and Latinis (Greek and Latin Literature). Question number seven, asked him to analyze this statement: "The ultimate test of the logical validity of a thought is its conceivableness." We do not know what Hopkins wrote in response. Coincidentally, however, one of the Moderators or examiners for the session was Balliol's William L. Newman, lecturer in modern and Greek history. He had been one of Hopkins' tutors for this very exam. According to Oxford regulations a tutor could not be the examiner of his own pupils, and therefore Newman would not have examined Hopkins at this time.

Nonetheless, a number of months before the exam Newman had set Hopkins the following practice question: "Distinguish between the *clearness* and *distinctness* of concepts and state the method by which each is attained." Hopkins' reply is preserved in manuscript at Campion Hall, Oxford, and he may have drawn upon this exercise in responding to the exam question. The first paragraph of the practice essay written by Hopkins and initialed by Newman illustrates the conjunction of Hopkins' formal studies and his keen interest in perception and colors.

> The clearness of a concept is the intelligent perception of the things it connotes, the distinctness that of the things it denotes. The following for instance is a distinct idea of primary colors—red, blue, and yellow. A concept is distincter the more it is divided; the vaguest concept as regards distinctness will be the *summum genus* divided into its immediate genera, the most distinct the *imum genus* divided into individuals, and an individual cannot by any process of thought be rendered a more distinct concept, though at the time it may be not at all a clear one. Division then is the process by which distinctness in concepts is attained.

Hopkins' study of logic would have prepared him to handle *summum genus* as the largest class into which a concept may be placed and *imum genus* as the narrowest class, in fact comprising a single item, the individual. Such distinctions inform Hopkins' way of classifying the various inscapes on the scale of natural objects (see chapter 3).

nations) from four Greek and four Latin authors of the student's choice, sight translations from Greek and Latin (translations that should "combine elegance with accuracy"), essays on questions in philology and criticism, and solutions to problems set in logic.

Logic—its ground claimed by both scientists and philosophers—was the keynote of the exam. Indeed, the *Oxford University Calendar* called the logic questions "indispensable" for the "highest honors." Hopkins faced a short but tough series of problems, ranging from the tortured byways of old empiricist conundrums to the latest concepts in science and philosophy. Of the former type is this dialogue between A and B, whose conversation mixes syllogisms and an old riddle: whether ideas of space occupy space.

> A: Whatever perishes is destroyed by the solution of its contexture and separation of its parts; nor can we conceive how that which has no parts and therefore admits no solution can be naturally corrupted or impaired.
>
> B: But nothing can be conceived without extension: what is extended must have parts: and what has parts may be destroyed.
>
> A: But an ideal form is no less real than material bulk; yet an ideal form has no extension. What space does the idea of a pyramid occupy more than the idea of a grain of corn? Or how can either idea suffer laceration? As is the effect, such is the cause: as thought, such is the power that thinks: a power impassible and indiscerptible.

At the point in the exam when he had to "explain the arguments" in this dialogue, Hopkins may have been tempted to believe, even if he was himself "impassible" (invulnerable) and "indiscerptible" (incapable of being broken into parts), that writing rhetorically rather than substantively was in fact encouraged at Oxford.

Hopkins and his fellow undergraduates in the 1860s prepared for questions like this by studying such texts as Mansel's edition of Aldrich's *Artis Logicae Compendium* ("the short way to the art of logic") and Jevons' *Elementary Lessons in Logic.* Jevons drilled students on questions taken from exams at Oxford and elsewhere. Since he was careful to set out issues in contemporary science, he constructed syllogistic drills on actual problems: "If light consisted of material particles it would possess momentum; it cannot therefore consist of material particles, for it does not possess momentum." Thus Jevons was a great help in negotiating the puzzles Oxford examiners enjoyed setting: "The *minimum visibile,*" Jevons stated, "is the least magnitude which can be seen." Which of the following statements follow logically, or are any of them fallacious? "No part of it alone is visible, and yet all parts of it must affect the mind in order that it may be visible; therefore, every part of it must affect the mind without being visible." Jevons would have been helpful as well for Hopkins' classmates who chose to pursue their arts degree in the school of natural science, for they had to handle questions about the solar spectrum and the polarization of light on the basis of the "undulatory" or wave theory of light, which argued that light has no "material particles."

Even though Mansel, an Oxford metaphysician, warned readers of his edition of Aldrich that "perversions" resulted from reducing the great tradition of Baconian or inductive science to syllogisms, most of the guidebooks that Hopkins and his peers consulted did precisely that. Perhaps in fairness to Mansel and Jevons, it should be noted that not a small percentage of the Oxford examiners did the same.

Hopkins' third exam was Greats, or the Second Public Examination in Literis Humanioribus, which began on June 7, 1867, the last day of the Easter term, and continued through the Trinity term, that is, the rest of June and early July. This exhausting exam was based on a set list of Greats books, which Hopkins copied into his journals from the *Oxford University Calendar* in 1864: "*Aristotle.* Rhetoric, Ethics, Politics. *Plato.* Republic. *Herodotus. Thucydides. Livy,* 10 books. *Tacitus.* Histories or 1st 12 books of Annals. *Bacon's* 'Novum Organon.' *Butler's* Sermons or *Analogy.*"

With such a range of materials it is not surprising that the list of questions for honors in Greats was impressive. Hopkins faced questions on selected periods of Greek and Roman history (e.g., "Compare the position given to women by Aristotle and Plato with their ultimate position in ancient civilization"), questions in political philosophy ("The effect of the practice of exile on the politics of Greece"), translations both into and from Greek and Latin poetry and prose, and essay topics in moral philosophy, logic, and the history of philosophy. Following is the entire set of questions that Hopkins had to answer under the rubric "History of Philosophy"; it will be apparent that these are questions in the history of science as well as philosophy:

1. The position and value of Bacon's *Novum Organon* in the history of scientific thought.
2. Judgment of Plato on the philosophers preceding Socrates.

3. Compare the influence of Philosophy upon Politics in Rome and Athens.
4. Trace the meaning of the word *psyche* in the Greek poets and philosophers.
5. Account for the failure of the Greeks in certain departments of science.
6. The influence of the Philosophy of an age upon its Poetry.

Hopkins was a double-first at Oxford, that is, he achieved first-class honors on both public examinations. Oxford legend has it that Jowett referred to him as the "star of Balliol." Even if this praise cannot now be substantiated, there is little doubt that almost twenty years later Jowett's recommendation that Hopkins be offered the Chair of Greek at Dublin's University College, part of the federation of colleges called the Royal University, carried some weight. Most of Hopkins' extensive and careful preparation for these exams has been preserved as his Oxford Essays, written for tutors over the almost three years of study between the Little Go and Greats. These essays are more than a record of an undergraduate's studies. In the first place they reflect the personal interests of the tutors, what could be called the unofficial curriculum, as well as topical issues in science and philosophy. In the second place they reveal Hopkins' apprenticeship in natural history, since his characteristic interests and distinctive phrasing when dealing with problems in philosophy often led him to insights about perception.

Even within the official curriculum—the set books for the exams—students often chose between the idealism of Plato's Forms and the empiricism of Aristotle's inductive science as they settled into the hard work for Mods and Greats. Pattison said that students usually expected Aristotle to rule the examiners, since it was harder "to frame a question on Plato." But Hopkins' exams were full of Plato; the coaching of Pater, who eventually wrote *Plato and Platonism* to Jowett's satisfaction, must have helped. Students could go either way on the exams, but they had to be consistent. The mixture of Platonic idealism and Aristotelian science in Hopkins' Oxford Essays indicates that he was practicing both.

The other, unofficial curriculum also had to be negotiated. Even the *Oxford University Calendar* recognized that necessity; after setting out the books needed for Greats in 1867, the calendar admitted that its "statements . . . are based upon usage only, which cannot be absolutely binding upon Examiners, and Students will do well to consult their Tutors about them." The tutors, whose personal interests were strong, and the lecturers, whose courses were optional, may have constituted a mix that at first sight was intimidating; but in the long run even faddish interests were of benefit to the honors students, who needed to be intellectually nimble to handle the exams. With a staunch Platonist like Jowett and a translator of Aristotle like Robert Williams as guides, Hopkins could meet the official curriculum head-on. With sceptics and modernists like Pater and Green as tutors, he could also entertain contemporary as well as maverick views on philosophical problems.

Beyond the thoroughness exhibited in his Oxford Essays, Hopkins' ability to handle both the official and unofficial interests of his tutors is evident in his recurring emphasis on matters of perception. In his study of Locke, for example, he recognized that native empiricism formed the basement of almost every Oxford philosophical edifice; yet he emphasized the role of the imagination. He tried to explain to Pater how "acts of apprehension apparently simple are largely influenced by the imagination." His example of motion as "the synthesis of a number of impressions of the same thing perceived in a number of different spots continuously" may have been influenced by the "faddish" Kant, who, wrote Hopkins, used *einbildung* (picture, image) to denote a similar "unity" or synthesis. He continued his analysis of the subjective nature of perception in another essay for Pater, on the Cyrenaics, fourth-century Greek precursors of the Epicureans. (Pater later used the Cyrenaics as the model for those who quest after the momentary pleasures of life in his novel *Marius the Epicurean,* published in 1882.) According to the Cyrenaics, Hopkins wrote, "we can be sure of nothing, but of having our own sensations, white and black, sweet and bitter." Sensations, furthermore, may be deceiving, for "in jaundice men see yellow and in ophthalmia red and drunkards and madmen see double."

He pursued these issues in his essays on both the ancients and the moderns. Even with Aristotle, the staple of Greats, he sought the personal and telling element. He had attended lectures on Aristotle's *Nichomachean Ethics* given by Robert Williams, one of his tutors and a fellow of Balliol, who went on to publish a standard translation of Aristotle. In book 6 on the intellectual virtues, Aristotle distinguishes between *phronēsis* (common sense or prudence) on the one hand and *aisthēsis* (sensation) and *nous* (intuition, intellectual understanding) on the other. Aristotle argues, in Williams' translation of a key passage published in 1869, that a boy can be a mathematician but not a philosopher or natural scientist. Such a youngster can perceive that "a particular figure is three-sided," for mathematical understanding is an act of sensation but not of prudence, which is a *moral* perception. Hopkins glossed this passage, using Aristotle's terms: "Perception then is *nous* treating the materials furnished it by sensation. . . . With regard to the triangle, *aisthēsis* in the sense of sensation sees three black strokes; in sense of perception, that is *nous,* sees a triangle, and *phronēsis,* common sense, sees that we must assume and call this a triangle."

Hopkins turned to the moderns, particularly to Kant, for a refinement of the Aristotelian and empiricist approaches to perception. The empiricists, he wrote, usually treated causation as "invariable sequence"; "a burned child dreads the fire" and understands that the cause of pain is the fire. Kant argued instead that the "connection" between "lighting a room and the room warming must be looked for in our minds, not in the things themselves." Kant tended, in Hopkins' view, to regard cause and effect as "coexisting." The arts, Hopkins continued, can supply us with a telling example:

> Suppose a white disk on a dark ground, say of a frescoed wall. On the disk are four dark pear shaped pieces, their points meeting at the center of the disk, their round ends touching the circumference, so that they make a sort of letter X. The figure made will be a quatrefoil. Its efficient cause is the draughtsman or architect, its material cause the dark color, its formal cause the four pieces because if there had been three it would have been a trefoil, and if five a cinquefoil. Here this point deserves notice, that causes cannot be counted. If the figure had five members we should cease to call it a quatrefoil at all, but if merely the curves of the foiling had been ever so little prolonged or rounded together it would no longer have been this quatrefoil.

Having selected this revealing optical illusion, Hopkins concluded with an analysis that today has become prominent as the figure/ground relationship in gestalt psychology:

> Now we have called the figure a quatrefoil, the figure so called is the effect in question, the white interstices left in the disk by their limiting and throwing up the foiling are prominent among the causes. The eye looking at a figure

> on a church wall might however be suddenly struck by the thought that not a quatrefoil but a Maltese cross was meant, a white cross thrown up on a dark ground. At once the sheaf of causes become the effect, the old effect, the quatrefoil, is scattered into a number of causes. Accordingly an effect is nothing but the way in which the mind ties together, not the sequences, but all the conditions it sees. A cause therefore is a condition of a thing considered as contrasted with the whole thing, an effect a whole as contrasted with its conditions, elements, or parts.

As we stare at Hopkins' drawing, our perceptions of quatrefoil and Maltese cross alternate. Hopkins has cleverly reminded us that the natural object and perceiving mind have a "stem of stress" that acts as a temporary bridge "between us and things." Even if our sensations are determined by atoms, even if our perceptions may shift, there is nonetheless a world of order beyond mere atoms. The logic of Oxford prepared Hopkins to accept this conclusion.

2 The Atoms of Lucretius

> The existence of the chemical atom, already quite a complex little world, seems very probable, and the description of the Lucretian atom is wonderfully applicable to it.
>
> —Fleeming Jenkin

The Fortuitous Concourse of Atoms

W. H. Mallock's *New Republic* (1877) portrayed a distraught aristocratic lady who had consulted an Anglican bishop about the "phase of infidelity" that was "passing over the nation" in the 1860s. The bishop was undismayed. "All the teachings of modern irreligious science," he said, were based on the atomists such as Epicurus and Democritus, and these men "had been long ago refuted." For reassurance he added that all the bishops were agreed on this point—in fact, it was the only point they agreed on.

Mallock's bishop spoke too soon. Nonetheless, Benjamin Brodie, the Oxford chemist, may have provided the bishop with at least one ally: Brodie himself. But not for religious reasons; Brodie was in the university museum busily trying to dismantle the atomic theory scientifically. His task was formidable, so strong had the orthodoxy of the "fortuitous concourse of atoms" grown. Exam questions on the atomic theory were becoming routine. Not too far from Brodie's lab in 1863 an Oxford undergraduate, let us say a passman for the natural science school, would have had to explain for his examiners "the application of the atomic theory to illustrate the laws of chemical combination."

Brodie and a few others finally instigated a series of atomist wars, an era of chemistry typified by the desperation of the chemist J. C. Brough, editor of the short-lived journal *The Laboratory.* Brough felt compelled to break into recitative to ease his pains:

I am dazed with the systems upraised
By each master of chemical knowledge,
Who seems to suppose that truth only grows
In the shadows of one little college.

These lines from his poem "Modern Chemistry" (1868) reflect his frustration in attempting to negotiate among competing theorists like Brodie and Crum Brown (another anti-Lucretian):

I've tried hard, but vainly, to realise plainly
Those bonds of atomic connection,
Which Crum Brown's clear vision discerns with precision
Projecting in every direction.
In fine, I'm confounded with doctrines expounded
By writers on chemical statics,
Whom jokers unruly may designate truly
As modern atomic fanatics.

Brough understood that the history of the atomic theory of matter in the nineteenth century had not been played out in chemical laboratories alone. From John Dalton, who in 1808 adopted the Greek concept of the atom to explain his experimental data, to Lord Kelvin (William Thomson), who in 1870 attempted to measure the size of atoms he could not see, laboratory work was of course essential in determining the validity of the theory. But the debate over the existence of atoms extended beyond scientific circles, engaging philosophers, literary figures, and even a translator.

This debate was therefore joined in both lecture hall and literary journal, and everywhere the key figure was Epicurus' disciple Lucretius, the first-century Latin poet and philosopher who somewhat immodestly set out in his poem *De Rerum Natura* ("On the Nature of Things") to explain the universe on the basis of laws governing the tiny particles of matter that for two thousand years or more have been called atoms. Poets, chemists, physicists, and biologists all claimed to be interpreters of atomism.

Victorian scientists were not the first to struggle over atoms. Only the Darwinian controversy surpassed the atomist debates in intensity; but the two soon combined as it became clear that Darwin's approach had strong atomist presuppositions and that chance or randomness was the basis for both the Lucretian universe and Darwinian natural selection. If reality was defined, in the words of the ancient atomists, as the "fortuitous concourse of atoms," then Darwinism and atomism enjoyed an unexpected kinship. Remember also that the Huxley-Wilberforce debate at Oxford had been touched off by Draper's question, Is man a "fortuitous concourse of atoms"? He had intended a negative answer, since he meant to argue that human history was guided by law, not chance.

The technical language of scientists soon became part of a culturewide debate on the philosophical issue of the constitution of matter. The paradigm of the atom was attacked in two ways. Brodie argued that a scientist should not name what cannot be seen, while Lord Kelvin maintained that the "solid hard atoms" of Lucretius could not account for the latest developments in research. Darwinism suffered a serious if temporary blow when scientists, including Darwin's own cousin, Francis Galton, criticized him for locating what we would call the unit of heredity in an atomist "gemmule" or traveling organic cell. When in 1864 H. A. J. Munro published his influential translation of Lucretius, rendering Lucretius' key term *primordia* as "first-beginnings" rather than "atoms," he plunged, perhaps innocently, into a debate that extended beyond the quiet halls of Oxford where students used their Munro as a crib for Mods.

Victorians argued incessantly and minutely about atomism. Some insisted on using the word *atom,* literally "uncuttable," while others preferred *ultimate particle,* which implied that no further division of the particle was possible. Lucretius' reconciliation of the determinism of his "fortuitous concourse of atoms" with his belief in free will also appealed to Victorians. Lucretius allowed the will to cause the "swerving" or *clinamen* of the course of moving atoms; otherwise all human and cosmic actions would be controlled by the chance clashing of the atoms. After 1860, whenever matter, free will, or Darwin became a topic of debate, the Lucretian atom inevitably was present.

Perhaps it was also inevitable that the poet laureate, always interested in science, would enter the debate. Tennyson may have offered his "Lucretius" in 1868 as a dramatic monologue in the manner of Browning to counter the fashionable pessimism of Matthew Arnold's popular poem about the fifth-century Greek philosopher, "Empedocles on Etna" (1852). Both Lucretius and Empedocles were materialists, prototypical natural scientists, and suicides. Victorian poets like Tennyson and Arnold, drawn to classical topics that highlighted their era's obsessions with the role of science and the development of moral conduct, found the lives of these ancient philosophers paradigmatic. Tennyson's contemporary reviewer in *Macmillan's Magazine* found them complementary: "Empedocles died because he could not find peace; Lucretius, because he had found and lost it."

Tennyson based his poem on the apocryphal story that Lucretius' wife, in a fit of jealous rage because her husband preferred poetry to her, gave him a love potion that deranged his senses. Rather than have his body's desires ruled by his mind, Lucretius committed suicide. This fanciful story solved a dramatic/philosophical problem for Tennyson. He knew that Lucretius never fulfilled a promise made in book 5 of *De Rerum Natura* to reconcile the belief that the gods are immortal with the conviction that everything in the universe is atomic. All Tennyson could do was follow the legend that Lucretius, driven insane by his wife's aphrodisiac, never properly finished his poem. Tennyson therefore closed his own poem with the following stanza, an open question:

> The Gods! The Gods!
> If all be atoms, how then should the Gods
> Being atomic not be dissoluble,
> Not follow the great law?

Tennyson's subject remained, however, somewhat intractable. Readers from both Tennyson's age and ours have received *De Rerum Natura* as an optimistic hymn to philosophy and science and their success in interpreting the universe. Resolutely materialistic, Lucretius accepted the gods only to make it fairly clear that the universe needs their intervention rarely if at all. Resolutely Victorian, Tennyson shifted Lucretius' drama from the realm of science to that of moral conduct. But the swerving of those atoms, the background noise of the poem, helped Lucretius to make, by the late 1850s, still another philosophical comeback.

The great early English philosophers and scientists, such as Francis Bacon, Thomas Hobbes, and Isaac Newton, had all thought highly of the Greek atomists in general and, in some cases, of Lucretius in particular. Lucretius' original popularity, however, had declined after the fall of Rome. His own success was founded on the substantial reputation of the fifth-century founders of Greek atomism, Leucippus and Democritus.

Although Aristotle offered a more worldly and materialistic philosophy than Plato, only the Epicureans maintained a strictly atomist orientation in metaphysics. Epicurus had followed Democritus in calling the building blocks of nature *atomoi,* atoms; but Lucretius called them *primordia.* He may have wished to avoid the Latin equivalent of *atom,* since the concept of "uncuttable" was already closely identified with Democritus. Moreover, by using the term *primordia,* he emphasized that these particles were the *only* things present at the beginning—that is, not even the gods were there.

Lucretius' theory became the focus of the debates on the structure of matter among scientists in the 1860s and later of the scientific-religious debates of the Darwinian controversy, primarily because it offered the most detailed, coherent, and convincing explanation of matter. Lucretian atoms could not be seen but their effects could be experienced; their motions did not depend on divine action, yet human will could influence their course; finally, their combinations could account for the properties of more complex materials.

De Rerum Natura is a didactic, argumentative poem and quite dialectical, as Lucretius first takes up and then rejects alternative views in preparation for his own (see p. 40). He describes the "first-beginnings" as incredibly small balls, invisible to the eye, each with tiny hooks. Why will light but not rain pass through translucent objects? Because the particles of light are smaller than those that form rain. Why does wine but not oil flow swiftly through a strainer? Either because the particles of oil are larger or because their hooks become more entangled. The smooth, round atoms of honey please the tongue, while the sharply barbed atoms of wormwood tear their way into our sense organs.

Aside from their hooks, the properties of Lucretius' atoms coincided with Dalton's experimental and theoretical work. His revival of the Lucretian atom also signaled his philosophical acceptance of seventeenth-century corpuscular theories of matter. Dalton refined this Newtonian heritage, for Newton's famous "Queries" at the end of the *Opticks* (1706) offered the following orthodox passage identifying God as the creator of the particles of matter:

> It seems probable to me, that God in the Beginning form'd Matter in solid, massy, hard, impenetrable, moveable articles, of such Sizes and Figures, and

The Lucretian Universe of Atoms

The principles that form the heart of Lucretius' system fairly leap off the pages of book 1 of *De Rerum Natura* because of their succinct and vivid nature. In the left column below is Munro's translation of the six important principles, singled out by John Tyndall as the central premises of his dramatic Belfast Address of 1874. Those principles are restated in modern terms in the right column.

1. Nothing can be produced from nothing.	1. The explicit anti-Genesis principle which holds that matter must come from matter (not from God, who creates it "from nothing").
2. Both the elements out of which everything can be produced and the manner in which all things combine are done without the gods.	2. There is not divine origin or control over the natural world.
3. Nature dissolves everything back into its first bodies and does not annihilate things.	3. Atoms persist (cannot be destroyed).
4. The first-beginnings of things cannot be seen.	4. Atoms are submicroscopic.
5. There is also void in things.	5. Atoms are separated by space. (But most Victorians believed in the ether, a kind of fluid that connected all matter.)
6. Bodies . . . are partly first-beginnings of things, partly those which are formed of a union of first-beginnings.	6. Matter consists of atoms or combinations of atoms (molecules).

> with such other Properties, and in such Proportion to Space, as most conduced to the end for which he formed them; and that these primitive Particles being Solids, are incomparably harder than any porous Bodies compounded of them; even so hard, as never to wear or break in pieces; no ordinary Power being able to divide what God himself made one in the first Creation.

Here, for almost the last time, were the Lucretian atom and the purposes of a Christian God resolutely joined by a scientist.

Dalton, of course, was not interested in teleology. He needed the atoms for his explanation of what has come to be called the Law of Multiple Proportions. He drew circular symbols for the elements (see pp. 42–43). While he never said that his symbols actually imitated the shape of the Greek atoms, his drawings in *A New System of Chemical Philosophy* (1808) certainly have the appearance of small balls. He did use other terms such as *elements* and *ultimate particles.* But in his more assertive moments, such as his lecture to the Royal Institution in 1810, he usually insisted on *atoms:* "I have chosen the word *atom* to signify these ultimate particles, in preference to *particle, molecule,* or any other diminutive term, because I conceive it is much more expressive: it includes in itself the notion of *indivisible,* which the other terms do not."

Dalton, however, was not always so clear and unwavering. His note to the drawings seems specific enough: "This plate . . . contains the arbitrary marks or signs chosen to represent the several chemical elements or ultimate particles." Water was a "binary compound of hydrogen and oxygen," represented in his drawing by a single circle each for hydrogen and oxygen. Although a drawing like this was eventually "corrected" by others (with *two* circles for hydrogen), the circles of Dalton's drawings informed the paradigm of the atomic theory throughout the nineteenth century.

Thus Dalton's resolution seems not to have been as hard as his atoms. Other drawings were labeled as "pictures" of the atoms' actual configurations. Although "simple" atoms were "denoted by a small circle," the "combinations" of as many as three or more "particles" might result in a situation in which "the particles of the same kind repel each other, and therefore take their stations accordingly." Dalton's version of alcohol, for example, consisted of three atoms of carbon and one of hydrogen. His diagram actually represented *how* the atoms would be positioned in the molecule (see pp. 42–43).

Drawing Atoms

Contemporary studies of the ruling paradigms or conceptual models of scientific disciplines often reveal that the way a model or image is pictured influences the progress of research. Rosalind Franklin's inability or slowness to see a helical structure in her microphotographs certainly provided Watson and Crick with the opportunity to see that structure in her photos. Bohr's planetary model of the atom was too static to accommodate evidence of the changing energy levels that would be represented by the quantum concepts of atomic structure.

When Dalton set out in 1808 to illustrate his research on atoms, he drew circles, as if he were imitating Lucretian round atoms. In his drawings an empty circle represented oxygen, a circle with a dot hydrogen, and a dark circle carbon. He used a very broad definition of atom here, but the configurations certainly suggest a Lucretian system:

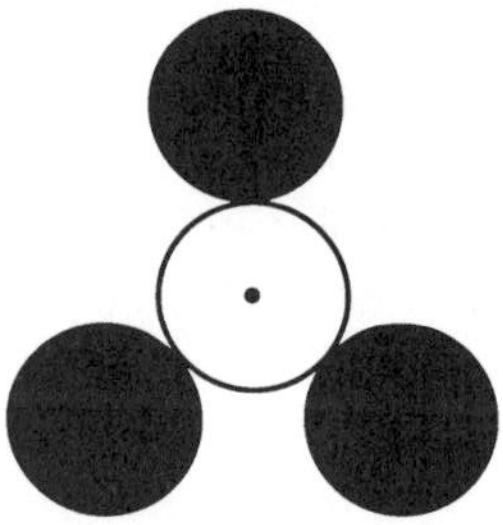

Alcohol according to Dalton (C_3H)

Brodie's challenge to traditional atomism criticized this tendency to imagine round atoms. In the modern atomic formula the dissociation, or breakdown, of hydrochloric acid into hydrogen and chlorine gas is usually represented in this way:

$$2HCl \xrightarrow{\text{heat}} H_2 + Cl_2$$

In Brodie's atomic calculus of 1867, $\alpha = 1 =$ the unit of space (1000 cubic centimeters) occupied by the gas hydrogen, and $\chi =$ chlorine gas. The dissociation of hydrochloric acid was therefore written in this way:

$$2\,\alpha\,\chi = \alpha + \alpha\,\chi^2$$

The resulting $\alpha\,\chi^2$ is the "alpha chi square" of J. C. Broughs' poem. In 1872 the organic chemist Charles Wright agreed with Brodie's critique. When chemists, Wright argued, draw the symbols for water as in the following diagram, they are suggesting "the theory of the existence of finite indivisible portions of matter, and a notion as to this mode of union or connection":

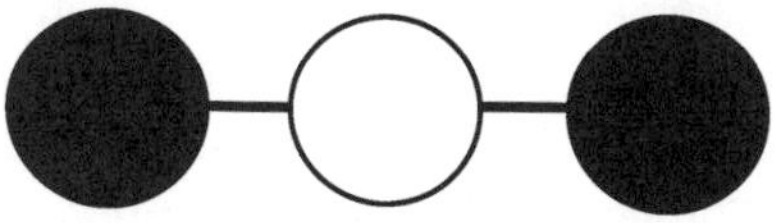

An atomist's drawing of water

Instead, according to Wright, water should be defined as that which contains "2 of hydrogen and 1 of oxygen" or "9 parts by weight yield 8 of oxygen and one of hydrogen," that is, without any reference whatever to atomic circles.

Dalton's atomic theory dominated English scientific thought for fifty years. Fleeming Jenkin, professor of engineering at the University of London and an occasional collaborator on research with Lord Kelvin, acknowledged Lucretius "as the clear expositor of a very remarkable theory of the constitution of matter" in an influential essay in the *North British Review* in 1868. Only Sir Benjamin Brodie, Fleeming whispered, had "broached ideas which seem independent if not subversive of the simple atomic faith." Brodie had in fact actively campaigned for an "atomic calculus," a full-scale alternative to the atomic theory that preserved Dalton's Law of Multiple Proportions as an operational analysis of chemical reactions while jettisoning the invisible atom. By avoiding "atomic symbols," he told the Royal Society in 1866, scientists would no longer have to adopt "atomic doctrines." Algebra, he said, would replace atomism. "A system of marks and combinations of letters" would accurately represent the "realities of nature." Chemists might think they were using atoms the way statisticians use balls, to illustrate probabilities, but "molecules and atoms" were only the "suggestions of fancy."

Mathematical equations rather than circles would henceforth represent chemical interactions. The dissociation of hydrochloric acid, for example, should be interpreted, not as two molecules of acid (each made up of an atom of hydrogen and an atom of chlorine) decomposing into molecules of hydrogen and chlorine gas (each made up of paired atoms), but as a chemical operation in which two volumes of acid decompose into equal volumes of hydrogen and chlorine gas. Brodie's symbol for hydrogen α (alpha) represents the unit 1 or the mathematical equivalent of a unit of space taken to be fixed at 1 liter or 1000 cubic centimeters. In Brodie's notation H and Cl become α and χ, and HCl becomes $\alpha\chi^2$ (alpha chi square). The sleight of hand that simultaneously made Lucretian atoms disappear and Brodie's space become operational called forth Clerk Maxwell's jibe, at an 1867 Chemical Society meeting in London, that from then on whenever he saw the symbol α he would know that it did not mean "hydrogen" but "make hydrogen." We are perhaps no better algebraists today than was J. C. Brough:

I turn for instruction to Brodie's production,
  But stick at the famous equations
Which make chlorine fare as "alpha chi square,"
  Or the product of three operations.
It may be the case that the "unit of space"
  Requires symbolic expression;
But I cannot extract any notions exact
  From Sir Benjamin's daring aggression.

When *Chemical News* published Brodie's speech to the Chemical Society in 1867 under the title "The Chemistry of the Future," his scathing critique of the atomists became general news. He had especially singled out the assumption that atoms were actually like the proto–Tinker Toy models of wires and sticks that were used routinely in the 1860s—as Tinker Toys are to this day—to represent atomic structures. Such Glyptic Formulae—the name under which they were marketed at the time—are now standard museum pieces in exhibits of the history of the atomic theory. Perhaps it was the very set now at the Old Ashmolean Museum of the History of Science at Oxford that caused Sir Benjamin so much discomfort. In any case he believed that only algebraic notation, not "model balls," should represent the "facts of chemistry."

Chemists in the late 1860s and 1870s reacted to Brodie's critique in various ways. Charles Wright, an organic chemist who defended Brodie's calculus against the atomists, said that the question of an ultimate particle was the province of philosophers, not chemists. The very use of the terms *atom* and *molecule* begged the question, substituting theory for fact. He divided the contestants into two groups. Some chemists used *atom* as a term for "a material something, possessed of dimensions in space mass and time," while others used it "as a simple number or ratio not possessed of such dimensions." In the first case the formula H_2O states "facts," since a volume of steam contains two volumes of hydrogen and one of oxygen. In the second, the "pictorial symbol" (as on p. 43) "represents the theory of the existence of finite indivisible portions of matter." In short, then, to use the word *atoms* or to draw circular figures is to risk the materialist assumption—that ultimate particles exist.

When in 1873 Alexander W. Williamson raised this issue in his inaugural address as president of the BAAS, his line was as hard as his favorite particles. Even the few opponents of atomism, he said, were "unconsciously guided" by its theory. Without atomism chemistry was "nothing more than a confused and useless heap of materials." The triumph of the Lucretian atom seemed assured as Williamson isolated, more or less disdainfully, "some few chemists" and philosophers who argued that "there are no atoms, but that matter is infinitely divisible."

But he could not chase the critics away. When Clerk Maxwell's long entry on "Atom" for the ninth edition of the *Encyclopedia Britannica* appeared in 1878, it gave a generous review to Lord Kelvin's "vortex ring" or "vortex atom." The Lucretian atom, Maxwell wrote, satisfied the demands of the atomic theory inasmuch as it accounted "for the permanence of the properties of bodies," but it failed to explain "the vibrations of a molecule as revealed by the spectroscope." Kelvin's advocacy of a vortex ring followed closely the research of Hermann von Helmholtz, who, while studying the motion of particles in a fluid, noted that a "filament" of particles not only tended to persist but also formed a ring with the properties of elasticity and mobility, two qualities that Kelvin believed the Lucretian atom lacked. Although Kelvin used the terms *vortex ring* and *vortex atom* interchangeably, his goal was to redefine the traditional term *atom* as the unit of combination of vortex rings. Having done experiments with smoke rings, he told Helmholtz that "if two vortex-rings were once created in a perfect fluid," like the ether, and if they passed "through each other like links of a chain, they never could come into collision, or break one another, [but] they would form an indestructible atom; every variety of combinations might exist." Such a vortex ring "would be as solid as the solid hard atoms assumed by Lucretius and his followers (and predecessors) to account for the permanent properties of bodies . . . and the differences of the characters."

In this particular contest among paradigms, a compromise won out. Henry Roscoe, an earlier supporter of Brodie's calculus against Williamson's atomism, showed the middle way. "The existence of atoms," he told fellow chemists at a BAAS meeting in 1870, "cannot be *proved* by chemical phenomena"; yet the atomic theory could explain some very knotty problems in chemistry. Isomerism, the existence of compounds with the same atomic formula but with different properties because of various arrangements of the same atoms, can only be explained by the atomic theory: "How otherwise than by a different arrangement of the single constituent particles are we to account for several distinct substances in which the proportions of carbon, hydrogen, and oxygen are the same?" Roscoe was a great compromiser. The term *particles* echoed the atomists, while *proportions* was a significant nod towards the Brodie faction. In fact an isomeric model circulated in 1874, J. H. van't Hoff's tetrahedron, was the first convincing three-dimensional representation of atomic structure, placing carbon at the center and various bonding groups at the corners. Eventually Brodie's operations lost the field entirely to the Lucretian atom, which within forty years was replaced, in turn, by Bohr's paradigm of a nuclear atom with planetary orbits. But that is the history of another era.

The Eternity of Matter

The atomist controversy inevitably spilled over into other fields of science, such as biology. Darwinism in particular became a focus because of its atomist presuppositions. Within his overall argument for evolution by natural selection, Darwin had proposed a theory he called "pangenesis," which attempted to explain how characteristics of adults are passed on to future generations, occasionally even "leaping over" one generation. The "gemmules" or organic particles released from each organ of the body journeyed through the bloodstream to collect in the reproductive organs for eventual transmission to offspring. Natural selection itself had an atomist cast: random or chance variations, like the random movements of Lucretian atoms, led to the survival of certain species. But even apart from the submicroscopic level, Darwin was always in trouble with the orthodox. His opponents felt rather than read contentiousness in his writings. Although only one sentence in *The Origin of Species* seemed to parody "the word" of Genesis—"Light will be thrown on the origin of man and his history"—the orthodox suspected that Darwinism meant a world that was not divinely ordered. They knew in their hearts what was coming in *The Descent of Man* (1871): an arboreal creature, not Adam, was our ancestor.

The Huxley-Wilberforce debate at Oxford did address Darwin's atomism; but the personal battle between Huxley and Bishop Wilberforce somewhat overshadowed both Draper's speech, which concluded that the "production, life, and death of an organic particle in the person answers to the production, life, and death of a person in the nation," and Brodie's criticism of Darwin's gemmule or "primordial germ," which "had not been demonstrated to have existed."

After his Oxford encounter with the bishop, Huxley, aided by another excellent physicist, John Tyndall, went on to defend Darwin's ideas before professional and popular audiences. Both faced formidable Anglican opposition as well as a hostile press, at least at first. But Huxley considered their greatest foe to be the Catholic Church, which he indicted for what he regarded as its blind opposition to science in remarks he made at a public meeting on scientific education in 1869: "In addition to the truth of the doctrine of evolution, one of its greatest merits in my eyes, is the fact that it occupies a position of complete and irreconcilable antagonism to the vigorous and consistent enemy of the highest intellectual, moral, and social life of mankind, the Catholic Church."

Such vehemence against a church with relatively few members on English soil may seem peculiar, but several factors made the Catholic

Church Huxley's special target. In the first place, the most cogent critique of natural selection came from St. George Mivart, a leading comparative anatomist, evolutionist, and Catholic convert who had been a student of both Huxley and Richard Owen, the two senior comparative anatomists in England. Not incidentally, these two men were opponents on Darwinian issues, since Owen consistently took an obscurantist if not hostile view of Darwin's ideas. In the second place, a leading group of Jesuit writers, that is, the Stonyhurst Philosophers (among whom Hopkins should be counted as an important if relatively unpublished member), devoted their considerable talents to criticizing the materialist and inevitably atomist basis of Darwin's ideas. Third, in 1869 Pope Pius IX had convened in Rome the first Vatican Council of the bishops of the Catholic Church since the sixteenth century, ostensibly to affirm the pope as the infallible ruler of the Church, but also to condemn such modern attacks on Genesis as evolutionary theory.

The Stonyhurst Philosophers and the first Vatican Council are more properly the subjects of chapter 4, but in any case it was Mivart's critique that caused the greatest stir in the Darwinian camp. Even the principal Darwinian was worried. In a private letter in 1871, Darwin wrote of his fear that Mivart's writings might swing the pendulum against natural selection or at the very least that they might "have a most potent influence" against his work. Mivart attacked on two fronts. He said that he accepted Darwin's theory of natural selection, albeit as only one of a number of natural laws, "as yet undiscovered," that govern evolution. God's *supernatural* act of creation, as outlined in Genesis, was unique, nevertheless; while the "*natural* action of God in the physical world" takes place according to such laws as natural selection. Hence God—a decidedly un-Lucretian God—had created something from nothing. Such generally theological remarks as these Darwin could perhaps disregard.

The second aspect of Mivart's critique, however, was more difficult to ignore. Darwin had accepted, in Mivart's words, "absolute organic atoms," his gemmules, which were "utterly invisible, intangible, indeed, in the words of Mr. Darwin, inconceivable" (see pp. 50–51). *The Origin of Species* did not discuss organic atoms, but Darwin's next book, *The Variation of Animals and Plants under Domestication* (1868), did. By enlarging upon his chapter on variation in *The Origin of Species,* Darwin developed his theory of pangenesis, by which organic atoms or gemmules are responsible for what we would now call the coding of characteristics passed from ancestors to offspring. Mivart criticized pangenesis in 1869 in a series of articles for *The Month,* the Jesuit journal of theological and contemporary issues. He was keen to undercut Darwin's revolutionary breakthrough by making a jibe at contemporary atomists: "It is remarkable how little is really new under the sun, how the same or similar conceptions crop up again and again. Some speculators appear now inclined to return once more to the fortuitous concourse of atoms of Democritus—for that each animal is merely the result of the physically selected aggregation of his component atoms, is the most recent (pangenetic) development of the Darwinian hypothesis."

Pangenesis—even the term itself would have caused tremors of discontent among the orthodox. Darwin had set himself a difficult question in *The Variation of Animals and Plants under Domestication:* How does a specific feature present in an ancestor suddenly appear in a later generation? Pangenesis, Darwin wrote, involves cells releasing "minute granules or atoms, which circulate freely throughout the system, and when supplied with proper nutriment multiply by self-division, subsequently becoming developed into cells like those from which they were derived." These gemmules therefore create the ova, spermatozoa, and pollen grains as the animals or plants reproduce themselves, but they are also "capable of transmission in a dormant state to successive generations."

In the later edition of *The Variation of Animals and Plants* (1885) Darwin rejected Mivart's criticism that gemmules were the product of an atomist's scientific imagination. He went on to protest too much, it seems, for despite his denial gemmules bore a distinctly atomist resemblance to similar concepts proposed by other scientists, such as Owen's germ cells or Herbert Spencer's physiological units (see pp. 50–51). Darwin did, however, drop all references to atoms in the later edition, changing "minute atoms," for example, to "minute granules." Eventually he refrained as much as possible from discussion of pangenesis, in part because in the 1870s Francis Galton, by means of experiments with rabbit transfusions, disproved the notion that gemmules could somehow be transmitted through the bloodstream.

Why had Darwin held on to atomist concepts for so long? Even as early as 1839 in his private notebooks he was wrestling with the materi-

Was Darwin an Atomist?

The young Darwin, as his notebooks make reasonably clear, was practically a materialist. He believed that the basis of life was the atom; but how it could lead to "modes of subjective action" like thought baffled him. The mature or public Darwin, who published *The Variation of Plants and Animals under Domestication* in 1868, certainly wrote as if he were an atomist: "All organic units . . . throw off free and minute atoms of their contents, that is, gemmules." After Jenkin's and Galton's criticisms of pangenesis, however, Darwin pulled back from overtly atomist theories and, in fact, edited out references to atoms in the 1885 edition of *The Variation of Animals and Plants under Domestication*.

The drive to satisfy the dilemma of inherited characteristics atomistically was authentic and widespread. Numerous scientists both before and after the period when Darwin offered his theory of pangenesis tried to identify what we would now call a mechanism of heredity. Darwin himself was aware of the most significant forerunners of his gemmules. In the eighteenth century the French scientists Buffon and Bonnet offered "organic molecules" and "germs," respectively; Darwin's contemporaries Richard Owen and Herbert Spencer offered "germ cells" and "physiological units" in their turn. All were theoretical precursors of the gene, but the Victorian emphasis on its material structure may have delayed the precise description of the gene as, in L. C. Dunn's term, an operational unit.

Why did Darwin abandon his atomism? Criticism from other scientists may have been sufficient, although in a letter to *Nature* in 1871 commenting on Galton's transfusion experiments, Darwin asserted that pangenesis had not yet "received its death blow." Galton's experiments proved that gemmules were not transmitted by the blood; but it remained a distinct possibility, Darwin wrote, that they were transmitted "[from] cell to cell, independently of the presence of vessels."

Perhaps equally compelling was the public identification of atomism with materialism and scepticism. Many other brilliant Victorians, studying the atoms of Lucretius too closely, felt the grounds of their faith slipping from under them. Only Darwin was spared Mallock's satiric pen in *The New Republic* (1877). Mr. Stockton, the fictional

Tyndall, explained to the assembled guests in Mallock's novel that "the Alps looked grander, and the sky bluer than ever, to those who truly realised the atomic theory." Mr. Storks, the fictional Huxley, was described as "great on the physical basis of life and the imaginative basis of God." Darwin endeavored throughout his life *not* to become such a target of satire, especially on the sensitive issues of materialism and scepticism.

alist implications of his speculations. He differentiated between force as an objective phenomenon of "particles of matter" and thoughts or perceptions as "modes of subjective action—they are known only by internal consciousness and have no objective aspect." In short, he wrote, "we cannot see an atom think." Thought should imply "the existence of something in addition to matter," because "the objects of thought have no reference to place." Only atoms or particles, as he sometimes called them, seemed to solve the problem of the constitution of the ultimate stuff of nature; and he seems to have accepted at this early date the idea of permanent, extremely small pieces of matter that somehow—no one knew how—could lead to thought. "All that can be said," he concluded, "[is] that thought and organization [of matter] run in a parallel series." Speculation of this kind unsettled Darwin, and he did his best to avoid such philosophical issues, at least in public, for the rest of his life. Huxley, on the contrary, would never let go of such nagging questions. He wrote to Mivart in 1885 that the next big step in philosophy would be "to show the evolution of intellect from sense." But such a step proved elusive.

The contemporary philosophers who came to be labeled as positivists, followers of Auguste Comte's *Course of Positive Philosophy* (translated by G. H. Lewes in 1853), believed they could finesse that step. John Stuart Mill, a temporary convert to positivism, announced in 1865 that the "fundamental doctrine" of positivism was that "ultimate causes" remain "unknown and inscrutable to us." The proper study of philosophy begins only after one accepts that matter and thought exist and obey laws. Positivism fueled the atomist wars as well. When Brodie's speech attacking the atomic theory appeared in the *Chemical News* in 1867, the leading British positivist, F. O. Ward, wrote in the next issue that Comte had bestowed his blessing on the atomic theory only for inorganic chemistry. The "essence of natural phenomena," Ward stated, was unknowable, and such agnosticism apparently disposed of organic chemistry. Ward, warming to Brodie's approach, said that we could nonetheless study the "relations" and "conditions" of substances in order to modify or control them.

British scientists also had trouble with Comte's pronouncements against waves of light, which, like atoms, could not be observed. Positivists had thus alienated both Williamson, an early admirer of Comte who was a champion of the atomic theory, and Huxley, who had acquired a positivist label for his emphasis on reducing the mystery of protoplasm to laws in his famous essay "The Physical Basis of Life," published in the *Fortnightly Review* in 1869. Soon afterwards, Huxley called positivism "Catholicism minus Christianity" and charged Comte with a vast ignorance of science. The final blow came when William Whewell, the dean of the English philosophers of science, called positivism nothing more than a "further advance of the sensationalist school," that is, incapable of moving from data to induction. By the end of the 1860s Comte had broken off personal contact with Mill, whose lukewarm support marked the end of Comte's brief English popularity.

The effect of positivism on the Oxford curriculum was curious. It was viewed by many, including Hopkins, as the philosophical twin of atomism. Hopkins had even classified positivism together with Bacon and the rise of physical science as the middle stage in what he called the three "great seasons in the history of philosophy." Plato, Aristotle, and the medieval scholastics were the first, while the Hegelians were the third.

This middle stage in a sense provided the background for some of the atomist wars of the 1860s. Hopkins' studies included Lucretius and two of his English followers, Bacon and Hobbes. Guidebooks for new Oxford students in the 1860s recommended Lucretius as the Latin option for Mods, especially since Munro's translation helped students not only to construe the Latin but also to construct the scientific and philosophical arguments they needed while obeying the examiners' injunction to translate with "elegance and accuracy." Hopkins was already a reasonably accomplished classicist and linguist by September 1864, when he began practicing his Lucretian translations for the Second Public Exam.

In November two of the three passages set for Lucretius raised topical issues in physics and biology. Hopkins had to translate and annotate passages from *De Rerum Natura* that argued—I quote Munro's translation here—that there are "such things as are possessed of no parts and are of a least nature" (that is, that indivisible particles exist); that human beings are not composed of alternating layers of "first beginnings of body and mind" (that is, that both mind and body have their origins in atoms); and that the sun's motions vary both diurnally and annually. From this set of passages only the sun's motions would not be controversial.

For his Greats exam Hopkins worked on Bacon and Hobbes, the two seventeenth-century philosophers popular with Victorian atomists and sceptics. Bacon's *Novum Organum, or True Directions Concerning the Interpretation of Nature* (1620) marked the debut of modern science, although Bacon himself was no experimenter. Instead he attacked the scholastic logicians who loved to dispute by means of syllogisms. Even Aristotle was faulted for not consulting experience. Only the atomists, "the school of Democritus," went "further into nature." Bacon admired them because they were unseduced by systems, what he called the "Idols of the Theatre." Atomists, at least, attempted to "dissect" nature "into parts." Hobbes, Bacon's secretary for a time, carried his mentor's ideas into the political and psychological arenas, where Hopkins and others doubted the power of atomism to resolve certain issues.

As a companion piece to his essay on the Cyrenaics, Hopkins submitted to Robert Williams "The Moral System of Hobbes," an essay that portrayed Hobbes as a pure sensationalist for whom even "the mind . . . is matter." "Objects affect us by sensation," Hobbes would have argued according to Hopkins, and therefore "sensation . . . is motion—the motion of matter." "All knowledge," then, "is or [is] of sensation." Hopkins observed that such a psychology, especially such a narrow psychology, must lead to a narrow morality: "The same one principle, atomism, is enforced all through." Practical politics, by analogy, may also be tied to atomism. If the unit of thought or sensation is the atom, the unit of society is the individual. Furthermore, the unit of the state is the monarch—seventeenth-century atomism even protected the royal line.

How faddish, so to speak, was Hopkins' search for simple solutions to difficult problems in atomism? It is not easy to say, for Balliol's concerns certainly reflected those of Victorian culture in general. Pater was already a notorious spokesman for impressionism in art and Epicureanism in philosophy, both of which were thoroughly atomistic. One of Hopkins' fellow Balliol graduates, William Wallace, eventually published what became the standard account—and certainly a sympathetic one—of Lucretius' school, *Epicureanism* (1880).

Epicureanism had not acquired the somewhat decadent resonance it has today, for both Pater and Wallace wrote unashamedly about what was for them a philosophical topic, not a moral one. Of course Hopkins would not always separate the two. Pater, in fact, was surprised that his hedonistic conclusion to *The Renaissance: Studies in Art and Poetry* (1875) produced so strong a reaction among reviewers and other moralists. He was, he thought, doing what he had always done in his lectures and in his advice to undergraduates in the 1860s. Immerse yourself in the flux of impressions, he advised, for every "moment" of your "physical life" consists only of a group of atoms that impinge upon your consciousness. Since there are only so many of these "moments" of heightened awareness available in the quest to experience life to the fullest, the goal of life is "not the fruit of experience, but experience itself." Pater's intentions were, of course, aesthetic; but too great an emphasis on the "physical life" perhaps pitched him into a position he would rather not have defended publicly. In any case, by 1877, when Mallock satirized Pater as Mr. Rose in *The New Republic,* Pater was more than willing to drop the offending conclusion. In retrospect we can see that what Pater did was to shift the aesthetic response from artist to spectator. Ruskin, for example, almost always emphasized the artist's perception of the world and how that perception became art; Pater emphasized the spectator's perception of the finished work of art.

Pater never abandoned the atomism of the 1860s, although in his final work, *Marius the Epicurean* (1885), he portrayed the plight of a mature alter ego, Marius, whose aesthetic instincts were curiously both Cyrenaic and Catholic—most likely, as it turned out, Pater's own makeup in the end. Marius, "with the Cyrenaics of all ages," decides to "fill up the measure" of his allotted moments "with vivid sensations, and such intellectual apprehensions, as . . . are most like sensations." But Marius is torn, as the novel makes clear, between this Cyrenaic "pleasure of the ideal present, of the mystic *now*" and the comforting eternal mysticism of the community of Christians growing up around him in second-century

Rome. All but converted, Marius descends slowly towards death, celebrated as a martyr by the Christians as they give him the last rites.

To turn Cyrenaic philosophy or Epicureanism into primitive Christianity was certainly no easy task, but Pater's way was paved, as it were, by Wallace, the Balliol undergraduate who, like Hopkins, was close to both Jowett and Green and in fact eventually succeeded Green as Whyte's Professor of Moral Philosophy in 1882. Wallace had caused a bit of a stir with his favorable account of Epicureanism, since the philosophical outlook of his mentors scarcely lay in that direction. But Wallace avoided any taint of suspicion by appealing to science. Epicurean psychology, he argued, was as securely based on atomism as was contemporary physics. Furthermore, the Lucretian concept of *clinamen,* the swerving of atoms caused by an act of the will, made Lucretius' contribution to philosophy distinctive. Wallace even urged the adoption of Kelvin's vortex rings, for they allowed the "hard, dead thing" that was the Lucretian atom to become almost "instinct with life."

If Epicureanism was a fad, positivism a contemporary alternative that seemed altogether scientific, and atomism the common denominator of many of these trends, is it then surprising that Hopkins slipped towards Pater's brand of aestheticism, coming as it did from an Oxford tutor who lived so austere if not pure a life? Hopkins' most extensive aesthetic moment came in 1865 with "On the Origin of Beauty: A Platonic Dialogue." Using the form so dear to Jowett's heart, Hopkins attempted to dissect the concept of beauty. He was not entirely successful, perhaps inevitably coming to rest at the Paterian locus of beauty as a mental "apprehension" or perception of the "likeness and difference" of things. In the next chapter we shall return to the only section of this dialogue that Hopkins never abandoned: the analogical use of musical scales. Here we shall only recall that Pater's most famous aphorism was that "all arts aspire to the condition of music." Hopkins might have paraphrased this to read that science as well as art aspires to a musical analogy.

Hopkins returned to the Cyrenaic basis of Pater's thought in another undergraduate essay, "Connection of the Cyrenaic Philosophy with the Cyrenaic Morals," written for Robert Williams in 1867. He is not as critical of these philosophers for pursuing "a sum total of particular pleasures" as we might expect. In fact, he states explicitly, they are no more to be criticized for their hedonism than the utilitarians for their statistical or majority approach to happiness. Hopkins finds the sensationalism of the Cyrenaics limiting, yet their system, no less than Aristotle's, "is logical and complete."

The Cyrenaics and other sensationalists, in Hopkins' view, constantly emphasized only the passing sensation and the inevitably fading pleasure of the moment. And it was precisely this tendency of atomism to dwell on the immediate and momentary experience of sensations from which he recoiled. In "The Probable Future of Metaphysics" he writes of atomism viscerally, as if it were a social disease: "A form of atomism like a stiffness or sprain seems to hang upon and hamper our speculation: it is an overpowering, a disproportioned sense of personality." Most likely Hopkins made this cry of philosophical frustration to Green, who was his tutor in 1867 when this essay was written. But the triumph of atomism or materialism over idealism is not assured, Hopkins adds: "It will always be possible to show how science is atomic, not to be grasped and held together, 'scopeless,' without metaphysics: this alone [i.e. metaphysics] gives meaning to laws and sequences and causes and developments."

Hopkins' critique of contemporary science in this essay focuses on psychology and physiology, which have usurped the traditional role of epistemology as they "withdraw to themselves everything that is special and detailed in the action of the mind." Green himself may have been very close to Hopkins at this point; very soon after, he began to deliver lectures attacking G. H. Lewes and Herbert Spencer as the principal spokesmen for a new psychology. Hopkins regarded these men as too narrowly reliant on sense impressions in their explanations of how we perceive the world. He was groping for a theory of perception that would involve the mind's active participation in the perception of nature. Science "without metaphysics," as he wrote, was "scopeless," "atomic," that is, incoherent and without direction. Out in the field he sought instead the scapes (shapes) of nature and the special inspiration of inscapes. *Scopeless,* the key word in the above quotation, is the etymological equivalent of *scapeless,* although the famous linguist W. W. Skeat was not convinced when Hopkins opened a debate on these words with him many years later. Hopkins always wanted linguistic proof of his theories; but with or without such proof, he felt that without the mind's active participation in the discovery of special forms in nature and without the recognition that God's creative power sustained those forms—in brief, without inscape and instress—the atomist randomness of natural events, the anti-metaphysician's dream, would prevail.

In 1879 Hopkins' friend R. W. Dixon, poet and Anglican clergyman, told him that Milton and Lucretius "were the greatest writers of their kind in their language: and each has given a cosmogony in poetry: the one has perfectly expressed *Creation,* the other *The Eternity of Matter,* thus exhibiting the opposite theories." Unfortunately we do not have Hopkins' reply to this simple and elegant summary of a decade's atomist wars. But Victorian scientists and intellectuals, especially those in the forefront of the argument for the "eternity of matter," deployed their Lucretian terms selectively. Lucretius himself, bound by his philosophy, and Munro, bound by his Latin, used *primordia* and *first-beginnings* to denote the material fabric of the universe. Others, as we have seen, selected the alternatives closest to their physics and metaphysics. The *atom* was an extremely small, hard "ball"; *ultimate particle* stressed its indivisibility. But the stronger the emphasis on Lucretius, the greater the likelihood that Genesis would be contradicted. Those who stalked Darwinian targets knew that home truths were in real danger. And even a scientist like Brodie, who criticized the invisible atom, felt the need to remind his audience at the university museum in 1860 that the human mind is an image of the divine. Certainly Hopkins would have agreed.

3 Black Rain in Lancashire

> The whole difference between one who sees in the external world of Nature a paradise, and one to whom it is a barren desert, consists in *the open eye.* When once the attention has been awakened to the perception *in detail,* of the wonderful beauty and fitness, the endless variety of structure and form, the curious contrivances, relations, modifications, and compensations, that are manifested in God's marvellous works, a well of pleasure has been unsealed that is never closed again.
>
> —Philip and Emily Gosse

New Words, New Science

Works by Plato and Whewell would have made an odd if inevitable couple of books on any Oxford undergraduate's desk in the 1860s. Plato: otherworldly, disdainful of the world's phenomena, perhaps a mystic; William Whewell: commonsensical, a logician and empiricist—an odd pair, certainly, but they strike us today as curious allies in Hopkins' campaign against atomism. He could use Plato directly. In his essay "The Probable Future of Metaphysics," Hopkins suggested that the revival of "some shape of the Platonic Ideas" would lead a "new school of metaphysics" against the modern atomists. Invoking Plato's spirit was appropriate, for the Greek philosopher had himself criticized the ancient atomists. Perhaps from Robert Williams' lectures, perhaps from his own reading, Hopkins came to believe that Plato's philosophy was "not the vague dream of transcendentalism we are inclined to think it." And at that point in history, the decade of atomist wars, "Plato's relation to us" would be tonic. "It does us good to read him," Hopkins asserted, especially "against the atomism of Humery and Positivism."

Hopkins would have found Whewell's interest in precise language attractive. When he met the details of the world head-on, however, Whewell had a heavy hand. Anyone who looked at him then, or for that matter looks now, would know that the author of *The History of the Inductive Sciences* (1837) never had a mystical or Platonic thought. Facts and only facts fit neatly into Whewell's syllogisms. Although he was a Cambridge professor, his books provided numerous generations of Oxford students with handy references on the discipline and history of logic. Whewell's encyclopedic framework, unlike the discrete problems set by Mansel or Jevons for cramming, opened up a world of scientific and philosophical thought in process. He had written, for example, a series of aphorisms "concerning the language of science" for his *Philosophy of the Inductive Sciences* (1847). He proposed, among other things, that "in framing scientific terms, the appropriation of old words is preferable to the invention of new ones." Certainly Hopkins' own practice, as he set out to capture in prose his perceptions of nature, followed Whewell's recommendation, for *inscape* and *scape* appropriated a common and readily available root, as did *instress*. Hopkins had less success with other rare words he may have regarded as his own coinage, such as *offscape*, the most distant part of a landscape, and *cloudscape*, both of which, in fact, were already in current use; but then Whewell's own *thermotics*, *electrics*, and *tidology* for the study of heat, electricity, and the tides, respectively, have not gone the distance either. Certainly Hopkins would have appreciated Whewell's *idiopts*, "persons who have a peculiarity of vision," for Hopkins had written of such persons himself. To this day idiopts—the persons if not the word—have survived.

The Oxford years provided Hopkins with an arena in which his studies, his increasing concern about atomism, and his love of language and nuance all developed significantly. Language, philosophy, and nature converged in the creation of a special set of terms: *inscape*, *scape*, and *instress*. These represent the young philosopher's obsession with meticulous terminology. He needed these terms to describe phenomena he encountered as a natural historian who rambled, like so many of his contemporaries, in the fields. Even twenty years later, having tried with only occasional success to make his mark as a philosopher and amateur scientist, he echoed his earlier obsessions as he contemplated writing a study of rhythm. He wrote to Canon Dixon that his study would be "full of new words," for without them "there can be no new science."

The 1870s brought Hopkins to Stonyhurst College for the philosophate period of his training for the Jesuit priesthood. Because of Stonyhurst's scientific prominence, he was there well imbued with the traditional methods of the natural sciences: observation (in which, of course, he was already highly skilled), experimentation, and record keeping. His journals of the 1870s show his love for and mastery of natural description. The years at Stonyhurst provided him with access to one of the nation's leading meteorological stations and close contact with a Jesuit astronomer of international reputation, Stephen Joseph Perry (see p. 61). Stonyhurst made news throughout these years with its professional reports on weather phenomena as well as on extraordinary occurrences such as the black rain in Lancashire and the northern lights. Such dramatic and beautiful events strongly appealed to Hopkins, who turned his attention to these as well as other scientific oddities and set pieces such as rainbows that failed to exhibit the spectrum, "sun rays" that appeared in the evening (*rayons du crépuscule*), and the once-in-a-lifetime atmospheric displays of light caused by the Krakatoa volcanic eruptions of the 1880s. (All of these are discussed in detail below.)

Despite the professional environment of Stonyhurst, the Hopkins we meet in the *Journals* remains quite consistently both intellectual and quirky. He mixes his modes. "The view from the fields," he wrote laconically in 1865, "with psychological value. The sunset." Or two years later in the French countryside: "The scales of color in the landscape were more appreciable before than after sunrise: all was 'frank.'" Or in 1873 while still at Roehampton, south of London: "I counted in a bright rainbow two, perhaps three complete octaves, that is, three, perhaps four strikings of the keynote or nethermost red, counting from the outermost red rim: this of course is independent of a double bow, which this also happened to be." Or a year later, commenting on a Frederick Leighton painting: "There was in the picture a luscious chord of color." Psychological value, scales, octaves, chords: these are all metaphors or concepts borrowed from other fields of study, and used by Hopkins to organize his observations of nature. Such borrowings were supplemented and certainly enriched by his own coinages, for which he is now known. In 1868 he sees a "noble scape of stars" in the Swiss night; returning home to England he senses the "all-powerfulness of instress" in the Ely Cathedral windows; still later that same year in Richmond Park he sees "trees in the river . . . inscaped in distinctly projected, crisp, and almost hard rows of loaves."

S. J. Perry and the Stonyhurst Observatory

When Hopkins returned to Stonyhurst in the 1880s he boasted to his friend Robert Bridges of its scientific ambience. Stonyhurst, he wrote, had an observatory, laboratories, an anemometer, a sunshine gauge, and magnetic instruments. Bridges, who had become a doctor, would have been suitably impressed by this list, although he may already have been aware of Stonyhurst's considerable scientific reputation. A leading Victorian astronomer and solar scientist, Stephen Joseph Perry, was the director of Stonyhurst Observatory, a fellow of the Royal Society, and a close colleague of Norman Lockyer, the founding editor of *Nature.* Stonyhurst was twice named a principal observatory in major Victorian scientific programs. In 1858 it was chosen by Sir Edward Sabine for his magnetic survey of England, and in 1866 it was the Board of Trade's choice as one of seven main meteorological stations in Great Britain. The observatory published monthly the *Meteorological Report,* which contained astronomical and meteorological data as well as observations of wildflowers and seasonal changes in the landscape. In August 1882, when Hopkins returned to Stonyhurst as professor of classics, the BAAS honored Stonyhurst at its annual meeting in Southport by organizing a visit of the delegates to the observatory.

As a scientist Perry made many substantial contributions. His fields of expertise included solar and magnetic phenomena, especially sunspots and auroras; he was also preeminent in the uses of scientific drawing and photography. He was a math instructor for the younger boys at Stonyhurst as well as an active priest. He died on an expedition to the West Indies to photograph the eclipse of the sun in 1889.

Hopkins often visited Perry's observatory, especially when phenomena like an eclipse of the moon occurred. Perry, like Hopkins, was attracted to such phenomena and had a naturalist's feel for the local scene. He even kept a lemur for a pet. In May 1884 Perry reported to *Nature* in two letters that an "extraordinary darkness at midday" with black rain, black hail, and black snow had struck locally at Stonyhurst the month before, producing a darkness "the most intense that is remembered by any of the inhabitants." Perry noted that "a dense black cloud with a slightly yellowish tinge hung over the south-west sky" and that fourteen miles away—over Preston, the industrial model for Dickens' Coketown in *Hard Times*—"the darkness was very marked."

These perceptions, these new words, were informed by a view of the world, indeed a metaphysics, even if Hopkins' remarks appear off-hand and untheoretical. What theoretical underpinnings he himself articulated we shall examine shortly. But we should first of all be aware that it is the journal form itself which suggests that Hopkins' thoughts were incomplete or that he had neither the time nor the inclination to complete his observations. Such a judgment is not quite fair, because writing journals not only permits but encourages incompleteness. Published journals represent a contradiction in terms. They have been brought to the public because their author is famous, not because he or she perfected every thought. Hopkins' journals do not, for the most part, record failures in accomplishment but monitor ideas in progress, as he thinks with his quill. Victorian culture and family life helped to provide him with a keen sensitivity to both art and nature. The discipline of Stonyhurst, especially during his second tenure there in the 1880s, with the high standard of professional scientific work set by Perry and his assistant, A. J. Cortie, helped Hopkins to publish four scientific letters in *Nature,* the leading general science journal of his day.

Hopkins came of age at midcentury, when the Victorian middle class enthusiastically supported its naturalists and amateur scientists. Nineteenth-century natural history was a splendid field, filled with poets and professional scientists, passionate amateurs and weekenders, none of them afraid to get wet in tide pools stalking the wild sea anemone. Gilbert White's *Natural History of Selborne* (1788), albeit the work of an earlier century, nevertheless remained paradigmatic for the many naturalists who admired him. The freedom of these early naturalists to roam was echoed by their refusal to stick to the scientific point. John Leonard Knapp, inspired by White, published his *Journal of a Naturalist* in 1829. He noted, for example, that it was easy to find the dyer's weed in stone quarries everywhere during all seasons, for the plant will survive even a frost. He went on to add that its yellow dye might be extracted and used for export if farmers were careful to lay up a good supply of manure for the plant's extensive cultivation. No less down-to-earth were the Gosses, Philip and Emily, whose *Sea-Side Pleasures* (1853) caused such a run on the invertebrates of the Devonshire coast that professional scientists feared a depopulation of sea squirts. Philip Gosse's own *Naturalist's Rambles on the Devonshire Coast* (also 1853) urged readers to garner the odd "new medusoid" (jellyfish) but not to exhibit a too "coldly correct" attitude towards science because of the danger of losing "any pleasurable emotions beyond the mere acquisition of knowledge." Together the Gosses continued the Romantic tradition of reverence for nature. Those who perceive, they wrote, the "endless variety of structure and form, the curious contrivances, relations, modifications, and compensations" in God's "marvellous works" will receive great pleasure. The "beauty and variety were there before," they added, but the "beholder" has changed. This same joyful attitude became a familiar one for Hopkins.

His family, so typical of the Victorian middle class, encouraged both artistic and scientific tendencies in their children. Numerous family members sketched or drew extensively, and eventually two brothers, Arthur and Everard, became professional illustrators. Hopkins' father had strong mathematical and scientific interests as well as a small talent for poetry. In addition to a collection of poems and a volume on numbers, Manley Hopkins published an extensive work of natural history, *Hawaii* (1862), which provided documentation contradicting Darwin's views on coral reefs. He also conveyed to London society in 1874 the good news, received from Hopkins' uncle Charles in Hawaii, that the dodo was not extinct, a rare specimen having arrived in Hawaii from the Samoan Islands. (This was, alas, not true.) The Hopkins family library contained a number of strictly scientific books, some of historic interest, such as John Bonnycastle's *Introduction to Astronomy* (1787) with its variations on the Argument from Design ("the stars . . . are most probably systems analogous to the solar one") and Henry Morley's *Life of Jerome Cardan* (1854) with its emblematic tale of Cardan disputing with King Edward VI about the origin of comets, together with more recent, authoritative texts such as George Johnston's *History of the British Zoophytes* (1846), to which professionals and amateurs alike would turn to classify the day's catch from a tide pool.

Scientific and artistic currents thus mixed easily in Hopkins' early life. He was especially attracted to one intriguing speculation that crossed artistic and scientific lines: he argued, following some distinguished forerunners, that the colors of the rainbow were analogous to the notes on the musical scale.

The Rainbow of Sound

The analogy between the colors of the rainbow and the tones of the musical scale provided some of the motivation for the "new words" Hopkins needed to render the "scales of color in the landscape" or the "octaves" in the rainbow. Perhaps tempted by an undergraduate's desire to find a system that would explain rather different phenomena or perhaps simply responding to the trends in Victorian culture that developed the analogy in scientific and artistic circles, Hopkins extended an analogy originally popularized by Sir Isaac Newton in the seventeenth century.

When Newton gathered his data on the refraction of light by a prism, the comments he made in his *Opticks* were both experimental and paradigmatic. They were experimental insofar as he described simply what he saw: white light broke down into seven component colors. The conclusion he drew was paradigmatic: the schema of seven colors was analogous to the seven tones of the diatonic scale in music. (The diatonic scale proceeds by whole tones, the chromatic scale by half tones.) Query 14 of the *Opticks* presented the analogy in the form of a question, but other references in the book indicate that the question was rhetorical: "May not the harmony and discord of colors arise from the proportions of the vibrations propagated through the fibers of the optic nerves into the brain, as the harmony and discord of sounds arise from the proportions of the vibrations of the air?" Newton did not invent this analogy. Aristotle had written in *De Sensu* that "it is possible that colors may stand in relation to each other in the same manner as concords in music, for the colors which are (to each other) in proportion corresponding with the musical concords, are those which appear to be the most agreeable." But Newton's assertion that the colors and tones were exactly proportional invested the analogy with scientific authority. Furthermore, Newton's illustrations in the *Opticks* were rigorously mathematical. One of his diagrams was a circle with the colors of the spectrum assigned to the tones proportionally by area, while another superimposed tones on a linear rendering of an actual spectrum (see pp. 66–67).

One of Newton's early popularizers in the eighteenth century was Louis Bertrand Castel, a French Jesuit and fellow of the Royal Society of London, who exhibited an ocular harpsichord in London in 1757. The keys of this instrument "played" different colored tapes through which light passed. This palpable manifestation of the analogy was a spectacular example of pre-Romantic synaesthesia, but by the nineteenth century the analogy had become more decidedly cross-disciplinary.

The analogy was first popularized in England by an expert in color science, George Field, and at the same time in Germany by Goethe in his anti-Newtonian guide to color, *Zur Farbenlehre* (1810). Indirectly and somewhat later, the British painter J. M. W. Turner aroused interest in similar questions, in particular by two of his experimental canvases that "commented" specifically on Goethe's ideas.

By far the most popular exponent of the analogy was Field. He was a chemist, paint maker, and inventor who broadcast his ideas in a series of philosophical pamphlets and best-selling color guides. His essay *Chromatics* (1817) argued that the law of analogy was an imitation of God's "perfect system." The analogy between colors and musical tones was "like the universe . . . an absolute unity comprehending a relative infinity." Fortunately his other books were less mystical. In his *Aesthetics* (1820), for example, he superimposed his "chromatic" scale of colors on a diatonic scale of tones. Although music, he explained, is an art of time and painting an art of space, "the distance on the scale from sound to sound, and that from color to color, are equally *intervals.*" When "one of the semitones of the octave falls between the notes B and C, or blue and green, [these] colors are discordant, and require the intermediate *demitint* opposed to the semitone to satisfy the eye, to connect the octaves in series, and to complete the harmony of the scale." Field handily supplied a color chart to help move this theory into the practical realm: olive or dark green, tertiary colors, are needed to form the harmonious bridge between blue and green (see pp. 66–67). If that concord or harmonious bridge is achieved, he concluded, then both "depth and brilliancy" result. Field's inventions and color suggestions were more successful than his theories. His chromoscope, a tube mounted on a tripod, with an enlarging eyepiece and an objective lens that functioned as a Newtonian prism, together with his color guides sustained his reputation long after his death at midcentury. This combination of scientific technique, aesthetic ends, and philosophical context in his work represent Victorian thoroughness at its best.

Newton's achievements were not as popular with Goethe as with Field. Instead of Newton's definition of white light, Goethe offered a compli-

Scales of Color

Newton offered two different diagrams in his *Opticks* as representations of the relationship between the spectrum of white light and a musical or chromatic chord. To him the relationships were strictly mathematical, not analogical, since each space on the line or circle graphs represented one of the seven major colors of the spectrum:

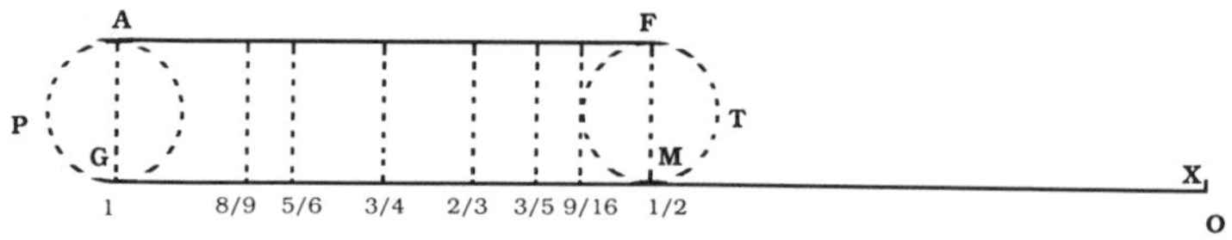

"The Rectilinear Sides MG and FA were by the said cross lines divided after the manner of a Musical Chord."

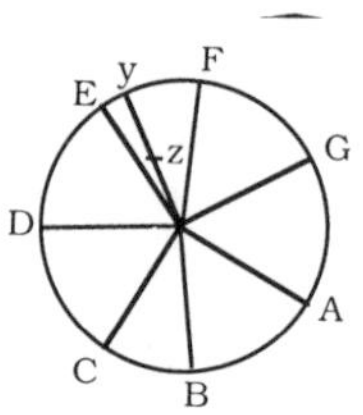

"A Circle ADF, . . . its Circumference into seven Parts DE, EF, FG, GA, AB, BC, CD, proportional to the seven Musical Tones or Intervals of the eight Sounds. . . ."

Newton did not discuss *why* it seemed not to matter whether the notes of the chord are compared to the segments of a line or to the areas of a circle, but perhaps it was obvious to him.

George Field, being a colorist, was more practical than Newton. He provided both a musical staff and a color chart. But, while he was practical enough to have them both engraved on the same plate, he did not include colors on the color chart of triangles that stretches diagonally across the staff. We must imagine, therefore, that on the musical staff below olive or dark green would be a "demitint" filling in one of the triangles on the third line from the bottom, to bridge the gap between blue and green, just as a semitone bridges the gap between notes C and B, which would have triangles colored blue and green, respectively:

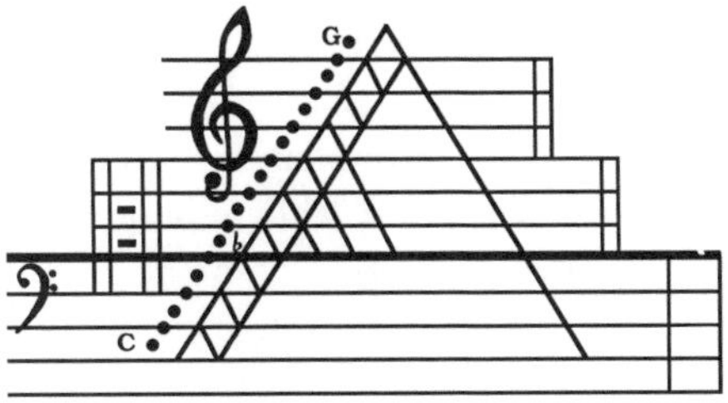

Field's musical staff and color chart (*Aesthetics,* 1820)

cated alternative that characterized light as a simple, uniform presence that results in color only by the interaction or intervention of what Goethe in *Zur Farbenlehre* called "opaques" or "mediae." The news of Newton's "errors" was brought to the attention of Victorians by two popular books published a decade apart. Sir Charles Eastlake, president of the Royal Academy, published *Goethe's Theory of Colors,* a translation of *Zur Farbenlehre,* in 1840; in 1855 G. H. Lewes published what became the standard explication of Goethe's ideas, his *Life of Goethe* (a book that the Hopkins family owned). Goethe believed, wrote Lewes, that "on the one hand there is Light, and on the other Darkness; if a semi-transparent medium be brought between the two, from these contrasts and this medium Colors are developed." Light seen through a "very slightly thickened" medium will appear yellow, further thickening will result in a yellow-red color, and still further "opaqueness" will turn the light ruby. Even Newton's color/sound analogy—indeed virtually all of Newton's diagrams and mathematics—infuriated Goethe, who preferred to believe that color tones are the product of light and darkness just as sound tones are the product of sound and silence.

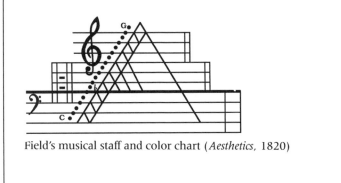

Turner is perhaps the best-known Victorian artist to confront head-on Goethe's criticisms of Newton, although on occasion Field himself had quoted Goethe's theories with some appreciation. Always attracted to analogies among the arts, and certainly, after Constable, the leading painter who was both artist and naturalist, Turner annotated his copy of Eastlake's translation of Goethe rather ambiguously. Soon afterwards, however, in 1843, he exhibited at the Royal Academy two controversial paintings, now at the Tate Gallery: *Light and Color (Goethe's Theory)—The Morning after the Deluge—Moses Writing the Book of Genesis* and *Shade and Darkness—The Evening of the Deluge.* They are exciting paintings, but their support of Goethe's theory is problematical. They embody, respectively, what Goethe called "plus" colors (yellow, orange, and red) and "minus" colors (blue-green, blue, and purple); and they certainly seem to be presenting light as if perceived through "opaques." Turner's biographer, Jack Lindsay, has called the paintings more an "homage to Goethe" than a strict illustration of his theory. Turner believed that the sun is the energizing source of all natural phenomena, and in fact offered the Newtonian rainbow as part of the poetic caption for the painting *Light and Color:* "[the] sun / Reflected her lost forms, each in prismatic guise / Hope's harbinger."

Perhaps Turner was not being precise enough when he wrote "reflected" instead of "refracted." In any case, by midcentury the study of the color/sound analogy passed from the artists to the scientists. In his translation of Goethe, Eastlake quoted with approval a scientist's remark that Newton "was betrayed by a passion for analogy, when he imagined that the primary colors are distributed over the spectrum after the proportions of the diatonic scale of music, since . . . intermediate spaces [in the spectrum] have really no precise and defined limits." Eastlake himself believed that such "fanciful analogies . . . have long been abandoned even by scientific authorities." Actually the situation was more complex. John Tyndall, a Victorian scientific expert on light and color, wrote in his critique of Goethe's book on color that Newton's "theory" of color was actually a "direct presentation of facts." White light is not *in theory* but is *actually* composed of "differently refrangible rays." Tyndall himself had little interest in the analogy, but one of his colleagues, another outstanding experimenter in light and sound, H. L. F. von Helmholtz, stated in *On the Sensations of Tone as a Physiological Basis for the Theory of Music*

(English edition 1877) that "the phenomena of mixed colors present considerable analogy to those of compound musical tones." The problem with achieving a purely scientific statement on the topic, Helmholtz concluded, lies in the fact that we neither "see the simple elements of our sensations of color" nor "rarely" do we hear "the sensation of tone, simple tones themselves." Nevertheless Newton had returned, in force.

Part of the background to Tyndall's and Helmholtz's work was the intense debate in the 1870s on the color/sound analogy in *Nature* and even (to a lesser extent) in *The Athenaeum,* a general review of the arts and sciences. The debate in *Nature* was sharper because one of the magazine's goals was to develop a debate between scientists and artists about the "truth" of painting, especially painting of natural subjects. Fairly regularly, for example, Norman Lockyer, the editor of *Nature,* reviewed shows at the Royal Academy, assessing their scientific accuracy; and a frequent contributor to *Nature* was the pre-Raphaelite painter John Brett, who wrote columns on astronomy and the relationship between science and art.

In 1870 W. F. Barrett, professor of experimental physics at the Royal College of Science in Dublin, had reopened the scientific debate on Newton's analogy. In "Correlation of Color and Music," a letter published in *Nature,* he stated that the ratios of the *extreme* tones of an octave and the *extreme* colors of the spectrum are "coincident," and that C corresponds to red, D to orange, and so forth: "The musical scale is thus literally a rainbow of sound." Critics of the analogy, in their replies to Barrett, pointed out some difficulties. One writer said he would not expect an analogy "between the effect of *simultaneous* sounds and the effect of *contiguous,* not *coincident,* colors." Another correspondent raised a "curious speculation": If the analogy is valid, what is "white sound"?

During this period Hopkins used the color/sound analogy in ways of his own. In the journal entries quoted above, the analogy is presupposed. In undergraduate essays at Oxford and later in his lecture notes when in 1873 he became professor of rhetoric at Roehampton, he developed an analysis of aesthetics that divided rhythm into chromatic ("transitional") and diatonic ("abrupt" or "marked") scales. His major contribution to prosody, "sprung rhythm," offers in a line of poetry "one stress [that] follows another running, without syllable between." Its rhythm was therefore diatonic. On the other hand, according to Hopkins,

The Great Chain of Being and Evolutionary Theory

Hopkins' interpretation of evolutionary development as a *chromatic* scale of scapes or species and of the traditional or pre-Darwinian view of the fixity of species as a *diatonic* scale followed two dominant paradigms of the eighteenth and early nineteenth centuries: the Great Chain of Being and the Argument from Design. The Great Chain of Being varied in some ways from authority to authority, but its essence remained the same. God had established a hierarchy of living forms with the angels on top, humans below them, and animals and plants still further down on the chain. With the exception of humans, each major class was in turn further divided, creating a spectrum of species or forms, each with enough similarities to place it near its cousins but sufficiently different to occupy a separate niche.

Darwin's scale of evolving species had not quite superseded the traditional view when Hopkins and other Oxford students studied for Greats the two key documents, both by Bishop Butler, of the Argument from Design: his *Sermons* (1726) and his *Analogy of Religion, Natural and Revealed, to the Constitution and Course of Nature* (1736). Butler argued that there is "an analogy or likeness between" that "system of things" we call nature and the Word of the Bible. That "scheme or system" is, of course, the Great Chain of Being, cunningly devised to place humans in the middle. Butler was fond of quoting Ecclesiastes to support his views. Since the son of Sirach said that "all things are double one against another, and God hath made nothing imperfect," we should expect to find such doubling or mirroring in the Great Chain as well. Human beings had bodies and souls, while angels were only spirit (souls if they had once been human) and animals only body.

Science, at least pre-Darwinian science, certainly "doubled" religion. The leading proponent of fixed types was James McCosh, professor of botany at Belfast's Queens College and later president of Princeton University, whose influential book, *The Typical Forms and Special Ends of Creation* (1855), was one of the last great monuments to the pre-Darwinian concepts of biology pioneered by followers of Goethe. McCosh argued that "adjustments" or adaptations in nature "are designed" and not the "casual nature of chance." Earlier, at a BAAS meeting in Belfast in 1852, McCosh explained that the ramification of plants (the arrangement of their branches) and their venation (the arrangement of veins in leaves) were analogous, since the angles of branches and veins were the same. Such a "unity of design" in plants would "enable the student of natural theology . . . to illustrate the order which reigns in the universe." Hopkins' mind moved in similar ways when he wrote in 1867 that the five stems of "a wonderful elm" he saw in Dartmoor were "*morphē mia*" or a single form. It was soon afterwards that he called those unique forms inscapes, diatonic occurrences on a scale of fixed species.

the traditional iambic line used unstressed syllables, which by analogy were the half steps or semitones in a chromatic rhythm. He quoted his own lines from "The Wreck of the Deutschland" to illustrate the difference between iambic and sprung rhythm. If in the following lines from stanza 2 the word "birch" were inserted between "lashed" and "rod," the effect of two stressed syllables running without a break would be lost: "I did say yes / O at lightning and lashed rod." Inserting "birch" restores a light stress, almost returning the line to an iambic or chromatic rhythm, with "birch" as a half step or halftone.

Hopkins also used these terms for more general categories of aesthetic perception. He described a "deepening color or a passing from one color into another" and "the change of note on a string of a violin or in a strain of wind" as chromatic phenomena, while a "collocation of colors" and "the change of note . . . on the keys of a piano" were diatonic phenomena.

By introducing "a strain of wind" into his aesthetic analysis, Hopkins was doing something that became his characteristic signature. Aesthetic judgments were by an easy shift of terms turned into comments on natural phenomena. His most distinctive modification of the color/sound analogy came at Oxford in some of his earliest remarks on evolutionary theory. Hopkins compared the diatonic scale to what we now call the Great Chain of Being and what Bishop Wilberforce and his supporters regarded as the "fixity of species" (see p. 70). If types or species were bound at fixed intervals on the chain like tones on the diatonic scale, they could not evolve from one position to another but would have an "absolute existence." Evolutionary theories, on the other hand, posited a scale of "pure chromatism" with no "fixed points" and allowed "accidental" variations (mutations?) like the sharps and flats of chromatic alteration on the musical scale. Here Hopkins was siding with pre-Darwinians like James McCosh (professor at Queen's College, Belfast, and later president of Princeton University), who argued in *The Typical Forms and Special Ends of Creation* (1855) for the notion, originated by Goethe, that species were fixed types that developed in imitation of an "archetype" of the species. For Hopkins such an archetype was quite close to "some shape of the Platonic Ideas" that he had hoped to use to worry the atomists.

The Scape of Things

Hopkins abandoned the chromatic/diatonic distinction in the 1870s. Perhaps he realized that he had tried to make it serve too many purposes. It may be, also, that *inscape* and *instress*, the new words he began to use, were sufficient. The color/sound analogy, in any case, helped define the characteristics of his distinctive coinages. Inscapes, for example, were diatonic; these marked, distinctive patterns were identified by Hopkins as dramatic exceptions to the usual flow of sensations in nature or art (see p. 73). Earlier at Oxford, he had described such phenomena as "certain forms which have a great hold on the mind and are always reappearing and seem imperishable." In his lectures on rhetoric, given at Roehampton in 1873–74, he attributed "brilliancy, starriness, quain, margaretting" to diatonic rhythm. These were words he usually associated with his perceptions of inscape and instress. "Swiss trees," he wrote in 1868, "are well inscaped—in quains" or wedge shapes. The "brilliancy, sort of starriness" of the instress of Stonyhurst primroses is "remarkable," he observed in 1871. Three years later, at a Royal Academy show in London, he noticed the "richness and grace" of a picture frame "margaretted with round arabesques in black," but "after much looking" he "did not find much inscape" in these sinuous lines of black beads.

Inscape and Wordsworth's "Spots of Time"

Wordsworth's "spot of time," an emotionally charged, significant incident, is the likeliest major literary forerunner of Hopkins' inscape, a pattern or shape perceived, often dramatically, against the backdrop of the natural world. In *The Prelude* Wordsworth designated as "spots of time" the "moments . . . scattered everywhere," especially in youth, which "retain / A renovating virtue," enabling the mind to be "nourished and invisibly repaired." In this autobiographical poem he recalled one such "spot of time" vividly. While quite young, he was riding in the Cumberland hills when suddenly he came upon the mysteriously carved letters of the name of a local murderer. Because of local superstition, this patch of ground was always kept clear of grass. His discomfort was reinforced by the perception of a girl on the hill above, who "seemed with difficult steps to force her way / Against the blowing wind." Although it was an "ordinary sight," this "spot of time" became invested with a "visionary dreariness" that remained with him long afterwards.

In 1865 Hopkins had read J. C. Shairp's essay on Wordsworth's "spots of time," which Shairp published in the *North British Review* in 1864 and reprinted in his *Studies in Poetry and Philosophy* in 1868. Wordsworth's tendency, Shairp stated, was to use an "ideal light" to bring out "vividly the real heart of nature, the inmost feeling, which is really there, and is recognized by Wordsworth's eye in virtue of the kinship between nature and his soul." Hopkins copied out this key passage from Shairp:

> Each scene in nature has in it a power of awakening, in every beholder of sensibility, an impression peculiar to itself, such as no other scene can exactly call up. This may be called the "heart" or "character" of that scene. It is quite analogous to, if somewhat vaguer than, the particular impression produced upon us by the presence of each individual man. Now the aggregate of the impressions produced by many scenes in nature, or rather the power in nature on a large scale of producing such impressions; is what, for want of another name, I have called the "heart" of nature.

Shairp, "for want of another name," should simply have used Wordsworth's "spot of time." Hopkins would have called that "impression peculiar" to "each scene in nature" inscape and the "power in nature . . . of producing such impressions" instress.

These coinages were the intellectual product of Hopkins' Oxford years, although as some of the quotations above indicate, he enthusiastically applied them to his observations of nature during the Stonyhurst years. The lovely and dramatic Lancashire countryside around Stonyhurst is more than sufficient reason for the "rambles of a naturalist" like Hopkins; but Stonyhurst was a sophisticated center of Victorian science as well. The speculations of his Oxford years easily found practical application as Hopkins wandered the Stonyhurst area, which included the Ribble Valley beneath the relatively low but rugged Pendle Hill, and made observations or even used the latest scientific apparatus of Stonyhurst Observatory.

Inscape, instress, and eventually another new word, *scape,* were not used in Hopkins' writings until 1868, the year after he left Oxford, but they represent tentative solutions to problems in epistemology that had been his concern for the three years he spent studying for Greats. The empiricists, he wrote in an unpublished essay in 1866, cannot explain why they focus on seeing and hearing only. He asked: "The sensations of the eye are given in space, those of the ear in time: why not a new form for each of the senses?" This "new form for each of the senses" became *scape,* roughly equivalent to an image of visual perception; at first Hopkins tended to use the two words synonymously. A word, he wrote in "Notes on the History of Greek Philosophy," conveys an "image (of sight or sound or *scapes* of the other senses)."

As his need for a term that would encompass a greater range of experience than *sensation* grew, Hopkins began to use *scape* to refer to an image that could be recalled and recreated in prose, poetry, or a sketch. In late December 1869, during his novitiate at Roehampton, he had been listening to the rector, Peter Gallwey, discuss methods of meditation, using the apostles as examples. As he listened, he was daydreaming. With his eyes closed he could nevertheless "see" an image of one of the apostles superimposed upon the image of a piece of wood. He had not consciously called up the image of the piece of wood and in fact only later remembered where he had seen it. It was like those "things which produce dead impressions, which the mind, either because you cannot make them out or because they were perceived across more engrossing thoughts, has made nothing of and brought into no scaping, that force themselves up in this way afterwards." "Scaping," the perception of form or shape, has been

Spectral Numbers

In 1887 Manley Hopkins, Gerard's father, published a popular account of mathematics and related topics called *The Cardinal Numbers.* The father included his son's account of what he called spectral numbers, numerals of different sizes and colors perceived across the "real" field of vision. These spectral numbers were quite like Hopkins' "dream images." This was one of Hopkins' rare appearances in print outside of *Nature.* He was simply following up a matter that had been taken up by Francis Galton in the pages of *Nature* in 1880 as an investigation of what Galton had called visualized numerals.

Galton's own busy "budget" (to use the Victorian term), a compendium of psychic probes and experiments titled *Inquiries into Human Faculty and Its Development* (1883), continued this investigation and added many more speculative and unusual forays, such as the "history of twins" and "color associations," that Hopkins would have appreciated. Hopkins called the engravings of the "visionary" numbers in Galton's book "very fantastic and interesting." They depicted the visions of the daughter of the novelist Charles Kingsley, Rosa Kingsley, who contributed a diagonal staircase of numbers from zero to one hundred, "with 40–50 in flaming orange; 50–60 in green," and so on. She was joined by Reverend George Henslowe, a student of Goethean botany, who saw a single red tulip become a double flower, then—as it lost its petals—watched it change into a rack of branched horns and finally a walking stick, all handsomely imagined and drawn.

Hopkins described his own "patterns" of numbers in his father's book. His smaller numbers were leaning. The higher numbers were in a "reach" or place of their own: "A million is in a clear light, far off, on the left. Still farther, and behind, scattered over a sort of vague landscape, are billions, trillions, and the rest—all to the left, in blocks, not in lines." Even Hopkins' number visions were Catholic and Dantean: "On the left of number *one* are a few minus numbers, and below it, swarms of fractions. The place where these appear is gloomy grass."

Unfortunately for Hopkins and his father a reviewer for *Nature* was not amused. He ignored the son's contributions and called into question most of the father's. He added that there would be no readers waiting impatiently for a second edition.

delayed, as the "dead impressions" of the piece of wood have not yet been organized into a perceptible form. Hopkins called them "dream-images," "brought upon that dark field" of the "shut eyelids" by a "reverse action of the visual nerves (the same will hold of the sounds, sensations of touch, etc. of dreams)." On other occasions he "imagined" related kinds of images—conjured up without an object to refer to—and called them "spectral numbers" (see p. 75).

In other instances where Hopkins used *scape* in his journals, we would most likely use the term *afterimage*. In June 1873 he recorded in his journals this observation of what he at first thought was a meteor that traveled from the near, or Stonyhurst, side of Pendle Hill and disappeared, after passing above the nearby village of Mitton, over the far side of the hill: "At two minutes to ten at night a greenish white meteor fell with a slow curve from right to left between this and Pendle over Mitton. I judged so because it seemed to pass this side of the crest of the hill but only a little way and then disappeared, so that perhaps I might be mistaken." The next night Hopkins realized that it had really been a piece of fireworks, as another fell, "but its seeming to pass the crest of Pendle is curious." He analyzed it as an afterimage phenomenon: "It may be because the eye taking up the well-marked motion and forestalling it carries the bright scape of the present and past motion (which lasts 1/8 of a second, they say) on to a part of the field where the motion itself has not or will not come." In effect the mind perceived a motion that did not in fact exist, by "creating" an afterimage of the fireworks passing "the crest of Pendle."

In July Hopkins described the lightning associated with a dramatic thunderstorm, which the local Lancashire folk regarded as uniquely "bright and terrible": "Flashes lacing two clouds above or the cloud and the earth started upon the eyes in live veins of rincing or riddling liquid white, inched and jagged as if it were the shivering of a bright riband string which had once been kept bound round a blade and danced back into its pleatings." The result? "Dull furry thickened scapes" of the forks of lightning were left after the alternating series of "strong thrills of light" and a "grey smother of darkness" affected the eyes.

Hopkins did not always need his new words for scientific observations. He was capable of observing natural phenomena with virtually the same eye to detail as the professional Stonyhurst scientists. Hopkins' prose has been widely praised in our time for its extravagant and revealing descriptive power, but we need to remember that elaborate and often metaphorical language was typical of much Victorian scientific writing, especially in meteorology and astronomy, both of which depended at that time on precise word painting. For example, on October 25, 1870, Hopkins saw at Stonyhurst a particularly striking manifestation of the aurora borealis or northern lights:

> A little before 7 in the evening a wonderful Aurora, the same that was seen at Rome (shortly after its seizure by the Italian government) and taken as a sign of God's anger.

He first sets the event in contemporary Catholic history: soon after the Vatican Council was adjourned, Rome was "invaded" by Garibaldi's forces. He then describes the aurora metaphorically:

> It gathered a little below the zenith, to the S.E. I think—a knot or crown, not a true circle, of dull blood-colored horns and dropped long red beams down the sky on every side, each impaling its lot of stars. An hour or so later its color was gone but there was still a pale crown in the same place: the skies were then clear and ashy and fresh with stars and there were flashes of or like sheet-lightning.

Perry and his associates at the observatory published a description of the same aurora in their national *Meteorological Report.* The professional scientists begin with more detail in terms of scientific data (time, compass direction, sky location):

> At 5:50 p.m. on the 25th, a band of red light forming a perfect arch was seen, the top slightly N of the Zenith, and resting E and W on the Horizon. In a few minutes the top of the arch was S of the Zenith, the western extremity fading and the eastern becoming brighter. At 5:55 streamers appeared to radiate from a point near β Cygni to 10° S of the Zenith. In the E a large patch remained intensely red, the rest faded gradually. At 6:25 it again burst forth with increased splendor covering almost the whole sky. The color was red, with the exception of a bright white streamer, which stretched from the radiating point near Cygnus to within 20° of the NNW horizon, where it was obscured by a bank of cloud.

With the exception of the star designations (β Cygni is the second brightest star in the constellation known as the Swan, just as β is the second letter in the Greek alphabet), Hopkins and the observatory staff proceed in similar ways. As the *Meteorological Report* continues, the use of metaphor increases:

> At 9:40 the white streamers were abruptly terminated by an arch extending E and W, and passing nearly through α Andromedae. The wave like motion of the streamers was instantly stopped on reaching this arch, and for a considerable time the rolling streams of light so suddenly checked, presented the appearance of a sea breaking on a level sandy shore.

A contemporary chromolithograph of a drawing of this October 25 aurora, available in J. Rand Capron's *Aurorae: Their Characters and Spectra* (1879), clearly corroborates the accuracy of both Hopkins and the observatory staff.

When Hopkins did use his new words, for observations of other transitory but striking phenomena, he became more evaluative and personal. Coggia's Comet appeared dramatically over England on July 12, 1874, and on a number of other nights that July:

> The comet—I have seen it at bedtime in the west, with head to the ground, white, a soft, well-shaped tail, not big: I felt a certain awe and instress, a feeling of strangeness, flight (it hangs like a shuttlecock at the height, before it falls), and of threatening.

Norman Lockyer, the editor of *Nature,* recorded his observations of Coggia's Comet for the London *Times.* His comments and his sketch of the comet as seen through a refracting telescope were published in *Nature:*

> Perhaps I can give the best idea of the appearance of the bright head in Mr. Newell's telescope, with a low power, by asking the reader to imagine a lady's fan opened out (160°) until each side is almost a prolongation of the other.

He then offered a comparison with another well-known contemporary comet:

> Now, if this comet, outside the circular outline of the fan, offered indications of other similar concentric circular outlines, astronomers would have recognized in it a great similarity to Donati's beautiful comet of 1858 with its "concentric envelopes."

Instead of "concentric envelopes," he saw "excentric" patterns that looked like "ears." "Such 'ears,'" Lockyer continued, "are to be observed in the comet, and they at times are but little dimmer than the fan." After continuing at greater length and with what would be considered greater scientific detail, he concluded that this event was a "magnificent and truly wonderful sight." For Hopkins the "awe and instress" of Coggia's Comet was a recognition of God's creative power in the universe, a belief that Lockyer might personally have shared but would not publicly have stated. Nonetheless, both accounts develop in part metaphorically. In modern terms Hopkins may be considered the smoother writer, for he has not mixed his metaphors quite as much as Lockyer; in any case, he was certainly ready to try his hand at more public scientific writing.

Evening Rays

Hopkins' first residence at Stonyhurst, his philosophate, ended in August 1873, when he was assigned to teach rhetoric at Manresa House, Roehampton, just south of London, where he had already served his novitiate from 1868 to 1870. The next decade, from 1873 through 1882, saw him assigned to numerous posts, most of them less than congenial and some, like St. Aloysius in Oxford, quite frustrating. This was a decade of intense religious and philosophical work for Hopkins and his friends in the Jesuits, and I have reserved the following chapter for a discussion of this period. But in order to show some of the continuity of his scientific work, culminating in two of the four letters he published in *Nature* in the 1880s, I shall now take up his observations of crepuscular or evening rays, which in the nineteenth century were called *rayons du crépuscule*. The precise extent to which contact with Stonyhurst scientists during his first residency there in the 1870s or his second one in the 1880s may have sharpened or developed his scientific skills is difficult to say. The fact remains that eventually he published four sophisticated pieces of analysis in the form of letters to *Nature*, a form also used by Stonyhurst scientists. Professional scientists, of course, would have supplemented such letters with further reports, published articles, and public presentations—modes significantly beyond the ability of amateur scientists like Hopkins (see pp. 80–81).

Rayons du crépuscule are an effect of reflected sunlight under certain conditions, some objective, others subjective. The result, with some

The Difference between Amateur and Professional Science: Tyndall and the White Rainbow

During a Christmas-day walk near Haslemere, Surrey, in 1883, John Tyndall and his wife observed a white rainbow, also known as Ulloa's Bow (named after the Spanish soldier who first described it). Tyndall wrote in his journal: "We walked along the new Portsmouth road accompanied by the bow which spanned the Punch Bowl. There was no color, but a distinct band of light on the outer circumference of which I noticed a slight ruddiness. We went up to the old Portsmouth road and, with a space of dark heather in front of us, Louisa exclaimed, 'The bow forms a circle meeting at my feet.' And there sure enough it was—the portion projected against the heather being very feeble but distinct."

Tyndall noted further that "had we not been working at the subject previously we should not have noticed it was a bow." This previous preparation included extensive laboratory and field research on the "two great standing enigmas of meteorology—the color of the sky and the polarisation of its light." His work was reported in a classic paper, "On Chemical Rays and the Structure and Light of the Sky" (1869), where he outlined his creation in the laboratory of experimental vapors that acted as miniature prisms refracting white light and his use of the Nicol prism on Primrose Hill, London, which demonstrated that the blue light of the heavens was polarized. It was this research that confirmed for many scientists a few years later that the spectacular sunsets of 1883–84 were the result of finely dispersed volcanic matter from the Krakatoa eruptions. Further preparation included his generous critique of Goethe's theory of color and light, delivered in 1880 at London's Royal Institution, where he nevertheless found few supporters of Goethe's ideas.

The immediate result of his and his wife's observations was an addendum to his long study of the rainbow and its "congeners" or similar phenomena, which he also delivered as a lecture at the Royal Institution in 1884. He drew on his journal directly, reworking the original entry to make it a little less personal. Louisa became his "companion," for example, but the major changes were additions. He briefly developed the history of various analyses of the white rainbow and more extensively explained how, back at his laboratory, he began experiments using the spray producer "employed to moisten the air in the Houses of Parliament" to recreate the white bow and other unusual solar phenomena.

Finally he popularized some of his findings in two places: his travel essays, including "Life in the Alps" (1887), and the letters column of the London *Times* (1888). The latter generated responses not only in the *Times* but in *Nature,* as other scientists, amateur and professional, contributed their own views on the white bow. Thus a cycle of scientific discourse, from journal writing to scientific papers to public response, was completed.

It was at this last stage of the cycle, in the letters column of *Nature,* that Hopkins himself intervened in the debates about *rayons du crépuscule.* It was the appropriate and inevitable stage for an amateur scientist, but, we should add, a limited one. Like Hopkins, Tyndall spent numerous weekends walking in the fields and recording his perceptions of nature in his (as-yet-unpublished) journals. But unlike Hopkins, Tyndall made extensive reviews of the scientific literature associated with the physics of light, carried out experiments in the lab and the field, and shared his theories with colleagues both at conferences and through extended scientific essays.

variations, is a dramatic pattern of alternating dark and light bands. The most commonly seen variation has been nicknamed Jacob's Ladder, in which sunbeams are separated by gaps in low clouds and are rendered visible because of dust or water particles in the air. (This is also called "sun drawing water.") The variations that Hopkins observed and studied over the years involve alternating white or light-colored beams and darker beams or streaks, which are shadows of clouds or even hills.

As early as July 1865 Hopkins had been fascinated by this phenomenon. In a drawing on a page of his early notebooks he noted "pale purple clouds with mysterious rosy edges, the coming between of which caused the spokes of light on the cloud." He repeats the drawing, becoming more assertive about the phenomenon but not yet naming it: "The clouds in the horizon caused the spokes." It may have been the patches of color that led him in the next few years to identify the phenomenon with rainbows, for he noted three years later, in 1868, that on a misty late afternoon in the hills of the Black Forest he saw "a low rainbow" crossed by "rays of shadow . . . and where they crossed it paled the color." He concluded that it was a "blue bow," echoing both a line from Shakespeare's *Tempest*, "with each end of thy blue bow" (4.1.80), and his own observations, made the preceding year at home in Highgate, of a rainbow dominated by the "deepest expression of color" in its "blue band edged by and ending in violet."

At Stonyhurst, looking towards Pendle Hill, Hopkins again recorded the phenomenon on May 24, 1871, identifying it once more with a rainbow:

> It was a glowing yellow sunset. . . . Now where a strong shadow lay in a slack between the two brows of Pendle appeared above the hill the same phenomenon I had seen twice before (once near Brussels), a wedge of light faintly edged, green on the right side, red on the left, as a rainbow would be, leaning to the right and skirting the brow of the hill with a glowing edge.

As he continued to observe, he tried to discover the true or "native" color of the phenomenon:

> Later when it was growing dark and the glow of the sunset was quite gone I noticed to the right of the spot a little—over Whalley—a rack of red cloud floating away, the red being I am persuaded a native color, in fact it could not have been borrowed, the sun having long set and the higher clouds behind it not having it.

Although the similarities between this phenomenon and the rainbow continued to distract Hopkins from correctly interpreting it, the blue and red tinges that he observed are in fact characteristic, according to the *Observer's Handbook* of the British Meteorological Office, of two of the three main classes of *rayons du crépuscule.* (Jacob's Ladder, the third class, does not usually have color.)

Within the year, however, Hopkins had begun to see the phenomenon as merely "rainbow-like." While on an evening walk near Bursledon, Hampshire, on September 17, he noticed the rays in the east:

> First definitely adverted to the V-shaped appearance in the sky opposite the sunset, the Ploughtail. The stilts seem on this side of the clouds when there

> are clouds. This day there were none and they were bars of dull blue. Now it seemed to me that as the sun sank lower beneath the horizon they fell over to the right, the south, which would agree with their being polar to the sun, which goes northwards by night as he souths by day, and adds weight to the reality of the phenomenon. And is not the rainbow-like phenomenon of May 24 the end of one of the stilts?

His final entry on the phenomenon in the journals came as he walked on the downs at Little Haldon near Dartmoor in August 1874:

> The distance, especially westward over Dartmoor, was dim and dark, some rain had fallen and there were fragments of a rainbow but a wedge of sunlight streamed down through a break in the clouds upon the valley: a hawk also was hanging on a hover.—I clearly saw then and also yesterday what I was once doubtful of at Bursledon—beams rising from the horizon in the east due opposite to the sunset: this was some time before sunset, yesterday was, I think after it. I think they are atmospheric merely.

This last entry was the most confident, although when he wrote his letters to *Nature* about the phenomenon almost ten years later, he slightly altered his interpretation that they were "atmospheric merely."

In 1882, when Hopkins was in the early stages of his second residency at Stonyhurst College—this time as a classics instructor—the columns of *Nature* began filling up with letters reporting unusual and striking solar phenomena. Scientific news in general found its way into reviews and other columns, but the letters section functioned as a kind of bulletin board. J. P. O'Reilly of the Royal College of Science in Dublin reported in July seeing "a sort of halo" of dark beams in the "east-south-east" sky late at night. "All those beams were *dark,*" he emphasized. Within a week another scientist, Sylvanus P. Thompson, then at Glasgow, reported that O'Reilly's "curious halo" was really an example of *rayons du crépuscule,* "frequently visible near sundown in the eastern sky." An astronomer from Shanghai, the Jesuit Marc Dechevrens, who had been trained at the Stonyhurst Observatory during Hopkins' philosophate there in the 1870s, wrote to *Nature* giving examples of *rayons du crépuscule* from the 1870s as well as from the seventeenth century. He "was rather at a loss," however, "to give a more satisfactory explanation" than "that the phenomenon is due to the atmospheric vapor."

Hopkins' two letters appeared a year apart, the first in November

1882. He replied to Dechevrens' observations that he had "several times" seen the "beams or spokes in the eastern sky about sunset, springing from a point opposite the sun." But the bulk of his letter concerned the process of perceiving such phenomena:

> There seems no reason why the phenomenon should not be common, and perhaps if looked out for it would be found to be. But who looks east at sunset? Something in the same way everybody has seen the rainbow; but the solar halo, which is really commoner, few people, not readers of scientific works, have ever seen at all. The appearance in question is due to cloud-shadows in an unusual perspective and in a clear sky; now shadow may not only be seen carried by misty, mealy, dusty, or smoky air near the ground, but even on almost every bright day, by seemingly clear air high overhead.

Hopkins then turned explicitly to Dechevrens' letter:

> Therefore, if this sunset phenomenon is much commoner in China, there must one would think, be some other reason for it than the sky of England is not heavily charged enough with vapor to carry shadow. Rather it is too much charged, and the edge of the shadow becomes lost with distance and with the thickening of the air towards the horizon before the convergence of the beams eastwards is marked enough to catch the eye.

"But who looks east at sunset?" Presumably only naturalists and poets!

Hopkins' second letter was much shorter and somewhat less scientific, more like his poetry and metaphorical prose: "Yesterday the sky was striped with cirrus cloud like the swaths of a hayfield; only in the east there was a bay or reach of clear blue sky, and in this the shadow-beams appeared, slender, colorless, and radiating every way like a fan wide open." Emphasizing that the phenomenon depended on the position of the observer, Hopkins said that it was "merely an effect of perspective but a strange and beautiful one." This careful analysis of the observer's subjectivity forms an important part of Hopkins' third and fourth letters to *Nature*, on the sunsets and other solar phenomena associated with the Krakatoa volcanic eruptions; but because these letters form a later part of a much more complex web of scientific assertion and discussion, I shall discuss them separately in chapter 5. During the 1870s, however, Hopkins' scientific interests inevitably mixed and sometimes clashed with larger trends in the scientific community outside the Jesuits.

4 The Stonyhurst Philosophers

In addition to the truth of the doctrine of evolution, one of its greatest merits in my eyes, is the fact that it occupies a position of complete and irreconcilable antagonism to the vigorous and consistent enemy of the highest intellectual, moral, and social life of mankind, the Catholic Church.

—T. H. Huxley quoted by John Rickaby

The "Plunge" into the Jesuits

The major Catholic event of the Victorian era was the Vatican Council of all the bishops of the Church, a meeting that codified as religious law the main theological and organizational ideas of Pius IX. The council convened in 1869 and adjourned a year later. The planning for the sessions and the debates themselves thus overlapped Hopkins' reception into the Catholic Church, his novitiate at Roehampton, and part of his philosophate at Stonyhurst. Catholics everywhere—Jesuits in particular, as we shall see—followed the controversial topics of the council, such as papal infallibility, with great interest. But the truly volatile Catholics were in the streets of Rome during the council. When one rebel inside the hall, Bishop Strossmayer of Germany, objected to Protestants being blamed for "systematic monstrosities" of radical thought and suggested that even the ideas of a freethinker like Leibniz or an anti-Jesuit church historian like Guizot were of value, a large number of his fellow bishops began shouting, "We condemn them all!" Some of the crowd in the streets, hearing an uproar, thought that Garibaldi and his satanic Red Shirts had broken into the hall in a drive to seize Rome. Others thought that the key doctrine of the council had finally been passed and started shouting, "Long live the infallible pope!" Both groups were wrong only temporarily: soon the Pope would be infallible, and soon Garibaldi would threaten Rome.

The English Jesuits, like other more philosophical Catholics, took the excitement of the council in stride. Nevertheless the political implications of the first Vatican Council were important to the English Jesuits, whose tenure on English soil had been problematic ever since the sixteenth century, when Jesuits such as Edmund Campion and Robert Southwell were martyred. Throughout the nineteenth century, Jesuits were still publicly vilified as agents of the Pope. In 1874 Hopkins spoke at the St. Beuno's debating club in support of a successful motion that addressed Prime Minister Gladstone's attack on papal infallibility as being incompatible with an Englishman's loyalty to the state. Hopkins' team argued that "in the present contest between Gladstone and Rome" Catholics had to face the matter squarely and accept that "the position of Catholics has been in no wise changed by the decrees of the Vatican Council," despite the dangers of such a belief's "being liable to misrepresentation."

The doctrine of papal infallibility holds that on matters of Church dogma, the pope cannot err. It was one of the two most important doctrines that marked the long tenure (1846–78) of Pius IX as pope. The other was the doctrine of the Immaculate Conception of Mary, promulgated in 1854. The convening of the Vatican Council, the first such meeting since the Council of Trent in the sixteenth century, was primarily a means of securing ratification of papal infallibility by the collective body of the Church. The Jesuits were part of the Ultramontane or pro-Roman majority of the Catholic hierarchy, who argued that both doctrines had been part of Catholic tradition for centuries. The potential for a papal dictatorship was contested by the minority or liberal wing of the Church, represented in England by Newman (not yet a cardinal) together with his supporters and kindred spirits and in continental Europe by the "Gallican opposition," the strong, independent French Church. For these groups the Immaculate Conception of Mary was one thing, an infallible pope quite another. A select number of Jesuits who took a fourth vow of direct obedience to the pope were bound by duty to defend the decisions of the Vatican Council.

Throughout 1869 and 1870 Hopkins and his fellow novices heard at refectory (mealtime) all the news of Vatican I published by the major Catholic newspaper in England, *The Tablet,* and in December 1870, as so-called philosophers at Stonyhurst, they were read Cardinal Manning's *The*

Vatican Council . . . A Pastoral Letter, which contained the key decisions of the council. The motion at St. Beuno's that Hopkins favored indicates that the Jesuits were well aware of the political implications of the council. And certainly the doctrines Pius IX insisted on were part of his own political drive to strengthen the papacy and, in particular, his temporal control over the Papal States of Rome in view of the pressures of Garibaldi and the Italian unification movement. But we shall here be concerned mainly with the doctrinal, rather than political, implications of the reign of Pius IX. The doctrine of the Immaculate Conception encouraged deeper study of the Incarnation, while the doctrine of papal infallibility sought to counteract the rise of so-called Protestant rationalism and scientific materialism by establishing a source of absolute truth.

The council passed two "dogmatic constitutions" supported by canon law that were to be enforced by threat of anathema or excommunication. One, *De Ecclesia Christi* ("Concerning the Church of Christ"), defined papal infallibility; the other, of direct interest to scientists and philosophers, was *De Fide Catholica* ("Concerning the Catholic Faith"). Through *De Fide Catholica* the Church hoped to rescue the minds of those who "have sunk into the abyss of Pantheism, Materialism, and Atheism." It reaffirmed Genesis—certainly nothing new—and specifically condemned anyone who would "affirm that except matter, nothing exists" or anyone who would say "that the substance and essence of God and all things is one and the same." Clearly no Catholic could be a follower of Lucretius with respect to these issues. Furthermore, and here I quote the canon law in full, it disallowed one version of evolution:

> If any one shall say that finite things, both corporeal and spiritual, or at least spiritual, have emanated from the divine substance; or that the divine essence by the manifestation and evolution of itself became all things; or, lastly, that God is universal or indefinite being, which by determining itself constitutes the universality of all things, distinct according to genera, species and individuals; let him be anathema.

Despite the arcane language, the message was clear: a theory suggesting that God did not create everything from nothing would be difficult to support without grave consequences. Finally, the council reaffirmed the central role of miracles, a decision that would disturb British scientists as much as the decision on evolution:

> If any one shall say that miracles are impossible, and therefore that all the accounts regarding them, even those contained in Holy Scripture, are to be dismissed as fabulous or mythical; or that miracles can never be known with certainty, and that the divine origin of Christianity cannot be proved by them; let him be anathema.

In the decades following Vatican I, significant and substantial philosophical work, often in large part a continuation of council's decisions, was carried out by four English Jesuits: the brothers Rickaby (Joseph and John), Richard F. Clarke, and Herbert Lucas. All of these Jesuits were Hopkins' friends and associates, and their work in many cases paralleled Hopkin's own interests. I call this group the Stonyhurst Philosophers, in part because this was the actual designation they received in the second stage or philosophate of their Jesuit training at St. Mary's Hall at Stonyhurst, and in part because in their mature years several of them not only became professors of philosophy at Stonyhurst but also launched the Stonyhurst Philosophical Series of texts on theology, logic, and epistemology. Like Hopkins, the Stonyhurst Philosophers were all recent Catholics, converts or the sons of converts. They were in agreement with one of the key themes of Hopkins' Oxford Essays, that contemporary philosophers, under the guise of scientific objectivity, had established materialism as the only issue for metaphysics. At Oxford Hopkins had identified two principal antagonists. The Stonyhurst Philosophers eventually criticized the atomists, Hopkins' main target, who held that the ultimate stuff of both body and mind was purely physical, and the positivists, followers of Comte, who argued that only the knowledge of phenomena, and not of their ultimate cause or purpose, was possible.

Not by coincidence Hopkins' philosophate turned out to be in good measure a continuation of the major issues in Oxford philosophy of the 1860s. As Huxley and Tyndall became more and more successful in presenting Darwin's ideas and their own vision of a materialist science, the English Jesuits stepped up their attacks on atomism and positivism. At Oxford in 1868, in his essay "The Probable Future of Metaphysics," Hopkins had called for a "new school of metaphysics" formed from "some shape of the Platonic Ideas" to meet the challenge of atomism. In 1874 his Stonyhurst colleague and friend, Richard F. Clarke, announced in an essay in *The Month,* "On Analogy," that he and others of "the metaphysical school" were especially on the alert to counter the positivists. Hopkins' and Clarke's use of the same phrase symbolizes a shared, if implicit, set of philosophical goals that were not simply imposed on Hopkins and his colleagues by the rigors of Jesuit training but that grew out of their common engagement with fundamental problems concerning the relationship of science and philosophy in the 1860s and 1870s.

Hopkins and his colleagues had mentors within the Jesuit order; the Stonyhurst Philosophers continued the work of a number of strong leaders and intellectuals, most of whom had been their and Hopkins' superiors at one time or another. This senior group also consisted of converts, and with one exception (John Morris) all were Oxford converts. These older Jesuits, almost all of whom were associated with Stonyhurst as well, had already begun the struggle for a new Catholic philosophy. Thomas Harper was professor of philosophy at Stonyhurst in the 1870s; John Morris was professor of Church history and canon law at Stonyhurst; Edward Purbrick was rector of Stonyhurst in the 1870s and later head or Father Provincial of the English Province of the Jesuits; and Henry Coleridge was editor of *The Month* and probably the first Jesuit Hopkins ever met.

Because these two generations of English Jesuits had strong ties to Oxford, they shared Hopkins' concern, often expressed in his letters, for their Puseyite and High Anglican friends who had come close to converting but for one reason or another had not done so or, in some cases, had backslid. Coleridge was at Balliol in the 1840s and was a slightly late convert to Newman's Oxford Movement. In his "Personal Recollections of an Old Oxonian," published in *The Month* in 1866, he talked openly of those men of the Balliol common room who did become Catholics and those who did not. The latter, he opined, should have become Jesuits or Dominicans because "those who had in them the making of saints . . . have been dwarfed for want of room to expand." Such men, with "simple-minded and generous" hearts, often "touched by the recital of misfortune, and moved to the most self-denying sacrifices for its relief," had become Protestant rectors rather than Catholic Missionaries of Charity.

Coleridge's memories of potential converts who had slipped away were emotional. Richard F. Clarke's meditation on his days of conversion in the 1860s was more intellectual. When he came to write his volume for the

Stonyhurst Philosophical Series, *Logic* (1889), he emphasized that he knew from personal experience how important a Catholic text would be:

> Converts to the Catholic Church trained in the English colleges and universities have unconsciously drunk in a number of principles, some true, some false, from their earliest years, and are often not a little puzzled to discern the true from the false. Perhaps in their early days Hamilton and Jevons, Mansel or Veitch, had represented to them the orthodox school, and Mill and Spenser and Hegel a more consistent and at the same time more sceptical system.

Clarke realized that many of these young converts had just recently wrestled with Jevons or one of the other guides as they crammed for Greats or the Cambridge University equivalent. He would provide a guide to these "rival claimants" for truth.

The keynote of Clarke's preface was really scepticism. In a series of essays on Catholics at Oxford for *The Month,* he analyzed the period from 1860 to 1885, when many men had come to Oxford to read for honors but had "fallen under the influence of sceptical teachers and sceptical books." At first the students arrived "full of religious enthusiasm and High Church notions and practices." Physically they settled close to Canon Liddon at Christ Church, while spiritually they were "determined adherents of the Catholic view of Anglicanism." These pathetic sheep were soon lost, however, for Oxford tutors knew that "however enthusiastic at first," these students would soon fall away "when they began to read for Greats, and modern philosophy imbued them with ideas directly or indirectly subversive of the opinions of their early days." Clarke named only one name, Mark Pattison, rector of Lincoln College, but alert readers familiar with Oxford might venture to guess that he also meant tutors like Walter Pater and T. H. Green and professors like Max Müller, all of whom embraced at least one of the "fashionable" forms of paganism on Clarke's inventory: "Agnosticism, Buddhism, Comtism, Hegelianism." It was really, he argued, a very short step from scepticism to agnosticism. The difference between the Oxford of the 1840s and the Oxford of the 1880s was that the latter "had lost its hold on the supernatural."

How did Hopkins avoid such a misstep? He had contact with the intellectual pagans Clarke feared. He walked the very paths Coleridge outlined. Yet his journey from Oxford to Stonyhurst exemplifies that of a young man who successfully, in Catholic terms, avoided the pitfalls Coleridge and Clarke described. Outwardly Hopkins' passage from the 1860s to the 1870s appears radically discontinuous; but there was a natural progression in his philosophical and scientific interests. The transition from the aesthetic and High Church undergraduate world of Oxford to the intensely ascetic novitiate at the Jesuits' Manresa House in Roehampton was no doubt eased by Hopkins' nine-month teaching stint at Newman's Oratory School near Birmingham. Whether Hopkins and Newman both knew this to be only a way station on Hopkins' road to the priesthood or whether Hopkins was not yet suited for a teaching post has been a matter of debate. In any case, after a tour of Switzerland with his friend Ed Bond—Hopkins knew that a Jesuit could not legally travel there—he entered the first stage of his long training to become a Jesuit.

Hopkins' decision to join the Jesuits caused some tremors at Oxford. His philosophical contacts at Oxford fall roughly into three groups: the Platonists, specifically those in Jowett's domain at Balliol; antiempiricists like Green (regarded by many as a sceptic); and aesthetes like Pater (with his atomist metaphysics). Despite Hopkins' close academic contact with Jowett and Pater, his social life was also tied to Green's circle of students, in particular R. L. Nettleship, eventually a fellow of Balliol, and Henry Scott Holland, eventually canon of St. Paul's. In December 1868, Nettleship and Holland had received a rare invitation to a reading or study "party" with Green at Shanklin on the Isle of Wight. On their return trip to Oxford they visited Hopkins at Roehampton. Holland and Green exchanged letters about that visit. The vehemence of Green's letters to Holland together with Nettleship's professed interest in working among the poor in the East End of London suggest that Oxford may have come close to losing several more of her sons to the Church of Rome.

Green's and Hopkins' relationship had a curiously circular quality to it (see p. 92). When Hopkins joined the Jesuits, Green said that he "liked" Hopkins "very much" but "never had his intimacy." In his early days at Oxford Hopkins sent a scathing note to his mother about a "wicked" act: a beech in the Balliol quad had been cut down, "its destruction . . . owing to the Fellows Green and Newman. The former is of a rather offensive style of infidelity, and naturally dislikes the beauties of nature." This emotional reaction was tempered by a more considered judgment

T. H. Green on the Incarnation

After leaving Oxford Hopkins' contact with Green was minimal; yet both men, from quite different religious orientations, held remarkably similar views on the Incarnation. Perhaps some cross-fertilization took place, or it may be simply that minds trained in Oxford philosophy and logic approached a problem in similar ways.

Hopkins believed that the Incarnation was "prior" to the creation of the angels and human beings. This Scotist view contradicted the idea that the Incarnation became necessary because of the Fall of the angels and humans. Christopher Devlin, the editor of Hopkins' religious writings, called Hopkins' interpretation his "most startling and original theological innovation": Hopkins "split" the great declaration of St. John—"The Word was made Flesh / and came to dwell among us"—into two events. The first event Hopkins called *ensarkōsis,* "the taking of flesh," which represented Christ's "entry as a creature into the angelic world." The second event was *enanthropēsis,* "the becoming man," which represented the historical Christ's entry into human time.

Green ended up with views close to Hopkins', although the professor of moral philosophy certainly didn't begin there. In the 1870s Green's teachings had taken on a more sceptical cast, as he sought a spiritual role for Christianity to replace the historical reality he doubted. Arnold Toynbee, Green's student and friend, described Green's desire to fix "an intellectual position for the Christian faith which should not be called in question by every advance in historical evidence and in physical science." Toynbee concluded, perhaps with irony, that while "other thinkers have assailed the orthodox foundations of religion to overthrow it, Mr. Green assailed them to save it."

Green lectured on the Fourth Gospel of John in the mid-1870s. Balliol undergraduates heard him say that the clause "the Word became Flesh" did not mean that the Word "became human," since Christ in his divine and human natures had existed from eternity—more or less the Scotist position. Rather, the clause means that He became "the object of sense, or apprehensible to the senses." Thus when the Apostle says, "we beheld his glory," he means both a "sensuous" seeing and a "spiritual" seeing. Green argued this position convincingly by analyzing the Greek words for "seeing" and "beholding"; but the real issue for him was a "belief in a person now spiritually present to and in us."

of Green almost twenty years later, in 1882, when he wrote to his friend Baillie about Green's death: "I always liked and admired poor Green. He seemed to me upright in mind and life. . . . His fortune fell first on Knox and then on Hegel and he was meant for better things. Probably if he lived longer he would have written something that would have done the same." This, in the end, was a generous assessment for Hopkins to have made, as Green's contemporary reputation as a religious sceptic had hardly changed over the years, whatever his feeling for "the beauties of nature."

Despite this reputation Green did not react to Hopkins' conversion in 1866 and his admission to the Jesuits in 1868 on strictly philosophical grounds. His rather extraordinary remarks about Hopkins came in his reply to a letter from Holland about the Roehampton visit. We have from him more than a simple reaction to Hopkins' decision. Instead we read, perhaps between the lines, of the alternatives available to sensitive, religious Balliol undergraduates like Hopkins, Nettleship, and Holland: "I am glad that you and Nettleship saw Hopkins. A step such as he has taken, though I can't quite admit it to be heroic, must needs be painful, and its pain should not be aggravated—as it is pretty sure to be—by separation from old friends." Green continued, emphasizing Newman's role as a spiritual but somewhat spurious ideal:

> I imagine him [Hopkins]—perhaps inevitably—to be one of these, like his ideal J. H. Newman, who instead of simply opening themselves to the revelation of God in the reasonable world, are fain to put themselves into an attitude—saintly, it is true, but still an attitude. True citizenship "as unto the Lord" (which includes all morality) I reckon higher than "saintliness" in the technical sense. The "superior young man" of these days, however, does not seem to understand it, but hugs his own "refined pleasures" or (which is but a higher form of the same) his personal sanctity. Whence, and not from heterodoxy, ruin threatens Christian society.

Holland and Nettleship, who from all accounts were not so very different from Hopkins as undergraduates, must have reeled a bit when they considered Green's remarks. They doubtless recognized the allusion to the Paterian type of student who "hugs his own 'refined pleasures'"; but what were they to make of Green's cutting remarks about "personal sanctity," surely a common enough ideal in their generation? Holland, with resolute frankness, wrote back to Green that he would "try and digest" these remarks on Hopkins, but that he, Holland, had a "lurking admiration for Jesuitry" and wondered if, given a certain "loyalty to Society," such "institutions of ascetic co-operation" could not supply "some wants of Society."

So bold a confession from Holland provoked a long, impassioned letter from Green. It was Green's version of *askēsis,* discipline or training. He accepted "ascetic co-operation," he wrote, as long as Jesuits or Catholics weren't in charge of it. Instead of their "monastic form," he hoped for a "new Christianity" that would supply "new forms of religious society or a gradual absorption of all such forms in simple religious citizenship." Green must have realized that he was holding out only the vaguest possibility of some future "organization," for he urged the adoption of a "waiting spirit" and "making the best of the institutions among which one finds oneself, to follow the lead of the foremost ideas in the world." In short, although he was not quite this blunt, he was advising his protégés to remain in the monastic imitations known as British colleges. The alternative—Hopkins' attitude of "saintly aspiration" and "a plunge into a society, resting on an untenable theory"—was not acceptable.

Why was Green so vehement? Perhaps it was simply Protestant prejudice against Catholics. Perhaps it was Hopkins' choice of the Jesuits. Or perhaps—and here I believe we are closest to the truth—Green recognized that Hopkins' decisions represented a logical development of certain religious and philosophical tendencies in Balliol undergraduates. Their earnestness, their brilliance, and the search for suitable outlets for their talents would lead many of them out of Oxford into Catholic and—for Green—other unacceptable religious ways.

But Green did not need to fear for Nettleship and Holland. They did not "plunge" into societies "resting" on "untenable" theories. Nettleship became another Green, a hard-working, respectable Oxford philosopher. Holland became a professional Anglican, eventually rising to become canon of St. Paul's. And Green himself? In Mrs. Ward's novel *Robert Elsmere* he became Professor Gray, whose protégé, Elsmere, realizes that "miracles do not happen" and gathers a "new company of Jesus" to work in a poor district of London.

Despite *his* plunge Hopkins retained close emotional and intellectual ties to Oxford. He returned there for one frustrating year as a priest at St. Aloysius, just a five-minute walk from Balliol. He had renewed contact with Pater but, he later regretted, insufficient time with Green. Like many of his fellow converts, he never quite lost the qualities he had developed at Oxford. And Oxford itself retained a powerful hold on these new Catholics. The 1880s witnessed an extended debate among Catholics on the role British universities should play in Catholic higher education. Hopkins' friend Clarke argued for a Catholic presence at Oxford and against setting up separate Catholic universities. Joseph Rickaby, who replaced Clarke as head of the Catholic hall that was finally established at Oxford in 1896, noted that Clarke was a man who still "kept so much of the Oxford manner about him" despite an absence of twenty-six years.

The Stonyhurst Philosophers were thus a generation of Catholic converts who were more than willing to take their chances at Oxford. Their superiors had not necessarily agreed. In 1869 Edward Purbrick used the occasion of his rebuttal in *The Month* to one of Huxley's successful "lay sermons," "On the Physical Basis of Life," to argue against sending Catholic youths to Oxford and other British universities. Huxley's speech, which had been published in the *Fortnightly Review,* was an attempt to refute the charge that he was a materialist, despite his avowed intention to continue using "materialist terminology." This compromise galled Purbrick. Even if Huxley refused to be called a materialist, taking "refuge in absolute scepticism" about knowing anything finally about matter or spirit, he nonetheless taught "the elaboration of thought by a process of molecular change"; he believed, in short, that somehow moving atoms lead to thought. Purbrick did not hesitate, then, to draw his conclusion. Without a Catholic university or at least a Catholic professor at his side, the student would face alone a curriculum that demanded a close and thorough knowledge "of the Mills, the Bains, the Huxleys of the day." Purbrick's view, however, forceful as it was, did not in the end prevail.

With love, then, as well as a certain amount of fear, the Stonyhurst Philosophers and Hopkins maintained a close but critical relationship with Oxford. The core of their concern varied. Sometimes it was scepticism, sometimes materialism, and sometimes even sceptical materialism. All the Stonyhurst Philosophers, with the exception of Hopkins, were prolific published writers. Hopkins, certainly more casually at times, tried his hand at the same topics: Darwinism, free will versus determinism, and of course materialism. They published extensively in *The Month*, which had in 1865 acquired its first Jesuit editor, Henry Coleridge, who remained in charge until he was succeeded in 1881 by Clarke. It was Coleridge who rejected both of Hopkins' shipwreck poems in the 1870s; it was Clarke who published Hopkins' notes and modern English version of a medieval hymn, "Angelus ad Virginem," in 1882.

In addition to their similarities in terms of conversion, Oxford background, and philosophical orientation, Hopkins and his fellow Jesuits formed a distinct social unit within the English Catholic world. They lived in a rigorous and controlled environment, which was designed, Clarke wrote in "The Training of a Jesuit," to foster "that spirit of implicit and unquestioning obedience which is the aim of the Society of Jesus to cultivate more than any other virtue in her sons." At Stonyhurst their theological training was combative, as in an Oxford debating society. The "philosophers" took turns being either exponents of the truth of a Catholic doctrine or the objicients, who "did their best to hunt out difficulties which [might] puzzle" the defenders. The objicients could borrow the sceptical weapons of contemporary philosophers such as Mill or Mansel or elder stalwarts such as Descartes, Locke, or Hegel to strengthen their mock attacks on Catholic doctrine. By this means, Clarke argued, the young Jesuits were provided "with a complete defense against difficulties which otherwise are likely to puzzle the Catholic controversialist." Thus this circle of debate during the Stonyhurst philosophate, coupled with the tradition of daily oral reading at mealtimes of current and timely literature—sometimes articles from the Catholic press and almost always articles from *The Month*—provided Hopkins and his colleagues with a grasp of contemporary problems, both theological and worldly.

During the more advanced or theologate period of his Jesuit training at St. Beuno's, Hopkins also participated in the debating club and the English Academy, a paper-reading club. The records from both indicate his active engagement with philosophy, theology, and science. Hopkins argued, for example, in the debating club in 1874 against the following motion: "Philosophy is more useful against the errors of the day than either science or theology." Two years later, he also argued against the following: "That *The Month* cannot command the influence which is worthy of the Society unless our Scholastics practice theological writing." Hopkins' side lost both motions, no doubt solidifying his reputation as a quixotic but earnest debater. In 1877 speakers at the English Academy took up such subjects as evolution, the nebular or star-cluster theory of creation, and the "claims of primitive man to an earlier age than Adam." It is clear that a Jesuit-in-training could not avoid at least some of the thorniest problems concerning the relationship of science and religion in the Darwinian era. Years later, in 1903, Joseph Rickaby felt that the time devoted to science was nonetheless inadequate. In response to questions about the quality of St. Beuno's theologate, he recommended greater emphasis on "biology exclusively . . . simple but fundamental questions on points vital to psychology and theology, e.g., sensation, infusion of soul, the theory of evolution of species, and perhaps some points touching on moral theology, which a priest ought to know."

Thus the intellectual atmosphere in which these Stonyhurst men lived was potentially as stimulating as that at any British university. They were under the intense strain, both religious and personal, that constitutes life in any restricted and highly disciplined order. Yet, at the same time, they were aware in considerable depth of the major philosophical and scientific problems of the world outside.

The New School of Metaphysics

The primary locus of the Stonyhurst Philosophers' work on contemporary philosophical, theological, and scientific problems in the 1870s and 1880s was *The Month*. Although we shall concentrate on one decade of their lively campaign, the 1870s, we should note that the four principal members of this group contributed almost two hundred fifty essays to *The Month* from 1870 to 1930. All four covered theological subjects in general, but each had specific interests as well. Clarke concentrated on Oxford University: its organization, philosophy (especially the Greeks), and relationship to Catholic education; he also wrote on scepticism generally. Both Rickaby and Lucas wrote on the relationship between science and religion, with Joseph also addressing topics in Greek philosophy while John concentrated his fire on Huxley and the evolutionists. Lucas worked on Huxley, too, as well as on issues in contemporary psychology, especially the problem of free will versus determinism, which Hopkins picked up more privately in the 1880s. Hopkins, who died young, at forty-four, never had the opportunity of a long career, as did his Stonyhurst associates. We have only a partial but significant record of his thoughts on these problems, to which we shall turn in the last two sections of this chapter. The leitmotif of the majority of the Stonyhurst Philosophers' essays in *The Month* was the abuse of rational thought or, in a word, scepticism.

Their recurring targets were Huxley and Tyndall. These two men were the foremost popular speakers on Darwinism and the materialist approach to philosophical problems, they were themselves religiously suspect (although Huxley's famous coinage, *agnosticism,* was not struck publicly until 1889), and they loved good arguments. John Rickaby distilled this list into one statement: the two men exhibited the high "degree of passionate hostility" characteristic of "the way which non-believers approach the question of religion." Huxley had already gained national attention in 1860 when he clashed with Wilberforce. The spark of their meeting had been a relatively innocuous speech by John William Draper, the American evolutionist and positivist. The Stonyhurst Philosophers, however, did not find him so innocuous. Draper's *Human Physiology* (1856), already a standard text in America, was gaining adherents in England, as it promised "to treat physiology as a branch of Physical Science; to exclude from it all purely speculative doctrines and ideas, the relics of a philosophy (if such it can be called) which flourished in the Middle Ages." At Stonyhurst it was indeed "called" philosophy by the Jesuits, whose scholastic approach was founded on the very medieval Thomas Aquinas. One of Huxley's boasts was that he had bested St. George Mivart, the Catholic evolutionist, by using scholastic philosophy to undermine Catholic opinions.

But the events that really brought a Stonyhurst school of metaphysics to life were the keynote speeches made at annual meetings of the BAAS: Huxley's in 1870 and Tyndall's in 1874. Huxley used the occasion of his presidential address to the BAAS in 1870 to reaffirm the "great doctrine of Biogenesis," that life engenders life. But no word with "genesis" as a root could possibly escape controversy in the nineteenth century. In fact "abiogenesis"—life arising from nonliving material, or "spontaneous generation"—had been in the news just a few months before. H. Carlton

Bastian, professor of biology at University College, London, had published a series of articles in *Nature* in which he announced that the spontaneous generation of bacteria inside hermetically sealed containers of fluid had taken place. Bastian classified matter into two forms: crystalline or static and colloidal or dynamic (living). His most important experimental "discovery" was that under certain conditions the crystalline state may change into the colloidal. Huxley and others rushed to demonstrate the flaws in Bastian's experiments, and after a flurry of letters in *Nature*, his work was discredited.

Four years later, in 1874, Tyndall's Belfast Address, as it was soon called everywhere, became more notorious than Huxley's speech, for it raised issues that went beyond the scientific community alone. Tyndall arrayed Darwinism and Lucretian atomism on one side and the formidable Bishop Butler, who argued God's existence from design (e.g., any law that shows symmetry in the universe implies a Law-giver), on the other. F. A. Lange, a German philosopher on whose *History of Materialism* Tyndall relied for a number of his points, returned the compliment in a revealing preface to the English edition of his book:

> Tyndall's Address is, as it were, the official announcement of a new era for England, which plays so important a part in the History of Materialism. The old hollow truce between natural science and theology, which Huxley, and recently Darwin, had seriously shaken, is now broken, and men of science demand their right to follow out in all directions, undisturbed by any subsisting traditions, the consequences of their theory of the world.

Even if we allow for Teutonic exaggeration, Tyndall's speech in effect did to theology what Huxley and Darwin had done to Genesis. Tyndall employed an imaginary dialogue between Lucretius, the prototypical atomist and materialist, and Bishop Butler, the apologist for the orthodox view of divinity. Shrewdly combining the Darwinian hypothesis and atomic theory, Tyndall translated a passage from Lucretius explaining the "natural selection" of atoms:

> The interaction of the atoms throughout infinite time rendered all manner of combinations possible. Of these the fit ones persisted, while the unfit disappeared. Not after sage deliberations did the atoms station themselves in the right places, nor did they bargain what motions they should assume. From all eternity they have been driven together, and after trying motions and

> unions of all kinds, they fell at length into the arrangement out of which this system of things has been formed.

Only a very sleepy delegate that day in Belfast could have missed Tyndall's allusions here to the "survival of the fittest" and the "fortuitous concourse of atoms." And those who read it shortly thereafter—like Hopkins and the Stonyhurst Philosophers—saw it as a defense of a godless cosmogony, reversing Hopkins' remarkable expression "chance left free" but lacking "order" or "purpose."

Certainly the atomist principles by themselves were enough to make Hopkins, as he wrote to his mother soon after the speech was published, "most mad." We do not know the extent to which he exchanged views on Darwinism, Tyndall's speech, or atomism with the Stonyhurst Philosophers. He recorded a walk with Joseph Rickaby the same month as the letter to his mother was written and just a month before Rickaby's careful critique of the Belfast Address, "Professor Tyndall's Inaugural Address," appeared in *The Month.* Rickaby's task was actually made somewhat easier by Tyndall himself, who, despite his obvious preference for Lucretius, had to admit that one of Bishop Butler's major arguments was "unanswerable." How do "molecular processes" give rise to consciousness? The atomist found himself with a terrible dilemma. He had to posit "dead" atoms, "without sensation" and "without intelligence," which nevertheless combine somehow to form "sensation, thought, and emotion." From Lucretius to Newton, mechanical definitions of the universe depended on "such materialism"—an easy target for a clever bishop. Tyndall remained stubborn. He was, if necessary, prepared to "cross the boundary of experimental evidence" to assert that matter is "the promise and potency of terrestrial life."

Tyndall's concessions may have made Rickaby overconfident in his reply. After all, holding contradictory opinions doesn't always mean the loss of important friends. Rickaby tried to be generous. A physicist, he said, may apply the "known laws of mechanics to the atoms"; an evolutionist may argue that "vegetables and animals may have risen out of inorganic matter." But these scientists must recognize that God created atoms and that He created humans in a "supernatural state" as well. Rickaby concluded that the stubborn Tyndall had invited the public to leap over intellectual precipices "in order to come down" on the side of materialism: "There are those of us who would not like to play, Follow the Leader, with the Professor among the Alpine *crevasses;* still more loathe are we to play that game in a region where the chasms are more tremendous, and the leader himself looks afraid." Rickaby was alluding to Tyndall's well-known and generally fearless climbing expeditions in the Swiss Alps. It may remind us that Hopkins and his friend Ed Bond had encountered Tyndall at the Matterhorn six years before. Of this potentially fascinating meeting only a few details have come down to us. Tyndall graciously treated Bond for an illness. Since the next hiking day was Sunday, Tyndall also arranged with his reluctant guide for a very early Mass, which Hopkins attended and which was probably a good idea: Tyndall's subsequent assault on the Matterhorn was successful.

Hopkins' criticisms of Tyndall's ideas were severe, although he found the address "interesting and eloquent." He told his mother that Tyndall refused to clarify either the "obscure origin" of humans or their destiny and, in a cutting remark when directed to a scientist, that "he has no sense of relative weights of authority": "He quotes Draper, Whewell and other respectable writers for or against Aristotle, Bacon, etc. as if it were just the same thing and you were keeping at the same level—the Lord Chief Justice rules this way, his parlormaid however says it should be the other, and so on." Hopkins could not resist, however, an aesthetic response to the closing lines of the address, when Tyndall spoke of the human need for knowledge and creativity, a need that would continue long after he and his listeners, "like streaks of morning cloud, shall have melted into the infinite azure of the past." Hopkins described these last words—"the infinite azure of the past"—as a "fine phrase." And, in a charitable way consistent with his reputation for gentleness, he concluded that, after all, Tyndall had been kind to him and Bond when they had all met fortuitously at the foot of the Matterhorn: "I fear he must be called an atheist but he is not a shameless one: I wish he might come round." Certainly Hopkins was more generous than John Rickaby was with Huxley: when Rickaby reviewed a biography of Huxley in 1901, he wondered if the departed sceptic and agnostic had in the end satisfied his Maker's demands. Rickaby concluded, without optimism, that Huxley may have "in his heart . . . believed enough to have been saved, though to us he has left no record of such sufficiency."

John Rickaby continued his brother's critique of the issues raised by

Tyndall in a series of essays on science and religion for *The Month* in 1877. Two of the essays, "Evolution and Involution" and "The Explanation of Miracles by Unknown Natural Forces," took a relatively liberal approach to difficult problems, given that the Vatican Council's strictures concerning topics such as evolution and miracles were explicit. Both essays attacked contemporary science for its atomist metaphysics and its mechanistic methodology. Rickaby attempted a daring linguistic maneuver by suggesting that there were two concepts we should accept: involution and evolution. Involution was the movement from the heterogeneous and complex to the homogeneous and simple, as in the development of the human tongue, where three different processes—speech, taste, and swallowing—are combined into one organ. Evolution was the countermovement, evident in the development of complex organisms from simpler forms. Here Rickaby again took up the anti-atomist crusade, arguing that it was not yet a "demonstrated truth, that all matter is reducible to one simple, elementary atom, endowed with one simple, elementary force; and that all variety in the material universe is the mere result of [the] combination" of Lucretian atoms. Evolution as an "action" should be recognized, but evolution as a "god" must give way to a Law-giver Who is "behind all laws of matter" and is a "self-existent Being," defined by "certain attributes that are altogether wanting in evolved matter."

Rickaby's appeal from laws to a Law-giver was developed at greater length the following year, 1878, in another series of essays for *The Month*. He used the traditional Argument from Design, updating it ever so slightly from the eighteenth-century debate between the deists, who imagined God as a clockmaker who sets the universe going and then retires, and Bishop Butler. Instead of deists, there now were materialists in Darwinian armor, defending without rigor the idea of the long-ago evolution of life from inorganic matter. (This is indeed a tricky argument, to which we shall return.) No one, Rickaby contended, could prove that "matter is capable of self-organization," since "simple, independent atoms" could never account for the "marvellous complex unity of plan, which is found both in detail and in the universe viewed as a whole."

How could John Rickaby feel it "perfectly logical" to believe in the special creation of Genesis in view of the evidence presented by the evolutionists? If what he called the contemporary "reign of mist" prevented people from seeing that science had usurped the province of philosophy and theology, that was no reason to forget that the Catholic Church had not condemned natural selection (see pp. 104–5). The Church did insist that "molecules of matter are capable of being compounded into live substance under the manipulation of an intelligent being." Actually, Rickaby argued, if he had evidence of God's creation of the ascidians, such as sea squirts, who resemble squash with tentacles, and if the scientists countered with their "proof" that sea squirts and other animals "were evolved from primitive Monera" (protozoa such as the tiny shelled foraminifera ubiquitous on the sea floor), he would still believe in "direct creative interference." Rickaby's examples were carefully chosen. Some of his readers would know that the poor "primitive Monera" were in fact one of Huxley's specialties and were often included in evolutionary debates because their enormous fossil presence encouraged the idea of evolution from the sea. Huxley and Tyndall were victims, Rickaby argued, of sceptical intellects that "confound the intuition of necessary truths with the synchronizing of two series of nerve vibrations." In brief, they understood the mechanics of life but not life itself. They were examples of the "perversion of the intellect."

A strong position, but not unexpected if we consider the great importance Catholics of every era have placed on the intellect in accepting matters of faith. Herbert Lucas' essays in *The Month* took up some of the same questions at his colleagues but from a different angle. He concentrated on the determinism of an atomist approach to psychology and how it invalidated the traditional Christian view of free will. His argument was simple and direct, but he also used contemporary science to back up his claim that "the consenting act of the will is not determined by pre-existing circumstances." No scheme of induction formulated by a Bacon or a Mill could validate the analogy of the determinists, who believed that "because there is uniformity in external nature therefore there is uniformity in the fact of the mind." Even Dr. Alexander Bain, a spokesman for the determinists and one of Mill's heroes, had to admit in his book *Emotions and the Will* that there is "a lurking nest of irregularity" in matters of the will.

Lucas obviously enjoyed this quotation from Bain. Probably with equal pleasure he decided to bring in the determinists' own spokesman, Lucretius, to show the weakness of their position. Metaphysics, after

How "Liberal" Were the English Jesuits?

How liberal was the intellectual atmosphere in the Jesuit order during the 1870s and 1880s? It is difficult to say. One of Hopkins' superiors, Thomas Harper, professor of theology at St. Beuno's in the 1860s and professor of philosophy at Stonyhurst in the 1870s, preached a liberal sermon on the Incarnation in the summer of 1869 at the Farm Street Church of the Immaculate Conception, the central church of the English province. Hopkins was then still at his Roehampton novitiate, just south of the Thames. Harper's attitude on art, for example, was quite enlightened. As a result of the Apostle John's having actually seen and written about the Incarnate Word as Christ, the apostolic record has had a "vital influence on Esthetic, because it rendered God visible to the human senses." The material world "has become one vast symbol, and a vehicle for sacramental grace." Art has been redeemed. By giving "a marvellous testimony" on behalf of the eternal truths that matter symbolizes, art shares in "this universal regeneration of matter." A Christian artist or poet would certainly have been encouraged by this message.

On the other hand, another of Hopkins' superiors, Edward Purbrick, rector of Stonyhurst in the 1870s and head of the English Province of the Jesuits in the 1880s, preached a sermon at Stonyhurst, "On the Feast of the Immaculate Conception" (December 15, 1873), that exemplifies the authoritarian trends in Catholicism favored by Pius IX and the Vatican Council. Purbrick emphasized that the doctrines of the Immaculate Conception and Papal Infallibility would provide antidotes to the "rationalism" and "naturalism" of the era. The Immaculate Conception forcefully represented the strong Catholic position on original sin, a position necessary for a culture that "emancipates the flesh, glorifies nature, and proclaims the sovereignty of human reason." Without the absolute leadership of the pope, Catholics would be no better off than the parishioners of a vacated Anglican church who "wait with anxiety to learn what their new religion is to be." Even the magisterial London *Times* could hold out no hope for those unhappy parishioners, since the Church of England's new minister could look Roman Catholic from one side, Calvinist from another side, and Deist from a third.

It may be, on the one hand, that the Vatican Council tightened some lines of authority in the Jesuits. It may also be, on the other hand, that Hopkins and the Stonyhurst Philosophers had enough intellectual muscle to maintain some independent liberal views on controversial topics. They were, after all, some of the most brilliant converts of the 1850s and 1860s. Regardless, when in the 1880s Hopkins posted these "May Lines" on the statue of the Virgin Mary at Stonyhurst, he did so anonymously because it was the custom, not because he was afraid to admit authorship; their distinctive Scotist views of the Incarnation would have given him away in any case:

> O doubly predestined, you who from all eternity have been the Mother of Christ, predestined after the foreseeing of the merits of the Innocent One, a second time after the sins of our race—though the former privilege is the purer crown, yet it is the latter which the more readily brings home to the heart the gifts of God.

This paean, which Hopkins composed as a Latin poem, renders Mary as "doubly predestined" to be Christ's mother: once, if the Fall and the Redemption had not happened, and twice, because they did happen and thereby provided the arena for God's great mercy, that is, the sacrifice of His Son. Most Jesuits, indeed most Catholics, did not accept a double predestination for Mary. But for Hopkins a celebratory poem and controversial theology were not incompatible.

all, has often dictated the ground rules of debate about the will. Even Lucretius had to make his seemingly undeviating atoms "swerve," for unless "first-beginnings" (atoms) swerved, they would follow a predetermined path for the duration of time. Lucretius believed that the atoms did "break through the decrees of fate" and changed "the direction" of their movement when and where the mind so prompted.

Thus Lucretius himself criticized a determinism that would allow "that cause not follow cause from everlasting." Furthermore, noted Lucas, scientists like Fleeming Jenkin, professor of engineering at the University of London and a collaborator with Lord Kelvin, had accepted Lucretius' assertion that the will could "deflect" the atoms "in their onward path" and yet "add nothing sensible to nor take anything sensible from the energy of the universe." In short, Jenkin concluded—and Lucas quoted him with satisfaction—that while "the doctrines of the indestructibility of matter and of the conservation of energy seem at first sight" to help the determinists, the idea of the "deflection" or "swerving" of the will actually supports the opposing view.

Lucas realized that scientists had readily defended determinism because it did not violate the Law of the Conservation of Energy (the sum of the kinetic and potential energies of a system is constant). And therefore—ignoring miracles!—in order for the will to direct or cause motion, it must "produce an effect upon matter precisely similar to that which would be produced by some assignable physical force." With Jenkins' aid, and going another step further, Lucas introduced an even more controversial solution to the problem by borrowing Lord Kelvin's and Clerk Maxwell's "sorting demon," an imaginary being or trope used by the physicists to explain the new concept of entropy, that is, the dissipation of energy in nature. The demon was placed at the doorway of a partition in an imaginary vessel with the power to sort or redirect atoms coming his way. Kelvin said that "by operating selectively on individual atoms he can reverse the natural dissipation of energy" that follows from the "fortuitous concourse of atoms" in nature. When atoms move randomly, they eventually lose "motivity" or their potential energy. The demon does no work, but he alters the conditions inside the closed vessel so that the atoms are "capable of doing work by mere *guidance* applied by finite intelligence." Lucas suggested substituting the soul for the sorting demon, a "flow of blood" for a "rain of atoms," and the human brain for the imaginary vessel. Then the "supposed interference in voluntary action with the law of conservation [of energy] may not only be *insensible,* that is incapable of detection by any means at our disposal, but it may also be temporary and even momentary."

This was using Lucretius to "atomize" the Lucretians. At the same time it provided a way out for those scientists who felt that free will was simply not a scientific issue at all. According to Lucas, if the leading physicists of the land could imagine a sorting demon who caused atoms to swerve, then he, Lucas, could certainly imagine the faculty of free will, which did the same thing inasmuch as both acted without violating the Law of the Conservation of Energy. Lucas may even have given Lord

Kelvin a jolt. Although Lord Kelvin did not refer to the Stonyhurst Philosophers by name, he may have been reacting to their philosophical commotion in his Friday night lecture at the Royal Institution in London in 1879, when he hastened to add to his comments on entropy that the sorting demon was "merely mechanical" and "was not invented to help us deal with questions regarding the influence of life and of mind on the motions of matter, questions essentially beyond the range of mere dynamics." Perhaps if he had said that the demon was "merely metaphorical," he might not have sounded so defensive.

Possibly tempted by his good fortune in discovering allies both ancient and modern, Lucas went still further, citing recent experiments with heat and muscle power that suggested the human body might *not* be governed by the Law of the Conservation of Energy. He also noted that other experiments with blood flow in the cerebral hemispheres of the brain suggested that such flow caused bodily movement. The soul could regulate that blood flow just as the sorting demon could regulate the "flow" of atoms. He admitted that these experiments were not yet conclusive, but one can imagine many a reader seeing the grin of the Cheshire Cat hanging in the air as Lucas completed his citations of the latest scientific support for free will.

Holy Wells and Prayer Gauges

Besides free will, the issue of miracles would inevitably cause debates among scientists and religious writers. The chief supporter on the Catholic side was formidable: by mid century Newman's enthusiasm for miracles was already prodigious. "Miracles are not only not unlikely," he wrote in "The Present Position of Catholics in 1851," "they are positively likely." He noted that "certainly the Catholic Church, from east to west, from north to south, is . . . hung with miracles." In Italy, he went on, painted Madonnas would often nod at those who came to admire a likeness that might briefly come alive. Annually the dried blood of St. Januarius (a relic) would liquify. Newman also mentioned St. Winefride's Well as "the scene of wonders even in our unbelieving country," for ever since the seventh century, miraculous cures had been worked by the spring that rose at the Welsh site of her attempted beheading.

In the mid-1840s, after the Oxford Movement had completed its major work of bringing numerous Anglicans to the brink of conversion to the Catholic Church, Newman had set himself and others the task of studying and cultivating the miraculous. He conceived a project, which became *The Lives of the English Saints,* that would combine history and devotion: "Doctrinal questions need not enter. As to miracles, I think they may be treated as matters of faith—credible according to their evidence." He wanted to attract the attention of those of his associates who were rapidly approaching Rome by emphasizing the national and medieval church of England. He was not very successful; but then in 1845, the final year of publication of the multivolume *Lives,* he was resolutely Romeward bound himself.

The sceptical Mark Pattison, rector of Lincoln College, Oxford, who stopped well short of Rome, was also a contributor to the *Lives,* and his comments on his association with Newman during the 1840s reveal just how Catholic the whole business must have been. Pattison had been to Paris for the first time in 1843, hoping to find some intellectual Catholics who "might be of a better mental stamp" than his home-grown Catholics. He found, he was sorry to admit, a "spirit of credulity so vulgar" that the "religious people . . . believed every miraculous story which was brought in, and simply because it was miraculous." That same kind of spirit he found back at Newman's home base near Birmingham, which he characterized as having "a lurking fondness for stories of miracles." In his own life of St. Ninian, the fifth-century apostle of the southern Picts, even Pattison equivocated on the issue of miracles. Since everyone during Ninian's life believed in them, Pattison wrote, we should look upon them "as things to be expected," without worrying seriously about the "physical facts" in the case. What mattered about St. Ninian's life was the "sanctity" of his religious community. We should also not concern ourselves too much, Pattison added, about the unusual finds of seashells on mountaintops, since "recent investigations" make us doubt that they were left there after the "deluge."

These bits of science and scepticism seeping into Pattison's prose were really more characteristic of Victorian scientists. Almost invariably they took up the question of the miraculous. Regardless of their personal lack of belief in miracles, perhaps even because of such a lack, professional scientists like Francis Galton, Huxley, and Tyndall felt obliged to test hypotheses about miracles and to investigate related claims of "theocratic intervention," as Galton called the general class of phenomena. Since all three, despite their different fields—Galton a psychologist, Huxley a zoologist, and Tyndall a physicist—shared the materialist view canonized by Huxley's phrase "the physical basis of life," they appreciated neither nonphysical bases of life nor spiritual suspensions of known physical laws.

Galton was a scientist given to asking difficult questions. We have already met him briefly as the man who asked his own cousin, Darwin, embarrassing questions about gemmules. Galton asked more embarrassing questions in the *Fortnightly Review* in 1872. If prayers really work, why don't insurance companies charge ministers less? Why do banks with pious stockholders sometimes fail? Why do Quakers, "who are the most devout and most shrewd men of business," not rely on prayers to make themselves even more successful? The religious reader who managed to finish Galton's essay "Statistical Inquiries into the Efficacy of Prayer" might well have prayed that Galton's tongue be stuck in his throat and not in his cheek. And not surprisingly, Galton's offer to classify fractures and amputations into classes, the "markedly religious and piously befriended" and the "remarkably cold-hearted and neglected"—medical sheep and goats, as it were—in order to see who would walk first, was not immediately taken up by either the medical or the religious community.

One person who did respond to Galton's proposal was Tyndall, who advocated a "prayer gauge" that would test "the efficacy of prayer on a selected hospital ward." Tyndall made his offer at London's Metaphysical Society, an unusual forum of scientists and literati, Catholics and Protestants. Huxley, the third scientist who at the same society took an active role in criticizing what he regarded as the vogue for miracles in English religious culture, complained that scientific investigators "jealous" of their time simply could not bring themselves to pursue the verification of miracles both "sparse and rare."

Huxley himself did, however, expend some further investigative effort. For at least two decades, from the early 1870s on, he published his and others' evidence that Moses was in fact a person about one-tenth real and nine-tenths fictional—despite the Bible's admonition, he added, that the world is not "haunted by swarms of evil spirits." Any of the essays later reprinted in *Science and the Christian Tradition* (1892) speak for Huxley's tenacity in pursuit of what he believed was the pseudomiraculous; but one, "The Value of Witness to the Miraculous" (1889), exposed most acutely the contradiction at the heart of the belief in miracles. If a Christian, Huxley asked, cannot believe in the miracles recounted in a tenth-century copy of an account written by Eginhard, the ninth-century abbot of Charlemagne's court, how then could such a Christian "profess to believe in stories of a like character, which are found in documents" as uncertain and unattributed as the Gospels and the Acts of the Apostles? Like many successful debaters, Huxley already knew the answer to his question. Eginhard, in his scrupulous way, had reported that the populace *believed* that the earthly remains of various Roman martyrs sweated blood and caused the lame to walk. Unfortunately, to his horror, Eginhard had discovered that these remains had in fact been stolen from garden-variety tombs to satisfy the need for relics to consecrate his church in Germany.

During his theologate at St. Beuno's, Hopkins was also tempted to bring science into the service of religion. He had become quite fascinated by the miraculous cures associated with St. Winefride's Well, in the town now called Holywell, about ten miles from his college. He recommended to Bridges the account of the well in Alban Butler's *Lives of the Fathers, Martyrs and Other Principal Saints,* an enormous and well-known eighteenth-century encyclopedia, still popularly referred to as Butler's *Lives* in Hopkins' day. In the seventh century, Winefride, a young Welsh noblewoman, was accosted by Caradoc, a local prince's son; having rebuffed his attempt to marry her, she also resisted his more direct assault and tried to escape to the church of her uncle, Beuno. Caradoc caught her and chopped off her head. Beuno, who had rushed from his church, restored her head to her body and brought her back to life. At the spot where her head fell arose a spring. Into a nearby crack in the earth Beuno sent Caradoc to his doom. At the site of the well, wrote Butler, "pebble stones and large parts of the rock in the bottom" were "stained with red streaks, and with moss growing on the sides under water, which renders a sweet fragrant smell." He quoted an eighteenth-century doctor who told of "the green-scented moss" that was "frequently applied to ulcerated wounds with signal success." A little suprisingly, given his respect for miracles, Butler hedged his spiritual bet at this point:

"Nevertheless," he wrote, "in the use of natural remedies we ought by prayer always to have recourse to God, the Almighty Physician."

In 1874 Hopkins and a fellow "theologian," Clement Barraud, traveled to the well and bathed there: "The sight of the water in the well," Hopkins wrote, "as clear as glass, greenish like beryl or aquamarine, trembling at the surface with the force of the springs, and shaping out the five foils of the well quite drew and held my eyes to it." Hopkins was moved by the realization of how a "sensible thing" like the well was capable of "uttering the spiritual reason of its being." He wanted his father, who was a marine claims investigator, mathematician, and certainly no soft touch, to accept evidence of an "alleged cure of a case of rupture" effected by water from the well. Hopkins sent the young man involved "searching questions" but received no answers. When he "heard of another cure having just been worked in London by the moss or water," he vowed to inquire about that.

St. Winefride's story became very important to Hopkins. To some extent his reaction to the miracles associated with her story may have reflected the Jesuits' defense of the Vatican Council's position on miracles. On a more down-to-earth level, the natural elements of the scene at St. Winefride's Well appealed to him. By the 1870s it was situated in a lovely little valley; yet before the miraculous spring erupted in the seventh century, the vicinity was known as Sechnant or Sychnant, Welsh words for a "dry valley" or "dry riverbed." Winefride's uncle, Beuno, the namesake of Hopkins' theologate college, was such a "mythological center to the Welsh," Hopkins explained to a sceptical Bridges, that any "odd marks on cattle were called Beuno's marks." Hopkins wrote fragments of an extended closet-verse drama about Winefride's struggle with her Byronic attacker, Caradoc ("Henceforth / In a wide world of defiance Caradoc lives alone") and about her miraculous valley:

> As long as men are mortal   and God merciful
> So long to this sweet spot,   this leafy lean-over,
> This Dry Dean, now no longer dry   nor dumb, but moist and musical
> With the uproll and the downcarol   of day and night delivering
> Water, which keeps thy name. . . .

After Hopkins' death in 1889, two Stonyhurst Philosophers continued to be interested in St. Winefride. Herbert Lucas provided an interim report on her legend, emphasizing that although her story was as yet "not proven," "one day" might bring "some unlooked-for confirmation of the story." Lucas was especially taken, as was Hopkins, with the original name of the valley, Sychnant, and argued on the basis of etymology for the accuracy of some of the details of Winefride's miraculous spring. A lesser-known Stonyhurst Philosopher, Michael Maher, who was not a friend of Hopkins (having joined the group as professor of psychology in the 1880s), argued in *The Month* that 1894 had, in "the number of cures wrought and of pilgrims who have visited the Well" exceeded "any decade during the last two hundred years." Even the London press, Maher noted, had found its way to the tiny Welsh village and had treated the "cures" with greater respect, even going so far eventually as to drop the quotation marks around "cures." His enthusiasm matched Hopkins': "The paths to the Well through the Vale of Sechnant had been worn bare by the feet of British and Celtic saints before either Norman or Dane landed in England."

To this day the well attracts visitors seeking cures. At least through the 1960s, guidebooks reported a "fine reddish moss," *Byssus iolithus,* growing on the steps of the well. The moss "appears like splodges of blood."

Darwin's Honeycomb

Believing in both miracles and evolution would have been difficult for any nineteenth-century Catholic naturalist. How were Hopkins' ideas about Darwinian science related to his philosophical interests and to the Stonyhurst Philosophers' work? The materials now available to us provide only two sources in which Hopkins wrote in some detail on evolution, the pre-eminent scientific controversy of the day: a letter to his mother (1874) and a letter to Bridges (1888). In his letter to his mother he combined a criticism of Darwin with his strong reaction to Tyndall's Belfast Address. By now the acceptance or rejection of Darwin's views on evolution has become a handy touchstone for progressive views on science and religion in the Victorian period. Judged in this somewhat limited way, Hopkins was not progressive; but a closer look at his critique of Darwinism reveals in him at least as much flexibility as in contemporary scientists who wished to accept Darwin's findings without altogether rejecting their traditional religious beliefs. Hopkins cited with approval St. George Mivart, the eminent scientist and Catholic, who had criticized Darwin's atomism and received favorable reviews in a number of scientific journals for his general commentary on Darwin's ideas.

While Hopkins' letter was more about Tyndall than Darwin, it touched on the problem of the mutability of species, which not only contradicted Genesis but also raised the question of the "descent" of human beings from inferior animals. *The Origin of Species* skirted the latter issue; only one sentence—"Light will be thrown on the origin of man and his history"—explicitly pointed the way towards Darwin's potentially more offensive study, *The Descent of Man*, published in 1871. In 1874 Hopkins apparently knew only Darwin's first book, unless he was being deliberately arch when he confessed to his mother that he did not know if Darwin had said that "man is descended from any ape or ascidian or maggot." He thought that Darwinism implied, rather, that man was descended "from the common ancestor of apes, the common ancestor of ascidians, the common ancestor of maggots, and so on." He found this alternative reassuring, since "these common ancestors, if lower animals, need not have been repulsive animals." (Perhaps Hopkins had never actually seen an ascidian or a maggot.) This was an aesthetic and not wholly accurate view of the matter, but it was a moderate's view and was no doubt gleaned from Mivart's *On the Genesis of Species* (1871), which Hopkins recommended to his mother as the work of an evolutionist who "combats downright Darwinism and is very orthodox."

Whether Mivart's orthodoxy was of the scientific or of the religious stripe Hopkins did not specify. Mivart's criticism of pangenesis, Darwin's atomist theory of what we now call heredity, had been reasonably successful. Certainly his attempts to square evolutionary theory with Catholic doctrine proceeded within the framework of the liberal theology characteristic of the Stonyhurst Philosophers. Pangenesis, however, was only one of the areas in which Mivart criticized Darwin. Likewise related to questions of inheritance was his argument that Darwin's gemmule could not maintain in offspring the "similar position to that which it occupied in the parents," that is, that each successive generation would be *less* likely to have a trait of the parents.

Two other, related areas of Mivart's critique reflect topical issues already taken up by the Stonyhurst Philosophers. In the first place, Mivart argued, there were really two ways to look at "creation." In Genesis, God's creation was "supernatural," because He carried out the "absolute organization of anything . . . without pre-existing means or material." In nature, however, God's creation was "derivative," because matter has "the potentiality to evolve from it, under suitable conditions, all the various forms it subsequently assumes." In Mivart's perspective, what was wonderful about "derivative" creation was its connection to his other area of criticism: spontaneous generation.

Since the creation of the universe and evolution were two different concepts, the only real issue was their relationship. And they were related, Mivart argued, because Professor Bastian had just shown that living matter could evolve from inorganic material. Mivart's use of Bastian's research set a very elegant trap for Huxley and Tyndall. If they believed that life evolved from inorganic materials "in a very remote period of the world's history," then why should this process not occur now (as in abiogenesis)? And if it did not occur now or could not now be experimentally repeated, why should we believe that it had happened in the past, however remote? If Bastian's experiments were successful, then Mivart's "derivative" creation was just as likely as Darwin's evolutionary theory.

Alas. Both Huxley and Tyndall carried the day against Bastian, as their experiments, particularly Tyndall's, debunked his work conclusively. Nevertheless Huxley, in his Liverpool Address, was honest enough to admit that it was "an act of philosophical faith" to believe that if he could "look beyond the abyss of geologically recorded time" he would "expect to be a witness of the evolution of living protoplasm from not-living matter." This, of course, was not quite the kind of faith the Stonyhurst Philosophers had in mind.

Mivart's acceptance of Darwin's mechanism of natural selection as one of a number of natural laws "as yet undiscovered" that govern evolution, together with his general critique of Darwin, earned him a measure of respect in an article featured in *Nature* in 1871. Mivart's arguments in *On the Genesis of Species,* the reviewer wrote, could not be disregarded, in view of his "cogency of reasoning," his "great knowledge of anatomical structure," and his "acknowledgement of the strength of his opponent's position." It was, therefore, up to every Darwinian "to satisfy himself that either Mr. Mivart's premises or his line of argument is unsound," for the next move must be for the advocates of natural selection to meet Mivart's objections. Actually, the principal Darwinian himself was worried. Darwin had written to a fellow scientist in 1871 that he feared Mivart's book might swing the pendulum against natural selection or at the very least "have a most potent influence" against his hypothesis. Although Darwin often exaggerated his opponents' successes, his personal copy of Mivart's book was much more heavily annotated than his brief published reply to Mivart's objections in the sixth edition of *The Origin of Species* would indicate. There he cavalierly suggested that Mivart's views would only help the reader "enter into the realms of miracle, and to leave those of science."

Hopkins' other extended comment on Darwinism may be found in a letter to Bridges written in 1888, part of a now-incomplete series of letters concerning the architecture of the honeycomb of hive bees and its relationship to Darwinism. In his chapter on instinct in *The Origin of Species* Darwin had analyzed how natural selection affected the development of cell making, from the simple, "irregularly" rounded cells of the solitary or "humble" (bumble) bee to the "extreme perfection" of the hexagonal cells of the honey (hive) bee. This was a key chapter for Darwin, who saw the natural selection of instincts as a potential difficulty for his overall theory. Tyndall, as it turned out, thought this chapter one of Darwin's best; in his Belfast Address he singled it out as an example of Darwin's "profound analytic and synthetic skill." There was a bonus here for Tyndall in that the development of this instinct implicitly provided for an attack on teleologists such as Bishop Butler, who would take the bee's instinct as an illustration of the technique of a "manlike Artificer" hidden behind His works in nature. This, as we shall see, is almost exactly what Hopkins felt about the issue.

Darwin had argued that the evolution of the hexagonal structure was directed towards the saving of wax, since a pattern of common hexagonal walls between cells is the optimal condition for that. With less time and energy devoted to building the storehouse, more time and energy would be available for making the stores (the honey). In his letter Hopkins did not take issue directly with Darwin's argument. Instead he questioned the cause of the hexagonal tendency, suggesting that it might be more than a "matter of mechanics": "Grant in the honey bee some principle of symmetry and uniformity and you have passed beyond mechanical necessity; and it is not clear that there may not be some special instinct determined to that shape of cell after all and which has at the present stage of the bee's condition, nothing to do with mechanics, but is like the specific songs of cuckoo and thrush." How much of Darwin he accepted here is unclear; it is likely, however, that Hopkins used "special instinct" in contradistinction to Darwin's own "instinct." A special instinct would then be a controlling force inherent in nature, like instress which an observer perceives suddenly, as in Hopkins' unfinished poem on the cuckoo:

> Repeat that, repeat,
> Cuckoo, bird, and open ear wells, heart-springs, delightfully sweet,
> With a ballad, with a ballad, a rebound
> Off trundled timber and scoops of the hillside ground, hollow hollow hollow ground:
> The whole landscape flushes on a sudden at a sound.

In the 1870s Hopkins had already asserted that phenomena were more than a "matter of mechanics." In this passage from the journals he was observing waves breaking on a seawall on the south coast of Devon: "The laps of running foam striking the sea-wall double on themselves and return in nearly the same order and shape in which they came. This is mechanical reflection and is the same as optical: indeed all nature is mechanical, but then it is not seen that mechanics contain that which is beyond mechanics." The seemingly random lapping of the waves really obeys laws and, beyond them, a Law-giver. While Hopkins never formulated a rebuttal to the atomism that was the basis for "mechanical necessity," the practice of discovering inscapes in nature provided him with a personal alternative: "All the world is full of inscape and chance left free to act falls into an order as well as purpose: looking out of my window I caught it in the random clods and broken heaps of snow made by the cast of a broom."

Unfortunately these passages are brief. If Hopkins had a particular analysis of "mechanics" in mind, it was either left unfinished or, more likely, left underdeveloped *and* unfinished. Only in his four letters to *Nature* did he achieve some measure of completeness as an amateur scientist. Whenever he set himself a larger task, such as a full-length study like those that all of his Stonyhurst colleagues had by the mid-1880s already written, he faltered. He wanted, for example, to write a book about the ether and light that would remedy a fault he perceived in scientific books. He was not worried that such books made people materialists, believing "in Matter more but in God less," but that they caused people to conceive "only of a world of formulas . . . towards which the outer world acts as a sort of feeder." The book he envisioned, however, which would combine his scientific and philosophical interests, he was unable by disposition or circumstance to write.

In scientific matters Hopkins generally followed the progressive lines of inquiry laid out by such men as Mivart. His practical scientific work—the letters to *Nature* discussed in chapters 3 and 5—obeyed the pattern set by the Jesuits in the nineteenth century throughout Europe. They carefully supported their internationally active scientists, who were for the most part astronomers or solar scientists. Few, if any, were naturalists, biologists, or chemists. This pattern may explain Hopkins' publications on solar phenomena and his public silence on other scientific matters that were also of interest to him. Although he did not publish his philosophical views, he was regarded by his friends and associates as an original and brilliant thinker. His interests and insights mark him as a conscientious albeit generally private Stonyhurst Philosopher. His accomplishments in scientific prose were well known in his order and, as we shall see, received publicity in some scientific circles as well.

5 The Spectacular Sunsets of the 1880s

As far as I have myself observed the Natural History of men, or women, either those who *can* write never do; and those who can see, never tell anybody what they have seen, while the people who can neither see, nor write, print volumes of their "speculations"!

—John Ruskin

The Krakatoa Eruptions

In Madras, India, in late 1883, the sun turned green. Near Hawaii blue sunlight woke the startled passengers of a steamer. In England the sun set in such a blaze of color that fire brigades all over the country went to the horizon in pursuit of nonexistent fires. In Switzerland a young boy (the Swiss psychoanalyst C. G. Jung) was carried in his father's arms to the western porch of their house to observe "the evening sky, shimmering in the most glorious green." Whether sunrise or sunset, east or west, spectacular solar phenomena dominated casual conversations and earnest scientific work alike throughout the mid-1880s. Very few doubted the cause. The volcano on the island of Krakatoa in the Straits of Java had erupted violently and uninterruptedly on August 26 and 27, 1883, bringing death and destruction to a vast area of the South Pacific and turning an inhabited island into a rocky wasteland. A few scientists who questioned what seemed to them a facile identification between the eruptions and extraordinary solar phenomena believed that it was impossible for volcanic dust to be ejected to the great heights and distances necessary for the stream of light from the sun to be affected. But the majority of Victorian scientists believed that an inordinate concentration of Krakatoa dust particles in the atmosphere had refracted the sun's light in novel ways requiring further investigation.

In *Nature* the flow of letters about *rayons du crépuscule* or "shadow-beams at sunset," to which Hopkins contributed, partially coincided with the dramatic solar effects reported in late 1883. Hopkins' second letter on the *rayons du crépuscule* appeared in November 1883, after the Krakatoa eruptions, although he did not mention them. In the same month as his second letter, further letters appeared discussing green and blue suns; observers also wrote about dramatic red glows, soon called "afterglows." W. Clement Ley, a nationally recognized meteorologist, and Annie Ley, his daughter and coworker, described both evening rays and red afterglows, implying a connection between the two. A number of other scientists, most notably C. Michie Smith, a meteorologist then in Madras, pointed out what was undeniably true, that both *rayons du crépuscule* and a green sun had been observed in years past.

Apparently such confusion goaded at least three prominent scientists into attempts at clearing up matters. C. Piazzi Smyth, astronomer royal for Scotland, wrote to *Nature* suggesting that the unusual solar effects might easily be the result of the dust from various meteor masses "rather than from a supposed continued ascent of one particular charge of volcanic dust from Java, full three months after the cessation of all violent disturbance there." Smyth's letter raised meteoric dust of its own as the first of two alternative hypotheses intended to account for the origin of the sunsets. The second hypothesis, a high concentration of water vapor in the atmosphere, was offered subsequently by Robert C. Leslie, a painter and Ruskin's friend. (This hypothesis will receive further comment below.) Early in 1884, C. J. Symons, a meteorologist and chairman of the Krakatoa Committee of the Royal Society, announced in *Nature* his committee's assignment to collect "the various accounts of the volcanic eruption at Krakatoa, and attendant phenomena," such as the fall of dust, pumice, and sulfurous vapors, unusual barometric readings, the "distances at which explosions were heard, and exceptional effects of light and color in the atmosphere." Although such a call for data would be routine in scientific circles in the modern era, in this case it surely gave the appearance of favoring the volcanic explanation for the unusual solar phenomena. Some adverse reaction, especially from anyone in C. Piazzi Smith's orbit, was inevitable. *Knowledge,* a short-lived magazine that treated *Nature* as an establishment rival, ran a letter stating that any data indicating that Krakatoa was not the explanation for the sunsets would be "burked" by Symons' "nice, impartial little association" and should be sent to *Knowledge* instead.

The most powerful analysis of the "recent sunrises and sunsets," by Norman Lockyer, was given prominent space in the London *Times.* Lockyer began by reminding his readers of the glorious reds associated with usual sunsets. These reds, he emphasized, are the result of the water vapor that at sunset forms part of the thickest layer of the atmosphere, blocking the blue and violet bands of white sunlight. With the blue and violet end of the spectrum removed, red is the color "seen at sunset under ordinary conditions." Under the extraordinary conditions brought about when the volcanic eruptions ejected enormous quantities of dust into the atmosphere, a significant layer of dust particles had been produced that would block the red component of sunlight. The result could be a green sun. Variations such as red sunsets and blue or green suns, Lockyer explained, were the result of sunlight passing through dust layers whose effective thickness would depend upon the angle at which the sun's rays approached the earth. At sunrise or sunset the sun's rays would hit these layers at a low angle and hence would travel through their greatest thickness.

In the end Lockyer's explanation was accepted, while both alternative hypotheses were rejected by the Krakatoa Committee of the Royal Society when it published its massive report, *The Eruption of Krakatoa and Subsequent Phenomena* (1888). Prior to that relatively late date of publication, scientists had already offered experimental data supporting Lockyer's views. Michael Faraday had completed experiments at the Royal Institution "which demonstrated the excessive divisibility of matter and the effect of finely divided particles on light," and Tyndall had carried Faraday's work forward by analyzing how the colors of the sky are determined by particles trapped in the atmosphere. And a German scientist, K. I. Kiessling, had refined their work by producing, experimentally, blue and green optical effects by passing light through dust clouds.

Hopkins was one of the earliest to criticize the alternative view offered in C. Piazzi Smyth's letter. Considering Smyth's rank in society as astronomer royal of Scotland, Hopkins' letter to *Nature* in January 1884, his first since the two *rayons du crépuscule* letters, was certainly bold if not downright aggressive. He wrote that "the body of evidence now brought in from all parts of the world must . . . by this time have convinced Mr. Piazzi Smyth that the late sunrises and sunsets do need some explanation, more particular than he was willing to give them." Hopkins then proceeded, in a long and rigorous argument of about two thousand words, to outline a rather dizzying array of phenomena, using his own observations and "those of others," including at least one unnamed member of the Stonyhurst Observatory staff. His letter attracted some attention in scientific circles, for it earned him the title of "observer" in the Royal Society's Krakatoa report, which reprinted parts of his letter.

The letter moves back and forth between the naturalist's detail and the painter's palette. In discussing the green phase of the phenomena, Hopkins wrote that "the green is between apple-green or pea-green (which are pure greens) and an olive (which is tertiary color)." His description of the curious nature of the red phase of the afterglow of the setting sun is also noteworthy, in part because of the precision of its details and in part because its reference to the "lusterless" quality of the light would be echoed in his last letter (of which more later). These sunsets differed from others, Hopkins wrote,

> in the nature of the glow, which is both intense and lusterless, and that both in the sky and in the earth. The glow is intense, this is what strikes everyone; it has prolonged the daylight, and optically changed the season; it bathes the whole sky, it is mistaken for the reflection of a great fire; at the sundown itself and southwards from that on December 4, I took a note of it as more like inflamed flesh than the lucid reds of ordinary sunsets. On the same evening the fields facing west glowed as if overlaid with yellow wax.

His renderings of unusual greens and his red "like inflamed flesh" are corroborated by two of the six pastel drawings included as illustrations to the Krakatoa report. The illustrations, which show the wide range of color of a sunset on November 26, 1883, a week before Hopkins' sunset, were done by William Ascroft, a member of the Royal Academy with scientific interests.

Hopkins continued his description of the December 4 sunset elsewhere in his letter, describing another phase of the afterglow as a very "impure" red:

> On the 4th it appeared brown, like a strong light behind tortoise shell, or Derbyshire alabaster. It has been well compared to the color of incandescent iron. Sometimes it appears like a mixture of chalk with sand and muddy earths. The pigments for it would be ochre and Indian red.

Again we have a fascinating corroboration of his color sense, for that phase of the December 4 sunset was captured in crayon by John Sanford Dyason, a professional meteorologist who drew colored sketches of sky conditions, exhibited under the title "The Chromatics of the Sky," by which he hoped to predict the weather.

Hopkins' penchant for transforming his observations into painterly lessons runs throughout this letter. In the passage in which we first read about the curious mixture of intense and lusterless light, he evokes a comparison with Rembrandt:

> The two things together, that is intensity of light and want of luster, give to objects on the earth the peculiar illumination which may be seen in studios and other well-like rooms, and which itself affects the practice of painters and may be seen in their works, notably Rembrandt's, disguising or freely showing the outlines or distinctions of things, but fetching out white surfaces and colored stuffs with a rich inward and seemingly self-luminous glow.

Hopkins' sensibility here displays itself in a remarkable rendering of the phenomena of the world without forcing or even acknowledging a distinction between science and art.

As a rule, a reference to Rembrandt would be unusual in a scientific journal, but under Lockyer's leadership *Nature* had always encouraged such cross-fertilization. Even in Piazzi Smyth's letter, which Hopkins criticized, the astronomer royal of Scotland felt compelled to give some advice to painters on the lessons to be learned from recent solar phenomena: "It is to be earnestly hoped, as an outcome of the late remarkable sunsets, and the great numbers of the public by whom they have been witnessed, that our painters will no longer be content to give us so generally mere afternoon pictures slightly yellow ochred and 'light red'-ed near the horizon before the sun goes down, as sunsets, but will more frequently paint the deep red afterglows at their richest."

The same mixture of artistic and scientific motive was evident in Ascroft's and Dyason's drawings. When the Royal Society was preparing his drawings for the Krakatoa report, Ascroft insisted that, in order to avoid the errors other publishers had made in printing J. M. W. Turner's remarkable color canvases, they order the printer to work only in "bright weather" so that the colors would be true. Dyason's work had always been more strictly scientific in intention; he called his drawings "photographic experiments" and a "faithful transcript of Nature." If Ascroft was a disciple of Turner, then Dyason followed Constable, who likewise regarded his drawings as experiments. Constable said in the 1830s that painting should not be considered "only as a poetic aspiration, but as a pursuit, *legitimate, scientific, and mechanical.*" Both Ascroft's and Dyason's drawings were exhibited at a number of Royal Society *conversazioni* or public meetings held at Carleton House, London, from 1884 through 1889; in 1886 Ascroft's drawings were exhibited with a selection by Perry of solar drawings from the Stonyhurst Observatory. The London *Times'* reviewer of the June 8, 1887, *conversazione* wrote that Ascroft's and Dyason's drawings demonstrated that "evidently science as well as art can find a use for . . . the evanescent glories of sunsets." It was an observation that Hopkins would have taken for granted.

The Blanched Sun

Scientist and artist soon contended with rather than complemented each other in the columns of *Nature,* but this time Hopkins supported the scientist. Ruskin, the greatest critic of art and society in the Victorian era (see p. 124), had secured his reputation in part with the publication of the multivolume study *Modern Painters* (1843–60), which included an analysis and defense of Turner's paintings. Ruskin had established himself as an expert on the artistic rendering of sunsets and other dramatic subjects of light and color that Turner loved—fires at sea, for example, and the conflict between industrial steam and natural forces. By the 1870s Ruskin had become convinced that traditional English sunsets were no longer to be seen. In 1884 he delivered two public lectures in London on what he called "the storm-cloud of the nineteenth century" or the "plague cloud," the meteorological phenomena, he said, that darkened England's physical and moral landscape. This "dry black veil," as he described it in 1871 in one of his letters of social analysis, reprinted as *Fors Clavigera,* looked "as if it were made of poisonous smoke"; it was, he concluded gloomily, more likely "made of dead men's souls."

There had in fact been an increase of smog in many areas of England during this period of heavy industrialization, as well as—and not merely

Ruskin's Career

In a number of ways Hopkins' and Ruskin's interests coincided. Both were avidly concerned with architecture and painting and both were amateur scientists. Ruskin seemed destined for a career as a scientist. In a sense he may be said to have begun and ended an astonishingly prolific career as an artistic and social critic by publishing articles not on art or society but on meteorology.

Ruskin had at first intended to be a geologist, modeling himself at Oxford after William Buckland, canon of Christ Church and a well-known geologist and mineralogist who was part of the early BAAS overlap of clergy and scientist (see p. 13). When he was twenty-five years old Ruskin published "Enquiries on the Causes of Color of the Water of the Rhine," which distinguished the color of the sea as an optical effect from the intrinsic color of fresh water. This, his first prose publication, appeared in 1834 in J. C. Loudon's *Magazine of Natural History,* where he continued to publish essays of primarily geological interest. He made his debut at the London Meteorological Society with a paper "On the Formation and Color of Such Clouds as Are Caused by the Agency of Mountains," which he read in 1837 but did not publish. His major statement on the beauty and utility of his field, "Remarks on the Present State of Meteorological Science" (1839), was published in the transactions of this society and reprinted as late as 1870 in *Symon's Monthly Meteorological Magazine,* the standard journal of weather reporting.

Even when his first piece of artistic analysis appeared in *The Poetry of Architecture* in 1837, he was still contributing scientific articles on problems of perspective, with geometric diagrams, to London's *Architecture Magazine.* By the late 1840s he had turned to the analysis and defense of Turner's paintings, but even in *Modern Painters* (1843–60) he illustrated such topics as Turner's clouds with diagrams of cloud structures and formations. By the 1880s, the decade of the Krakatoa eruptions, Ruskin believed that Turner's sunsets were gone forever.

by coincidence—a series of years of bad weather during which sunny days were at a premium. At Brantwood, Coniston Water, in Cumbria, Ruskin was but seventy miles from Stonyhurst when Perry described that remarkably black day in 1882. Ruskin's association of bad weather with a plaguelike visitation of God's wrath was his way of predicting the collapse of English civilization.

During his London lectures on the "storm-cloud of the nineteenth century" Ruskin, in typically dramatic fashion, displayed one of his own drawings, done at Brantwood, "of a sunset in entirely pure weather, above London smoke." It was a drawing, he asserted, of "one of the last pure sunsets" he had seen in 1876. Then, using a glass over the "pure" sunset, he smeared some ugly marks to demonstrate how he could have "blotted down . . . a bit of plague-cloud to put beside" this; but why bother? His listeners could walk outside and see such an ugly sunset every day. He added that even his garden was not growing properly anymore. (In fact, in his despondency he had neglected it.) The rhetorical conclusion of these lectures was the phrase "blanched sun, blighted grass, blinded man," which metaphorically joined the radical change in the sun's appearance, the decay in his garden, and the moral blindness in society. Citing biblical passages, Ruskin reiterated what "every seer of old predicted," that "physical gloom" mirrors the "moral gloom" of society.

Despite his lifelong dedication to science, Ruskin attacked the essence of scientific method by arguing that "observation by instruments or machines was useless." He had gone to consult the anemometer at Radcliffe Observatory at Oxford, but he rejected the data. "What is the use of scientific apparatus," he asked, "when it can't tell you whether [the wind] is a strong medicine, or a strong poison?"

When Ruskin delivered his lectures, he thought that the plague cloud with its effect on sunshine and the Krakatoa eruptions with their solar phenomena were no doubt related. A short time later, when the lectures were published, he added a note indicating that he realized there was those who believed that the eruptions had not caused the unusual solar effects. But for him, in any case, the issue of causation was not crucial. He believed that the plague cloud had blotted out traditional English sunsets more than a decade before Krakatoa erupted.

In fact the two sets of phenomena were not in every way unrelated, for a certain kind of Krakatoa sunset did fulfill his prophecy of a plague cloud choking off the sun's rays. Ruskin had told his London audience that the plague cloud "blanches" the sun "instead of reddening it." If his listeners were "in a hurry to see what the sun looks like" behind such a cloud, they had only to throw a silver coin, "a bad half crown," into a mixture of soap and water.

This description of a "blanched sun" corresponds to Bishop's ring, an atmospheric phenomenon associated with Krakatoa. Named after its first published observer, the Reverend Sereno Bishop of Hawaii, it is depicted in quite a few of Ascroft's drawings of sunsets executed in 1884, some of which were exhibited at the Royal Society. Ascroft's drawings captured this "blanching" effect beautifully, revealing, in Bishop's own words, the sun's "whitish corona" or "haze canopy." Bishop described the ring in greater detail in a prize-winning essay on the sunsets: "A conspicuous object when the sun is high has been from the first the opalescent silvery glow around the sun. This occupied a circle of 25° radius or more. The outer part develops a pinkish hue, which against the blue sky shows lilac or chocolate tints."

Bishop's description was matched by others in *Nature*. One notable contributor to the letters column was Robert C. Leslie, a painter and Ruskin's friend. His father, Charles R. Leslie, was a major painter and public figure in the early Victorian art world, counting both Constable and Turner as his intimate friends. His son grew up literally surrounded by Constable's clouds and Turner's sunsets. Leslie's letters on Krakatoa and associated phenomena appeared in *Nature* throughout the 1880s. Ruskin relied on his opinions and letters, both in his storm cloud lectures and in his autobiography, *Praeterita* (1885–89), to buttress his prophetic messages for England of impending artistic and social doom.

Leslie doubted the direct connection between Bishop's ring and the Krakatoa eruptions:

> I have watched the sky as an artist (out of London) for quite forty years, and feel sure that this corona, or blanching of the sun, has been a more persistent feature of late years than formerly. . . . The last very mild winter and the preceding one could have had no connection with the Krakatoa eruption, and I think we must now seek for an explanation of the present and past atmospheric phenomena in some increase of solar energy, and consequent lifting of vapor higher than usual.

Leslie's letters to *Nature* in 1884 differ markedly from those of other correspondents because Leslie, like Ruskin, believed that the unusual solar phenomena had occurred for years before Krakatoa erupted. Furthermore, he insisted on the use of "blanched," Ruskin's term, for the description of the sun at certain moments. Finally, although Ruskin himself believed apocalyptically that "the sun's going out," Leslie thought that there was "some increase of solar energy." On this last point he began to lose scientific credibility, as he even suggested at one point that everyone had been "muddling up cause and effect" and that the Krakatoa eruptions and the solar effects might have both been caused by an "actual increase of sun power."

But other correspondents, as well as Hopkins, disagreed with virtually all of Leslie's points. E. Douglass Archibald, who had observed halos for twenty years, believed that the "new" solar halo, that is, Bishop's ring, had "never been seen here before, at any rate within the last twenty years." He went on to describe it briefly: "I remember noting the halo in November, and calling the attention of my assistant to the beautiful salmon color it showed in the interstices of a mackerel sky, which shut off the direct glare of the sun." Today we would judge this description typical of Hopkins, perhaps not realizing that he and Archibald shared a common source: the word painting of Victorian naturalists.

Hopkins' fourth and final letter to *Nature,* published on October 30, 1884, contained sharp criticism of Leslie as Hopkins directly addressed the issue of Bishop's ring. Hopkins wrote that the phenomenon should not be called a halo, which is a clearly defined circle of color, rainbow-like, around the sun, nor a corona, which implies that the phenomenon is part of the sun. He noted that the ring's color was "sometimes rose, sometimes amber or buff" and that "towards sunset it becomes glaring, and white and sallow in hue."

Hopkins also argued for scientific objectivity over subjective judgment. Even though Ruskin and Leslie disagreed about the nature of the changes in solar energy, both men believed that the sun was actually changing in some dramatic way. Hopkins, like most of the astronomers and other letter writers to *Nature,* believed that the phenomena in question were meteorological or atmospheric, not cosmic:

> If there is going on, as Mr. Leslie thinks, an "increase of sun power," this ought to be both felt and measured by exact instruments, not by the untrustworthy impressions of the eye. Now Prof. Piazzi Smyth says that sunlight, as tested by the spectroscope, is weaker, not stronger, since the phenomena of last winter began. To set down variations in light and heat to changes in the

> sun when they may be explained by changes in our atmosphere, is like preferring the Ptolemaic to the Copernican system.

So much for Ruskin's preference for the eye over the scientific instrument! Without the context of Victorian science, Hopkins' remark about the "untrustworthy impressions of the eye" would seem out of character for him, the precise and careful observer of nature.

Hopkins concluded his letter with an impressive summary of the principal issues that had been debated in *Nature* for two years:

> It is . . . right and important to distinguish phenomena really new from old ones first observed under new circumstances which make people unusually observant. A sun seen as green or blue for hours together is a phenomenon only witnessed after the late Krakatoa eruptions (barring some rare reports of like appearances after like outbreaks, and under other exceptional conditions); but a sun which turns green or blue just at setting is, I believe, an old and, we may say, ordinary one, little remarked till lately.

His disinterested evaluation dominates this letter; and indeed modern meteorology—the British *Observer's Handbook,* for example—recognizes the phenomenon of the green flash, which occurs for a short duration only, as distinct from other "twilight colors," which last for varying lengths of time. In fact the green flash is objective; it is not an "optical effect" caused by a reaction in an "over-strained eye" observing the setting sun, as Hopkins thought. His old colleague Perry correctly determined that the green color associated with Krakatoa sunsets was "not due merely to contrast," but by the time he reached this conclusion, early in 1884, Hopkins had already moved to Dublin.

Hopkins the amateur scientist comes through clearly in this last letter. He offers an experiment in which the light from the sun's disk could remain white while surrounded by other colors: "It may be noticed that when a candle-flame is looked at through colored glass, though everything else behind the glass is strongly stained with the color, the flame is often nearly white." But Hopkins the poet is present as well. The afterglow he observed on an October night in Dublin was "bronzy near the earth; above like peach, or of the bluish color on ripe hazels." He also offered a speculative hypothesis regarding the problem that had bothered the astronomer Smyth and others. How could the ejected dust influence sunsets so many months after the original event? Hopkins' solution was novel: "It would seem as if the volcanic 'wrack' had become a satellite to the earth, like Saturn's rings, and was subject to phases, of which we are now witnessing a vivid one."

On scientific grounds there is little doubt that Hopkins' criticisms of Leslie were accurate and telling, and that in general his contributions to *Nature* were of a high standard. Leslie was without allies in *Nature*. Only Ruskin enthusiastically shared his views, but Ruskin's scientific star had fallen so low that his storm cloud lectures were openly ridiculed by W. Clement Ley in *Nature* early in 1884. Ley recommended that "those who sympathize" with Ruskin's theory of the "storm-cloud" should "study some of those little books [science primers] which are beginning to be the delight of our children." Ley accused Ruskin of being a representative of a Philistinism "which shows itself in opposition to scientific culture." Ruskin was vulnerable because of the subjectivity of his observations and his lack of records, since barometric gradients, wind force statistics, and other data favored by Ley and most if not all scientists were openly dismissed by Ruskin.

Perhaps it was easy, then, for the Royal Society's Krakatoa report to dismiss both Leslie and Ruskin, for none of Leslie's letters was cited despite the fact that *Nature* was a major source of data and alternative views on the origins of the sunsets did appear in the final report. The subsequent careers of Ruskin and Leslie were followed in the press, but their trajectories were very different. Leslie enjoyed some success as a painter and writer on marine subjects; Ruskin, however, soon passed into a terrible senility and probably insanity, never reappearing in public after the storm cloud lectures.

By the time of his fourth and last letter to *Nature*, Hopkins had already moved to Dublin, where he began the final phase of his short life and career. Encouraged by a faculty of brilliant and eccentric scholars, he addressed certain philosophical and theological problems. He turned to science less as an activity than as a source of metaphor. But then Dublin was not Stonyhurst.

Conclusion: A "Beautiful but Broken Arc"

> I am a Greek philosopher. . . . I shall never become a saint on my tack, no, though I lived a hundred years more. My occupations go to form such a character. I don't know how to change, and I can't make up my mind to desire to change.
>
> —Joseph Rickaby

"Progressive Science"

Hopkins, too, was trained at Oxford to become a "Greek philosopher." Perhaps, like his friend Joseph Rickaby, he couldn't change either. Like the ancient Greek philosophers, however, Hopkins, his fellow students, and later his fellow Stonyhurst Philosophers found it necessary to know science as well as philosophy. In the first place, science was news; the atomists and Darwinians saw to that. In the second place, an Oxford curriculum that included logic and the history of philosophy by definition, according to the Victorians, included science as well.

Hopkins' experience and fascination with science are a constant in his career. He remained a naturalist and amateur scientist throughout his life, as his letters to *Nature,* his journals, and his poems make clear. How he dealt with science, however, varied with his circumstances and interests. A range of attitudes towards science are apparent. At Oxford in the 1860s he saw science *as* science, a discipline with its own laws. As a priest and philosopher who returned to poetry in the 1870s, he sometimes treated science as art, the subject of poetry. And in the 1880s, even as he succeeded in publishing his own views on contemporary topics of science, he was at the same time pursuing science as a source of metaphor, science in the service of a higher calling, his philosophy and theology.

As an undergraduate Hopkins wrote two major Oxford Essays in which he demonstrated quite explicitly a sophisticated grasp of contemporary science. The first essay, "Distinguish Exactly between Deduction, Induction, Analogy, and Example," began as a routine exercise in philosophical terminology, covering material available to Oxford students in a number of commentaries, particularly those that focused on scientific method: Whewell's *History of the Inductive Sciences* (1837) and Mill's *System of Logic Ratiocinative and Inductive* (1843), for example. When Hopkins came to define "induction," he chose to illustrate a shortcut to induction called "example," in which "one or more instances are made to stand" for all possible instances. By induction, then, other instances of the same class may be assumed to resemble those instances chosen as examples. Hopkins' final paragraph cited a specific botanical example that had recently become a locus classicus in the field:

> Let us say all double roses are barren. It being impossible to reach this proposition by simple enumeration it must be formed upon a number of observed instances. But what right have we to make a proposition wider than the actual number observed? The question brings out the real nature of the inductive process and serves to put in a right light certain notions held about it in modern times. In becoming double a rose changes its generative organs into petals and we find that we are stating identical propositions: a double rose is one with an unusual number of petals: the number of petals is increased by the conversion of the stamens etc.: a rose without stamens etc. is barren.

Hopkins' botanical example was actually the heart of Goethe's major contribution to early nineteenth-century science. In plant development, according to Goethe, all the parts of a flower—petals and calyx together with the sexual organs, stamen and anther—develop from the primary or primordial leaf and are all variations of the leaf. Although Goethe published "On the Metamorphosis of Plants" in 1817, a full translation by Emily M. Cox did not appear until late 1863, in the *Journal of Botany, British and Foreign*. Hopkins did have access to G. H. Lewes' popular *Life and Works of Goethe* (1855), which was in his family's library, but Lewes did not go into the botanical detail of plant morphology that was to be found only in Cox's translation:

> In those flowers whose habit is to become double, we may trace this transition through all its changes. In Roses, among perfect colored petals, others may often be seen which are contracted both in the middle and at the side. This is occasioned by a little protuberance more or less resembling a perfect anther, and in the same proportion the whole petal assumes the form of a stamen. . . .
>
> When all the stamens are changed into petals, the flower produces no seed, but if any of the stamens are developed whilst the process by which the flower becomes double is going forward, fertilization may take place.

In his second essay, "The Tests of a Progressive Science," Hopkins also showed a grasp of contemporary scientific issues and an ability to place those issues in a theoretical framework. In the beginning of this short essay, Hopkins argued that one test of the development of a scientific field is whether it is inductive, that is, whether it explains "more facts":

> The discovery of a new species of willow or the observation of parthenogenesis in aphids two generations longer than had before been found possible shows little progressiveness in science; on the other hand the spectral analysis by which the chemical composition of non-terrestrial masses is made out is a development of optics which cannot be called supplemental but a complete widening or alteration of its beat.

The second test of a progressive science is deductive, "the more exact or the more comprehensive and rational treatment of facts":

> The advance of a science in this stage is to be looked for in development of method. This means the gathering of some of its facts and laws into groups which give new starting-points and postulates. The process meant is most conspicuously seen in mathematics: thus the properties of angles given in Euclid are in trigonometry thrown together into a new conception of the angle as a measure for a wide and alien field of matter. The change of view has in fact brought within our reach facts which the prior science was too cumbrous to treat of: and this change of view is paralleled in all the sciences where we can find a link or blending between a higher and a lower.

Hopkins' three examples—parthenogenesis and spectral analysis as examples of induction, a "new conception of the angle" as an example of deduction—were all topics of great interest in scientific circles during the 1850s and 1860s.

His first example, the extended generation of aphids by nonsexual reproduction, reflected the work of Richard Owen, whose standard essay, *On Parthenogenesis* (1849), introduced the term *parthenogenesis* into English. The plant lice known as aphids, according to Owen, provided the classic example of "virgin-birth." In an authoritative manner befitting his status as the outstanding comparative anatomist of his day, he explained for the first time the facts concerning the reproductive cycle of aphids:

> If the virgin progeny . . . be kept from any access to the male, each will again produce a brood of the same number of aphids: and carefully prosecuted experiments have shown that this procreation from a virgin mother will continue to the seventh, the ninth, or the eleventh generations before the spermatic virtue of the ancestral coitus has been exhausted.

Additional generations of little virgin aphids did not amount to much scientific progress, in Hopkins' view. More substantial, he argued, was the spectral analysis of heavenly bodies, that is, determining the composition of their matter by analyzing the spectrum or component bands of light emitted or reflected by these bodies. Such analysis was still controversial throughout the 1860s. The seminal work in spectral analysis had been accomplished in the 1850s through the collaboration of the German scientists Gustav Kirchhoff and Robert Bunsen. Kirchhoff's landmark paper, "On the Relation between the Radiating and Absorbing Powers of Different Bodies for Light and Heat," which analyzed the chemical constitution of "the sun and fixed stars," appeared in translation in the *Philosophical Magazine* in 1860 and inaugurated a decade of controversy over the composition of the sun.

Hopkins' mathematical example illustrating the "deductive" development of science is the most problematical of the three. Despite the reference to trigonometry, which Hopkins had studied, the only contemporary candidate for an "alien field of matter" is non-Euclidean geometry. This subject would certainly have provided a heady contrast to the normal Euclidean fare for Oxford undergraduates. The pangeometers, as the leading non-Euclideans were nicknamed, refused to accept Euclid's axiom on parallel lines, which states that through a given point only one line can be drawn parallel to a given line. Such daring forays into a "hyperspace" where parallel lines could meet and the sum of the angles of a triangle did not have to equal 180° shook the British world of mathematics in the mid-1860s. In 1865 Arthur Cayley, Sadlerian Professor of Pure Mathematics at Cambridge University, published a modest paper in the *Philosophical Magazine*, "Note on Lobatchewsky's Imaginary Geometry," concerning one of the Russian founders of this "new," impure math. Cayley was apologetic in this very early paper on the subject, scratching his head over his lack of understanding of Lobatchewsky's proof that the sum of the angles of a triangle can, "if not in nature at least in analysis," be less than 180°.

Hopkins certainly knew that trigonometry did not represent "new starting points and postulates." Only non-Euclidean geometry, with its assault on the axiom about parallel lines and its creation of spherical triangles, which did not behave as plane-surface triangles did, could be such "an alien field of matter." By the 1870s, in any case, non-Euclidean geometry had achieved general circulation and, one might add, respectability through such journals as *Nature* as well as the more broadly based *Academy*, another of Hopkins' usual reads.

The Oxford Essays thus reveal an undergraduate confident in his grasp of difficult contemporary scientific problems—in brief, an understanding of science as science. Certainly Hopkins never lost this understanding. His four letters to *Nature* in the 1880s demonstrate a commendable regard for scientific observation and method. But there was another side to Hopkins and science—when he turned his science into art.

Bright Sun and Black Boreas

Hopkins' poem "The Loss of the Eurydice" (1878) was his poetic response to the dramatic shipwreck of the *Eurydice*, a training ship of the Admiralty, in the English Channel just southeast of the Isle of Wight on March 24, 1878. Hopkins took both a scientific and a Catholic view of the wreck. This ship of Protestant souls was the victim of Providence in the form of such freakish weather that it foundered within minutes. A squall and snowstorm came at the ship so quickly and powerfully that it sank at once, yet one of the only two survivors testified that "the weather cleared up" almost immediately afterwards.

At the time of the shipwreck, Hopkins was carrying out pastoral duties at a church in Chesterfield, in the heart of the Midlands, quite a distance from the English Channel. Yet he depicted the events with such meteorological precision that he doubtless had consulted at least one of the reports filed about the freakish weather; the weather news in the London *Times* was scanty. Because of its thoroughness the most likely candidate is W. Clement Ley's report "The Eurydice Squall," published in the April 1878 issue of *Symon's Monthly Meteorological Report,* the standard journal in its field.

Ley's document supports the precision of detail with which Hopkins describes the storm in these stanzas (5–8) from the poem:

> No Atlantic squall overwrought her
> Or rearing billow of the Biscay water:
>   Home was hard at hand
> And the blow bore from land.
>
> And you were a liar, O blue March day.
> Bright sun lanced fire in the heavenly bay;
>   But what black Boreas wrecked her? he
> Came equipped, deadly-electric,
>
> A beetling, baldbright cloud thorough England
> Riding: there did storms not mingle? and
>   Hailropes hustle and grind their
> Heavengravel? wolfsnow, worlds of it, wind there?
>
> Now Carisbrook keep goes under in gloom:
> Now it overvaults Appledurcombe;
>   Now near by Ventnor town
> It hurls, hurls off Boniface Down.

The London *Times,* which Hopkins routinely read, described the squall as "a heavy bank of clouds . . . coming down from the northwest" with "a gale, accompanied by a blinding fall of snow . . . rushing from the highlands down Luccombe Chine." But Ley's report contained a richer compendium of facts that more closely match Hopkins' poem. Ley believed that the squall originated in the Northumberland and Cumberland hills; with a county-by-county chart of the squall's locations on March 24, including Perry of Stonyhurst as one observer, he documented a consistent movement from the northwest and north-northwest. Hopkins was familiar with the place-names of the Isle of Wight from his sketching excursions there in the 1860s, and he presents them in stanza 7 in a northwest to southeast line, the direction of the storm as it moved from Carisbrook Castle to the ruins of Appledurcombe House and finally to the coastal town of Ventnor at the base of Boniface Down.

Other details in stanzas 6 and 7 are corroborated by Ley's report. Ley noted that "very fine weather prevailed at 8 a.m. over nearly the whole of England" on the 24th, the "blue March day" Hopkins calls a "liar." Hopkins lets the lights and darks of the "black Boreas" or north wind and the "baldbright cloud" metaphorically represent the characteristically dense, dark storm cloud with bright edges. One of Ley's Surrey observers described "an enormous black cloud like a monster balloon," while a Worcester observer described it as "resembling a white wall." Ley himself, in Leicestershire, had recorded the storm "as a bank of dense white cirro-stratus" accompanied not only by hail and snow but also by violent winds and "complicated currents of air."

Years later, whenever scientists took up further discussion of this remarkable meteorological event, they were always careful to praise the accuracy of Ley's analysis. In the end Ley concluded that "meteorology, and not least of all, the principles of cloud observation" should "occupy a very large place in the education of seamen." Certainly Hopkins would have agreed, for the moral navigation he urged upon readers of "The Loss of the Eurydice," while capable perhaps of saving "three hundred souls," would not have been able to save three hundred lives.

The Archsnake of the Evolutionists

Hopkins' prose during the early 1880s was punctuated dramatically by a number of complex images or metaphors drawn from science, in particular from natural history. When his friend Coventry Patmore stated in "Love and Poetry," an article that appeared in the *St. James's Gazette* in 1886, that "natural sciences are definite, because they deal with laws which are not realities but conditions of realities," Hopkins was able to agree with him. But Patmore went even further: "The greatest and perhaps the only real use of natural science is to supply similes and parables for poets and theologians." Having read another article by his friend in the same newspaper, Hopkins applauded Patmore's "parable" of the carcass of a sheep found on a country lane. Patmore wrote that the carcass had been "transformed into a mass of the soft, white, malodorous grubs known to anglers by the name of gentles." The moral? Patmore feared that the "ordered state of England" was being transformed into the "pulsating mass of grubs" known as democracy.

However much Hopkins may have agreed with some of Patmore's reactionary politics, he expressed surprise at Patmore's absolute statements about the "real use of natural science." But in these years science did indeed come to serve Hopkins as a source of dramatic metaphors for his religious and philosophical thoughts. Thus we read of the "cleaves" of the pomegranate as selves; the serpent or the dragon as the "archsnake" or the archetypal reptilian of the evolutionists; and the "scale of being" as a scale of selves, some inclined to evil, others to Godhead.

Hopkins used the pomegranate in his meditations on St. Ignatius' *Spiritual Exercises* as a metaphor for the "infinity of possible strains of action and choice for each possible self" in this world. "God sees whole," he wrote, but "we see at best only one cleave." In 1885, after his arrival in Dublin, he appended to one of his meditations this beautiful and intriguing sentence: "Of human nature the whole pomegranate fell in Adam."

By the time Hopkins had devised his own audacious use of the pomegranate, that seedpod had acquired not only a Christian but also a sensual iconography. Both are no doubt related to the fruit's seediness, its "seedbed of being," in James Cotter's phrase. A contemporary *Handbook of Christian Symbolism* (1865) described it thus: "The pomegranate, burst open and displaying its seeds, was accepted by early artists as the emblem of the future life, and of hope in immortality." But in its sensual life the pomegranate ranged in the nineteenth century from Byron, who wrote in *Giaour* (1813) that "the young pomegranate's blossoms strew their bloom in blushes ever new," to Flaubert, who described his heroine in *Salammbô* (1886) as being "as rosy as a half-opened pomegranate."

No one who has seen Rossetti's painting (1877) of Proserpine with her once-bitten pomegranate is likely to doubt its sensual associations, especially since the model was the stunning Jane Morris. Although Hopkins' affinity with some of the Pre-Raphaelites has been well documented, he would not have been especially comfortable with the band of Rossetti, Morris, Burne-Jones, and Swinburne, whose conversation, as they painted the Oxford Union Debating Hall in 1857, turned to a description of Heaven as "a rose-garden full of stunners." The flippancy of the Pre-

Raphaelite brotherhood did not, however, keep Rossetti from attempting traditional Christian subjects. Before the image of Proserpine with her pomegranate finally emerged, Rossetti had intended to paint Jane Morris as Eve with an apple.

The image of Eve brings us back to Hopkins' sentence, "Of human nature the whole pomegranate fell in Adam." That is, according to Hopkins' metaphor, the original range of choice, of our "actual" and "possible" selves, was sorely diminished with Original Sin. The compensation is of course the Incarnation or, as Hopkins wrote, the "cleave" of the "sphere of divine being" to us, the "entrance of Christ on the world." It is in this context that Hopkins offered what Christopher Devlin called Hopkins' "most startling and original theological innovation" (see chapter 4). Hopkins the Scotist was recycling the terms of a fifth-century heretic, Apollinaris, by distinguishing between *ensarkōsis* ("the taking of flesh") and *enanthropēsis* ("the becoming man"). These terms separated "the word was made flesh" and "came to dwell among us" into two orders of time, the first angelic, the second human or historic time.

Hopkins had some curious University College documentation of his Scotist views. His old Oxford friend William Addis held a brief fellowship there in 1882. He had collaborated with one of Hopkins' current colleagues, Tom Arnold, Mrs. Humphrey Ward's father (see chapter 1), on the *Catholic Dictionary* (third edition 1884). The *Dictionary* explained the condemnation of Apollinaris as the result of his refusal to accept that "becoming man" gave Christ a human intelligence. The *Dictionary* also explained the Scotist view of the Incarnation, which Hopkins believed, that "the Word would have become man, even had there been no fall."

The necessity of the Incarnation provoked another of Hopkins' striking metaphors. The satanic snake of the Garden of Eden is at once both the archetypal dragon of Revelation and, according to the evolutionists, the reptilian ancestor of all the vertebrates. In a meditation on Satan's inability to "recognize" Mary and "Christ in the flesh," which led to his refusal to serve God and his eventual Fall, Hopkins suggested that Satan was "the *kosmokratōr,* the worldwielder," who attempted to seize nature for his own purposes. Nature was nonetheless redeemed, "making it still habitable by man." Lucifer's countermaneuver made use of "the red or fiery dragon" that was the "sign that appeared in heaven," according to Revelation, chapter 12. He pulled "a third of the angels" in "his train" and "with his tail . . . swept the third part of the stars down to the earth." Hopkins concluded that as the woman is compared to the Earth in the solar system, so the dragon is to the constellation Draco, the tail of which "sweeps through 120° or a third of the sphere and which winds round the pole." P. J. Treanor, S. J., an astronomer teaching at Balliol in the 1950s, has confirmed most of Hopkins' analysis of Draco, including the possibility that the imagery of the Book of Revelation was in fact based on the position of importance that Draco held in the sky in ancient times. The polestar, once in the head of Draco, symbolizes Satan's attempt to establish himself with "a throne and post of vantage and so wreathing nature" in a spiral, just as his Edenic snake "wreathed himself in the Garden round the Tree of Knowledge."

Hopkins carried his metaphor even further. As the "coil or spiral" is a "type of the Devil," so then is the dragon, "taken to be a reptile," a "symbol of the Devil." "So that," Hopkins argued, "if the Devil is symbolized as a snake he must be an archsnake and a dragon." Dragons are almost always reptiles: "Now among the vertebrates the reptiles go near to combine the qualities of the other classes in themselves and are, I think, taken by the Evolutionists as nearest the original vertebrate stem and as the point of departure for the rest." Reptiles gather "up the attributes of many creatures": they "sometimes have bat's wings," often are armored like crocodiles, sturgeons, or "lobsters and other crustacea," and display "colors like the dragonfly and other insects." This enormous variety really represents a satanic flaw. The dragon "symbolizes one who aiming at every perfection ends by being a monster, a 'fright'"—as if Satan had tried to seize the whole Chain of Being for himself.

Hopkins actually returned to the paradigm of the Great Chain of Being, refurbishing the analogy of the musical scale he had used so often in the 1860s and 1870s. As a metaphor no longer devoted strictly to inscapes or species, it came to represent for him a scale of "selves" or human "natures" that is "infinite up towards the divine." The old problem that the Stonyhurst Philosophers had grappled with returned. Human nature has a "freedom of pitch" or self-determination that "is in the chooser himself and his choosing faculty." God can "shift the self that lies in one to a higher, that is, better, pitch of itself; that is, to a pitch or determination of itself on the side of good." It was at this point in his meditation that Hopkins introduced the "cleaves" of the pomegranate as an additional metaphor for the "actual" and "possible" selves of human natures. With such metaphors, then, he attempted to resolve some of his most pressing theological problems (see p. 141).

"Papers, Writings or Notebooks, Sketches or What Not"

In 1884 Hopkins was dispatched to Dublin to help strengthen the classics faculty of University College, whose administration had been entrusted to the Jesuits as a special project. He began a period that, although extremely difficult for him personally, brought him into a university setting of brilliant if eccentric colleagues whose scientific and theological interests complemented his own.

Nevertheless Hopkins felt out of place in Dublin. His poems attest to that feeling; bad health plagued him and Irish politics dismayed him, while more of his spectacular and quixotic exploits eventually reached legendary status within the Society. He allowed himself, so one story went, to be dragged by the heels around the lecture table by students in order to illustrate Hector's fate at Troy. Others recalled that he would only lecture on material he knew would *not* be on the exams, since the extramural students were unable to attend his lectures but had to take the same exams as the attending students. And, as mentioned previously, he walked out of the honorary-degree ceremony for his old friend and colleague Stephen Perry because the music played was "God Save Ireland."

When his long-time Jesuit friends and colleagues donned the mask or persona of Plures to write their short biography of him for the *Dublin Review* in 1920, they were goaded to their task by what they felt were Bridges' unwarranted criticisms of Hopkins' relationship with the Society of Jesus. Bridges, they wrote, was "under the delusion . . . that Gerard caged himself in a religious prison amid the political Yahoos and clerics of Dublin like some bright plumaged songster in a bat-tenanted belfry." His "terrible sonnets," as a number of his Dublin poems have come to be known, did reveal a wrestling match with his own soul: "Not, I'll not, carrion comfort, Despair, not feast on thee." Plures' task was to add the perspective of Jesuit friends and colleagues "to the beautiful but broken arc" that Bridges had only begun to describe. Plures saw Hopkins' final Dublin years as a "tragedy," but only because sending this "English

Joseph Rickaby's Diary

In 1877 Joseph Rickaby wrote in his diary that he was inclined towards "the Scotist view of the Incarnation." But we should not hold too melodramatic a view of the matter. Rickaby's edition of the *Spiritual Exercises of St. Ignatius Loyola* (1915, with a second edition in 1936) was forthright in its author's Scotist belief in an Incarnation that was always to have been, "even antecedently to the sin of Adam."

Rickaby's diary constitutes a revealing parallel document to Hopkins' journals. Their careers were also in many ways parallel, except that Hopkins' untimely death cut short his career. Like Hopkins, Rickaby was at Stonyhurst in the early 1870s and at St. Beuno's in the mid-1870s, but he returned to Stonyhurst for the first major part of his career, as a professor of philosophy from 1877 to 1896. After a short stint in London at Farm Street, he spent the second major part of his career at Oxford, from the turn of the century until his death in 1935. His diary faithfully records his spiritual and emotional life for virtually every year from 1877 to 1926.

During a retreat in the 1880s he reflected on his youth: "After a pietist boyhood, aetat 20, 21, I should have become an infidel from Mill's philosophy. Aetat 23–25, I should have given myself up to my passions, but not finally, I have too much intellect. So I should have turned part aesthete, part social politician." This was presumably a close call; but as he revealed later on, in the 1890s, he was unable to grow fond of Oxford until he became a writer. Nevertheless, he worried in 1901 that his scholarship might make him into "that old scholar-squire" in *Robert Elsmere,* who was modeled on Mark Pattison of Lincoln College. Such a path would have been a "mistake."

Rickaby thus shared many of Hopkins' fears and aspirations. But in one way they were definitely unrelated: "I don't find God," Rickaby admitted, "in Nature." Instead Rickaby found himself agreeing with Newman, who, Rickaby asserted, found Nature opposed to God. Then, as if to realize that this was much too strong a statement, Rickaby pulled back. Nature "rather hides God than displays him. God lurks under Nature, and shall only be revealed when the veil of Nature is rent. Yet even on the veil are wrought certain figures of what is hidden beneath." Had his friend Hopkins neglected to remind him how inscapes flash out from the landscape when the beholder is suddenly moved by the instress of God?

mystic compounded of Benjamin Jowett and Duns Scotus" into Ireland was to "launch him into a further and stranger country" than if he had been sent to China.

Yet Hopkins persisted in his philosophical quest for answers on his own terms. He really did resemble Joseph Rickaby, who wrote in his diary of his reluctance or perhaps inability to change. Plures said of Hopkins that "the obvious he avoided like sin." Ruskin said of himself, in *Fors Clavigera*, that he had "the balanced union of artistic sensibility with scientific faculty, which enabled [him] to love Giotto, and learn from Galileo." To remain true to such a union Ruskin may have gone insane. Hopkins' eccentric ways may have been a somewhat smaller price to pay.

When Hopkins was at Stonyhurst, a porter had noticed him staring at brightly colored objects in the path. This "eccentricity" and "simple-mindedness" soon passed into Jesuit legend as the marks of Hopkins' "whimsical genius." And perhaps this is an accurate assessment. But what of a University College professor who opened his lectures on spherical trigonometry by peeling a potato for his class and cutting it into sections? That is precisely what John Casey, Hopkins' colleague and a mathematics professor, did on the first day of classes in 1884: "We sat round him in a cluster," Father Darlington, then a University College student, reported, "and the first thing he did was to bring out of his pocket a potato with a knife, and he commenced operations by cutting it into cubes." And Casey was supposedly a sophisticated mathematician!

Casey and Morgan Crofton were the mathematical stars of the University College faculty. Both men were fellows of the Royal Society, both wrote numerous scientific papers, and both were capable of introducing their broader views of spiritual life into that seemingly absolute realm of numbers. Casey had the reputation of being an excellent teacher; perhaps he was simply better with a paring knife. He believed that all first-rate mathematicians were believers in God; he told Father Darlington, "If ever I came across one who was not, I knew that he was a second-rater, and I was never deceived."

Crofton, when he came to sum up his ideas on probability for the ninth edition of the *Encyclopedia Britannica* in 1885, wrote of Newman's *Grammar of Assent* as he explained the differences between mathematical and "common" definitions of "certainty": "It is very difficult and often impossible, as is pointed out in the celebrated *Grammar of Assent*, to draw out the grounds on which the human mind in each case yields the conviction, or assent, which, according to Newman, admits of no degrees, and either is entire or is not at all." Perhaps it was appropriate to quote Newman here, for philosophical if not sentimental reasons. Like Hopkins, Crofton had been received into the Church by Newman himself, albeit a decade earlier, in the 1850s. But what is of special interest is Crofton's gloss on Newman, a quotation from the astronomer Herschel that appeared in the *Edinburgh Review* (1850): "There is a sort of *leap* which most men make from a high probability to absolute assurance . . . analogous to the sudden consilience, or springing into one, of the two images seen by binocular vision, when gradually brought within a certain proximity." Here again is science used as metaphor, but this time by a nationally known scientist.

Hopkins' letters from Dublin during his last years are strewn with various projects, scientific and otherwise, that he never finished. He wrote about placing "music and meter . . . on a scientific footing which will be final like the law of gravitation"; it was this project for which he told Bridges that he would need "new words, without which there can be no new science." He wrote to Dixon about a "popular account of Light and Ether," and still later mentioned a paper called "Statistics and Free Will," surely a topic only a Galton could master, although his viewpoint would not have been Hopkins'. And while these projects continued or, more likely, faltered, he was corresponding with others about Egyptian etymology and Chinese music. We see a mind churning with ideas, venting theories in letter after letter.

His early death in Dublin at age forty-four was indeed tragic, the destruction of so many of his personal papers in a whirlwind cleanup of his room very sad. The unpublished letters to his parents from his brothers, Arthur and Everard, are also poignant. Everard hoped that Father Wheeler, the Jesuit in charge of household tasks in Dublin, would give Hopkins' parents "his papers—his poems among them," as well as "a little rosary" Everard sent him at Christmas. Arthur wrote similarly, but with more detail: "I have only a few minutes to catch the post, but I write to remind you in case it may not have occurred to you, that before you leave Dublin it would be worth while to ask Father Wheeler for leave to look into any papers, writings or notebooks, sketches or what not that Gerard may have left. Probably they would be allowed to pass into your possession." Arthur added that he believed that Gerard had "kept a Diary," and that "if there are any little Devotional Books," his wife "would much like to have one."

But Father Wheeler burned most of the papers and "what not," reserving only the poems to send to Robert Bridges. What other papers in Hopkins' hand remain from this period are either letters that he had sent or the results of the foraging expeditions of other Jesuits in his residence who wished to save something of their eccentric colleague.

But if Hopkins was whimsical, eccentric, and original in his ways, he was no more so than many of his contemporaries within the Jesuit order. We have already looked briefly at some of his colleagues in Dublin. What of his old friends and the Stonyhurst Philosophers who survived him? Henry Marchant, for example, lived out his retirement at Stonyhurst, having published only two articles, one on weather reporting, the other on hypnotism. His room was filled with boxes of newspapers, magazines, books, old clothing, and bits of furniture, an arrangement that reminded the younger Jesuits there of the Roman catacombs. Still, those younger Jesuits came to him for instruction and advice because he kept up with the latest theories in physical science as well as speculations about the relationship of faith and science. He wrote but did not publish essays on the importance of radium as a paradigm of energy and the equivalence of energy and life.

Two of the men who signed themselves "Plures" had distinguished careers as Catholic writers, but they too came to be regarded as eccentrics. The same young Jesuits who visited Marchant's room at Stonyhurst also attended John Rickaby's classes in ethics, where they were not "surprized when something of St. Thomas Aquinas or Suarez was illustrated by a quotation from Lewis Carroll or an old *Punch* joke." He was particularly known as a perpetrator of "atrocious puns." Another Stonyhurst College student reminisced about his brother, Joseph Rickaby, known as a "brilliant, lively and eccentric man of the old school."

Marchant died in 1937 at age eighty-nine, John Rickaby in 1927 at eighty, and Joseph Rickaby in 1932 at eighty-seven. Hopkins died almost forty years before his Stonyhurst friends. His poetry made the journey to the twentieth century; he did not. His contemporaries saw his life as a "beautiful but broken arc"; they based their image on many of his views and activities that have been obscured over the years. That their image, together with the figure of Hopkins in this book, should be regarded as a new portrait of Hopkins is really an accident of literary history. In fact, as I hope is obvious by now, it is really an old portrait.

Notes

The six volumes of Hopkins' prose and poetry are cited by short title only; in the Sources they are listed and described fully under "Hopkins." All other published materials are cited by author or by title (if author is anonymous).

Preface

p. xiii "the stars themselves . . .": Manuscript, D.VI.6, Campion Hall

Introduction: The Portraits of Hopkins

p. 1 "Surely one vocation . . .": *Correspondence . . . Dixon,* 90
"long icicles . . .": *Journals,* 201
André Bremond: Ruggles, 124
"Everything bizarre . . .": Barraud, 159; another version in Denis Meadows, 142–43
p. 2 "was naturally somewhat eccentric . . .": *Journals,* 421
"Father Gerard's work . . .": Manuscript letter from Mrs. Frances de Paravicini, June 14, 1889, Bodleian; also in *Journals,* 301
p. 3 "All the world is full . . .": *Journals,* 230
"What philosophy good *or* bad . . .": *Further Letters,* 250
"A form of atomism . . .": *Journals,* 120
"I do not think . . .": *Journals,* 199
p. 5 As a young man Keating: Bischoff (1951–52), 556–57
p. 6 "Thirty years have passed . . .": Page, 47
"an English mystic . . .": Page, 52
Plures' gently ironic description: Page, 56
p. 7 neurasthenia: Page, 56

"I would not have done that . . .": Lahey, 142. Page, 55–56, has it paraphrased: "He would not have minded it, if it were not so wicked!"

Jesuit participation: Walsh, 202–15

a fraction of Clare's work: *Journals*, 63. Hopkins had read an unsigned essay on Clare's death, "A Luckless Poet," *Spectator*, May 28, 1864, 615–17, which quoted Clare's poem "I am."

Hopkins "had a keen eye . . .": *Journals*, 421

"full of new words . . .": *Letters to Bridges*, 254

p. 8 "What becomes of my verses . . .": *Correspondence . . . Dixon*, 150

"between an apple-green . . .": *Nature*, January 3, 1884; in *Correspondence . . . Dixon*, 164

"Note on green wheat . . .": *Journals*, 20

p. 9 "This has been a very beautiful day . . .": *Journals*, 242–43

1. Oxford and the Cockatrice's Den

p. 11 "From the mere analysis . . .": John Rickaby (March 1877), 284

"pink obscenity": Sulloway, 49

"vigorous horizontals": "To Oxford (ii)," *Poems*, 22

Brodie's influence: Vernon and Vernon, 61–62

"There, gentlemen . . .": Cox, 452–53

p. 12 Although the official reason: Vernon and Vernon, 42–44

Dr. Kidd . . . said: Vernon and Vernon, 44

In 1832 Ruskin's master: *Reports . . . BAAS* (1835), 104–7

"erection of an edifice . . .": Vernon and Vernon, 40

p. 14 "cockatrice's den": Vernon and Vernon, 57

while others attacked: Vernon and Vernon, 51

the vote of seventy to sixty-four: Vernon and Vernon, 58

"induce a mental habit . . .": Vernon and Vernon, 36

Rolleston, noted a contemporary: Vernon and Vernon, 63–64

Acland encouraged his friend: Vernon and Vernon, 74–81

p. 15 its interior should resemble: Vernon and Vernon, 57–58

The number of students sitting: Vernon and Vernon, 98

"dispute between science . . .": Pattison (1868), 275

An Oxford historian: Edward A. Freeman, 819

Since the "philosophical element . . .": Pattison (1868), 292, 297

These reforms: Edward A. Freeman, 821, 823

p. 16 Renan routinely describes: Renan, 257

Logic at Oxford: Nettleship (1901), 113
"Is it possible to deduce . . .": *Oxford University Examination Papers*, no. 69 (1867), 21

p. 17 Ruskin's spiritual handymen: Vernon and Vernon, 79–80
Lord Wrottlesbury emphasized: *Reports . . . BAAS* (1861), lviii

p. 18 Henslow, the section's chair: "British Association" (July 7, 1860), 26
"presented more differences . . .": "British Association" (July 7, 1860), 26
a key role in memory: Sagan, 69
"the gift of speech . . .": "British Association" (July 7, 1860), 26

p. 19 "chemical stinks": Vernon and Vernon, 55
although keen observers: Leonard Huxley, vol. 1, 182; Sidgwick, 434–35
Draper set out: *Reports . . . BAAS* (1861), 115
The Reverend Cresswell: "British Association" (July 14, 1860), 65
The unfortunate Mr. Dingle: Leonard Huxley, vol. 1, 196

p. 20 Darwin's "primordial germ . . .": "British Association" (July 14, 1860), 65
"What have they . . .": Freemantle, in Darwin (1888), vol. 2, 320–21
Huxley was reported: Sidgwick, 433–34
"With regard to the psychological . . .": "British Association" (July 14, 1860), 65
"You say that development . . .": Freemantle, in Darwin (1888), vol. 2, 320–21

p. 21 "He was not ashamed . . .": Sidgwick, 434
"had forgotten to behave . . .": Unpublished letter from Canon Farrar to Leonard Huxley, July 12, 1899, quoted in J. R. Lucas, 327. Lucas' article is a mine of information about the debate, but his conclusions—that the bishop was arguing scientifically and that the debate's "victory" did not go to the scientists—are untenable and, for the most part, are refuted by his own evidence. See Gould, who develops Lucas' position at great length, although he ignores the July 7 sparring match between Huxley and Owen. He also offers Balfour Stewart as a disinterested witness and "uncommitted scientist"; Stewart however, was quite a religious scientist, as his co-authorship of *The Unseen Universe* demonstrates. Still another angle comes from Alfred Newton, president of the biology section of the BAAS in 1887, when he gave his recollections of the debate in *Report . . . BAAS* (1888), 727: he said that the debate was a "drawn battle" and that it was only in the following year that Darwin's theory began its ascendancy.

Robert Fitzroy: "British Association" (July 14, 1860), 65. Himmelfarb, 291, has the Bible story, but writes (483 n. 12) that in Darwin's manuscripts there is a reference to the incident of "poor Fitzroy with the Bible," which Darwin believed had happened in another meeting during the same conference; see Darwin (1967), 210.

Sir John Lubbock reported: Sidgwick, 433–34

Dr. Joseph Hooker: "British Association" (July 14, 1860), 65

p. 22 an intellectual center: Rogers, 168 ("no doubt Balliol is the most distinguished college . . .")

all of whose students: Liddell, 59

"the Examination . . .": Stedman (1878), 223

"a sort of cloudy rumor . . .": Parkin, vol. 1, 290

"Here come I . . .": Cited as H. C. Beeching's poem in Grigson, 536, but there are other, slightly different versions reported (e.g., Jan Morris, 184).

p. 23 "system of quasi-scientific ethics": Mallock (1920), 82

"sceptical teachings": Mallock (1920), 80. The suicide in 1870 was Favour James Greg; see Elliott, 50.

"It is a great pity . . .": Geldart, 157

"plain living and high thinking . . .": Geldart, 138–40, 153–54

"gushed . . .": Geldart, 168, 170

p. 25 "university of Duns Scotus . . .": Pattison (1876), 82

Was Socrates a utilitarian?: Jowett, 212, 200–206

they complained: Liddell, 62; Nettleship (1882), 860

"ecclesiastical platform . . .": Pattison (1876), 93

p. 26 He saw the tutors: Clarke (1885), 353

Jowett's rise: Faber, 357

"lost its hold . . .": Clarke (1885), 358

saintly qualities: Unpublished letters from Hopkins' Oxford friends in the Bodleian: Frances de Paravicini (June 14, 1889), "saintliness"; Ed Bond (June 12, 1889), "fine spirituality"; also a letter from Friedrich von Hügel (June 24, 1889), the nuns "all felt that he must be a saint." Even allowing for Victorian piety, these would constitute the beginning of an impressive register of opinion.

"fashionable form of paganism . . .": Clarke (1885), 358

"I care for him . . .": *Letters to Bridges*, 31

ritualists: Geldart, 139

p. 27 Hopkins' first exam: *Oxford University Calendar* (1863)

Hopkins joked: *Further Letters*, 84

"Of all the religious sects . . .": Coleridge (1866), 54

"Oh, do let me . . .": Sutherland, 383

His second exam: *Oxford University Calendar* (1864)
This exam: *Oxford University Examination Papers,* no. 33 (1864)
p. 29 logic questions "indispensable . . .": *Oxford University Calendar* (1867), 106
dialogue between A and B: *Oxford University Examination Papers,* no. 33 (1864), 52
that writing rhetorically: Coleridge and Clarke, 104; similar judgment in Pattison (1876), 93
"If light consisted . . .": Jevons, 320
"The *minimum visibile* . . .": Jevons, 324
p. 30 the school of natural science: *Oxford University Examination Papers,* no. 8 (1863), 12
"perversions": Mansel, 222
Hopkins' third exam: *Oxford University Calendar,* 1867
"*Aristotle* . . .": *Journals,* 49; *Oxford University Calendar,* 1864
Hopkins faced questions: *Oxford University Examination Papers,* no. 69 (1867), 17, 19
the entire set of questions: *Oxford University Examination Papers,* no. 69 (1867), 22
p. 31 "star of Balliol": A legendary attribution. See Lahey, 43, and Gardner, in Hopkins, *Poems and Prose,* xxiii; more critically, Allsopp, 175 n. 54.
Jowett's recommendation: Page, 51
it was harder "to frame . . .": Pattison (1876), 90
they had to be consistent: Stedman (1887), 248
"statements . . . are based . . .": *Oxford University Calendar* (1867), 103
faddish interests: Clarke, quoted in Coleridge and Clarke (1869), 107
p. 32 "acts of apprehension . . .": Manuscript, D.III.5, Campion Hall
"the synthesis of a number . . .": Manuscript, D.III.5, Campion Hall
"we can be sure . . .": Manuscript, D.XI.2, Campion Hall
Aristotle argues: Aristotle (1869), 195–96
p. 33 "Perception then is *nous* . . .": Manuscript, M.II., Campion Hall
"invariable sequence . . .": Manuscript, D.VI.2, Campion Hall
"Suppose a white disk . . .": Manuscript, D.VI.2, Campion Hall. The figure here is not in Hopkins' own hand but is a copy of the original.
"Now we have called . . .": Manuscript, D.VI.2, Campion Hall
p. 34 "stem of stress . . .": *Journals,* 127

2. The Atoms of Lucretius

p. 35 "The existence . . .": Jenkin (1868), 241
"phase of infidelity . . .": Mallock (1908), 40
"the application of the atomic theory . . .": *Oxford University Examination Papers,* no. 17 (1863), 3
p. 36 "I am dazed . . .": Russell and Goodman, 120
"I've tried hard . . .": Russell and Goodman, 120
to measure the size of atoms: Kelvin (1870), 551–53; Kelvin (1889), vol. 1, 147–217
p. 37 Brodie argued: Brock, 150; Knight, 125
Lord Kelvin maintained: Kelvin (1867), 217–60
p. 38 "Empedocles died . . .": Jebb, 103
p. 39 "It seems probable to me . . .": Knight, 5–6
p. 41 He drew circular symbols: Jones and Cohen, 139–40, or Dampier, 98
"I have chosen . . .": Roscoe and Harden, 111
"This plate . . .": Jones and Cohen, 140, or Dampier, 99
Although "simple" atoms: Jones and Cohen, 139–40, or Dampier, 97
p. 43 "as the clear expositor . . .": Jenkin (1868), 241
By avoiding "atomic symbols . . .": Brodie (1866), 855–56
p. 44 "A system of marks . . .": Brodie (1866), 855
Clerk Maxwell's jibe: "Chemistry of the Future," 296
"I turn for instruction . . .": Russell and Goodman, 120
Such Glyptic Formulae: Brodie (1867), 296
p. 45 not "model balls . . .": Brodie (1867), 296
He divided the contestants: Brock, 141–42
Alexander W. Williamson: Williamson, 409
"for the permanence . . .": Maxwell (1878), 45
the research of Hermann von Helmholtz: Thomson, vol. 1, 510
p. 46 "if two vortex-rings . . .": Thomson, vol. 1, 514
"The existence of atoms . . .": Roscoe, 406
"How otherwise than by . . .": Roscoe, 406
J. H. van't Hoff's tetrahedron: Crosland, 265–67
p. 47 Darwin had proposed: See Darwin (1868), especially vol. 2.
"In addition to the truth . . .": Huxley (1893–94), vol. 3, 147
p. 48 In a private letter: J. W. Gruber, 77
Mivart attacked: Mivart (1871), 5, 252–53
Darwin had accepted: Mivart (1871), 217
p. 49 "It is remarkable . . .": Mivart (1869), 288
Pangenesis, Darwin wrote: Darwin (1868), vol. 2, 374
These gemmules: Darwin (1868), vol. 2, 402

In the later edition: Darwin (1885), vol. 2, 350 n. 1
Darwin did, however, drop: Darwin (1885), vol. 2, ch. 27, "Provisional Hypothesis of Pangenesis." See Galton (1871) and Geisen for the context of the debate on pangenesis.
Even as early as 1839: Howard E. Gruber, 397
p. 51 "we cannot see . . .": Howard E. Gruber, 398
"All that can be said . . .": Howard E. Gruber, 398
He wrote to Mivart: Leonard Huxley, vol. 2, 113
the "fundamental doctrine . . .": Mill (1865), 6
p. 51 The "essence of natural phenomena": F. O. Ward, 40
Huxley called positivism: Thomas Henry Huxley (1869), 141
The final blow came: Whewell (1837), 320–33
"great seasons . . .": *Journals,* 119
Guidebooks for new Oxford students: Stedman, 208
p. 53 Hopkins had to translate: *Oxford University Examination Papers,* no. 33 (1864)
"such things as are possessed . . .": Lucretius (1864), vol. 2, 28, 120, 241–42
Instead he attacked: Bacon (1963), 205–6
Only the atomists: Bacon (1963), 198
"The Moral System of Hobbes": Manuscript, D.XI.3, Campion Hall
p. 54 Immerse yourself: Pater, vol. 1, 233
"not the fruit of experience . . .": Pater, vol. 1, 236
Marius, "with the Cyrenaics . . .": Pater, vol. 2, 148
"pleasure of the ideal present . . .": Pater, vol. 2, 158
p. 55 Wallace even urged: Wallace (1880), 182
"likeness and difference" of things: *Journals,* 90
"Connection of the Cyrenaic Philosophy . . .": Manuscript, D.X1.2, Campion Hall
p. 56 "A form of atomism . . .": *Journals,* 120
"It will always . . .": *Journals,* 118
"withdraw to themselves . . .": *Journals,* 118
W. W. Skeat: *Further Letters,* 431–32
p. 57 Milton and Lucretius: *Correspondence . . . Dixon,* 18

3. Black Rain in Lancashire

p. 58 "The whole difference . . .": Gosse and Gosse, 8
"some shape of the Platonic Ideas . . .": *Journals,* 121
"not the vague dream . . .": Manuscript, D.VIII, Campion Hall

"Plato's relation to us . . .": Manuscript, D.VIII, Campion Hall

p. 59 "concerning the language of science . . .": Whewell (1843), vol. 2, 502
thermotics, electrics, and tidology: Whewell (1843), vol. 2, 508–9
idiopts: Whewell (1843), vol. 2, 509
"full of new words . . .": *Letters to Bridges,* 254

p. 60 "The view from the fields . . .": *Journals,* 71
"The scales of color . . .": *Journals,* 147
"I counted in a bright rainbow . . .": *Journals,* 237
"There was in the picture . . .": *Journals,* 246
"noble scape of stars . . .": *Journals,* 170
"all-powerfulness of instress . . .": *Journals,* 188
"trees in the river . . .": *Journals,* 189

p. 62 He noted: Knapp, 98–100

p. 63 "new medusoid . . .": Gosse (1853), 331
"coldly correct . . .": Gosse (1853), vi
"endless variety . . .": Gosse and Gosse, 8
His family: See Bump (1982).
the dodo was not extinct: "The Dodo Non-extinct," 21
The Hopkins family library: House and House (1975), 19
"the stars . . .": Bonnycastle, 305
its emblematic tale: Morley, vol. 2, 136–37

p. 64 Query 14 of the *Opticks*: Newton, 346
Aristotle had written: Goethe (1810), Eastlake's note BB
The keys of this instrument: Scholes, 206

p. 65 pre-Romantic synaesthesia: See von Erhardt-Siebold.
God's "perfect system . . .": Field (1817), 27
"the distance on the scale . . .": Field (1820), 204. Heuser, 20, 105, first pointed out the likely connection between Hopkins and Field.
"one of the semitones . . .": Field (1820), 203
Field handily supplied a color chart: Field (1817), example 9. See also Field (1835), plate 1 (figs. 2–3).
"depth and brilliancy": Field (1817), 204
chromoscope: Field (1817), 216–17

p. 67 Goethe believed: Lewes (1864), 337
Goethe, who preferred to believe: Lewes (1864), 342

p. 68 Turner annotated his copy: See Lindsay, 278–81.
but their support of Goethe's theory: Lindsay, 280–81
"plus" colors: Lindsay, 281
"homage to Goethe": Lindsay, 281
poetic caption: Lindsay, 281

Newton "was betrayed . . .": Goethe (1810), xii
"fanciful analogies . . .": Goethe (1810), xii
"direct presentation of facts . . .": Tyndall (1900), 66

p. 69 "the phenomena of mixed colors . . .": Helmholtz (1877), 64
"see the simple elements . . .": Helmholtz (1877), 64–65
"The musical scale . . .": Barrett, 286–87
"between the effect . . .": Monro, 362
"curious speculation . . .": Dean, 385. See *Nature* from January through June 1870 and September 1872 for numerous other letters concerning this issue.
"one stress . . .": *Correspondence . . . Dixon,* 23

p. 71 He quoted his own lines: *Letters to Bridges,* 46
"deepening color . . .": *Journals,* 76. Hopkins uses *intervallary* as a synonym for *diatonic.*

p. 72 "absolute existence": *Journals,* 120
"certain forms . . .": *Journals,* 120
"brilliancy, starriness . . .": *Journals,* 290
"Swiss trees . . .": *Journals,* 170
"brilliancy, sort of starriness . . .": *Journals,* 206
"richness and grace . . .": *Journals,* 246

p. 74 "The sensations of the eye . . .": Manuscript, D.VI.1, Campion Hall
"image (of sight . . .)": *Journals,* 125
As he listened: *Journals,* 194

p. 76 "At two minutes to ten . . .": *Journals,* 232
"It may be because . . .": *Journals,* 232
Hopkins described the lightning: *Journals,* 233–34
"Dull furry thickened scapes . . .": *Journals,* 234

p. 77 "A little before 7 . . .": *Journals,* 200–201
"It gathered . . .": *Journals,* 201
"At 5:50 p.m. . . .": *Stonyhurst Observatory* (October 1870), 25

p. 78 "At 9:40 . . .": *Stonyhurst Observatory* (October 1870), 25. For a similar description, see "Reports on Three Aurorae," 226–28.
"The comet . . .": *Journals,* 249
"Perhaps I can give . . .": Lockyer (July 23, 1874), 226
"Now, if this comet . . .": Lockyer (July 23, 1874), 226

p. 81 "sun drawing water": *Observer's Handbook,* 161
"pale purple clouds . . .": *Journals,* 65

p. 82 "a low rainbow . . .": *Journals,* 169
"deepest expression of color . . .": *Journals,* 148
"It was a glowing yellow sunset . . .": *Journals,* 210

two of three main classes: *Observer's Handbook,* 161
"First definitely adverted . . .": *Journals,* 216
p. 83 "The distance . . .": *Journals,* 252
"a sort of halo . . .": O'Reilly, 268
"frequently visible . . .": Thompson, 293
He "was rather at a loss . . .": Dechevrens, 31
p. 84 "There seems no reason . . .": *Correspondence . . . Dixon,* 161
"Yesterday the sky . . .": *Correspondence . . . Dixon,* 162

4. The Stonyhurst Philosophers

p. 85 "In addition to the truth . . .": John Rickaby (1876), 197
When one rebel: Quirinus, 386–87
p. 86 In 1874 Hopkins spoke: Thomas, 247
Throughout 1869 and 1870: Thomas, 219–21, 228
p. 87 "have sunk into the abyss . . .": Manning, 194, 201
"If any one shall say that finite things . . .": Manning, 201
p. 88 "If any one shall say that miracles . . .": Manning, 202
the Stonyhurst Philosophers: See unsigned note, "Stonyhurst Series of Philosophical Manuals," 243. This series, eventually called the Stonyhurst Philosophical Series, was written by those who had "lectured on philosophy either at the College or St. Mary's Hall, and all, with a single exception, [had] made their own course of Philosophical studies at the latter place." Two other Stonyhurst Philosophers, Michael Maher (professor of mental and moral philosophy at Stonyhurst College) and Bernard Boedder (professor of natural theology at St. Mary's Hall) wrote books included in the series, but they had no personal connection with Hopkins.
"new school of metaphysics . . .": Hopkins' phrase is in *Journals,* 121; Clarke's is in Clarke (1874), 179.
p. 89 "those who had in them . . .": Coleridge (1866), 58–59
p. 90 "Converts to the Catholic Church . . .": Clarke (1889), preface
"fallen under the influence . . .": This and all quotations following are from Clarke (1885), 353, 358.
p. 91 Hopkins knew: *Further Letters,* 53
he "liked" Hopkins: Holland, 29
a "wicked" act: *Further Letters,* 83
p. 93 "I always liked . . .": *Further Letters,* 249
"I am glad . . .": Holland, 29–30

"I imagine him . . .": Holland, 29–30
p. 94 "try and digest . . .": Holland, 30
He accepted: Holland, 31–33
"miracles do not happen . . .": Mrs. Humphrey Ward (1888), 388
p. 95 "kept so much of the Oxford manner . . .": Joseph Rickaby (1900), 338
This compromise galled: Purbrick (1869), 414–15, 418–19
p. 96 "that spirit . . .": Clarke (1896), 219, 221
"Philosophy is more useful . . .": Thomas, 247
"That *The Month* . . .": Thomas, 252
p. 97 In 1877 speakers: Thomas, 173
Years later, in 1903: Joseph Rickaby, manuscript, January 19, 1903, Archives, English Province
p. 98 John Rickaby distilled: John Rickaby (October 1876), 197
"to treat physiology . . .": Draper (1858), v
"great doctrine of Biogenesis": Thomas Henry Huxley (1870), 404
p. 99 Bastian classified matter: Bastian (July 14, 1870), 220, 228
"Tyndall's Address . . .": Lange, vol. 2, 363–64
"The interaction of the atoms . . .": Tyndall (1874), 32
p. 100 "most mad": *Further Letters,* 128
"unanswerable": Tyndall (1900), 169
"molecular processes": Tyndall (1900), 167–68
Tyndall . . . "cross the boundary . . .": Tyndall (1900), 191
Rickaby tried to be generous: Joseph Rickaby (October 1874), 219–21
p. 101 "There are those of us . . .": Joseph Rickaby (October 1874), 216
Hopkins . . . encountered Tyndall: *Journals,* 182; *Further Letters,* 128. Tyndall (1896), 275–76, describes the mass but does not mention Hopkins or Bond.
"He quotes Draper . . .": *Further Letters,* 128
"fine phrase": *Further Letters,* 128
Rickaby concluded: John Rickaby (1901), 28
p. 102 Involution was: John Rickaby (March 1877), 273
Rickaby again: John Rickaby (March 1877), 279, 282
"matter is capable of self-organization . . .": John Rickaby (May 1878), 45, 43
"perfectly logical": John Rickaby (March 1877), 284
p. 103 "molecules of matter . . .": John Rickaby (October 1876), 197
"were evolved from primitive Monera . . .": John Rickaby (November 1876), 294–95
Huxley's specialities: See Thomas Henry Huxley (1878), 73, 4 n. 1.

"confound the intuition . . .": John Rickaby (1879), 46–47
"the consenting act of the will . . .": Lucas (February 1878), 242
"because there is uniformity . . .": Lucas (February 1878), 246
"a lurking nest of irregularity": Lucas (February 1878), 247

p. 105 "break through the decrees . . .": Lucas (June 1878), 243, quotes this passage from Lucretius (book 2, 251ff.) in Latin, but the translation I have used is Munro, vol. 2, 63.

p. 106 "the doctrines . . .": Lucas (June 1878), 249
"produce an effect . . .": Lucas (June 1878), 248
Maxwell's "sorting demon": Lucas (June 1878), 250
"by operating selectively . . .": Kelvin (1889), vol. 1, 138
"capable of doing work . . .": Maxwell, quoted in Lucas (June 1878), 250–51
Lucas suggested: Lucas (June 1878), 251

p. 107 Although Lord Kelvin did not refer: Kelvin (1889), vol. 1, 141
Lucas went still further: Lucas (June 1878), 254–56
"Miracles are not only . . .": Newman, 375, 371–72

p. 108 "Doctrinal questions . . .": Holmes (1966), 529
"might be of a better . . .": Pattison (1885), 211
"a lurking fondness . . .": Pattison (1885), 212
"as things to be expected . . .": A. W. Hutton, vol. 5, 322–23

p. 109 "theocratic intervention": A chapter with this title is found only in the 1883 edition of Galton's *Inquiries.*
If prayers really work: Galton (August 1872), 133–34, 127–28
"markedly religious . . .": Galton (1872), 127–28
"prayer gauge . . .": See Tyndall and Thompson; the phrase "prayer-gauge" appears in R. H. Hutton, 181.
Huxley, the third scientist: R. H. Hutton, 183–84
"haunted by swarms . . .": Thomas Henry Huxley (1893–94), vol. 5, ix, xiii

p. 110 If a Christian, Huxley asked: Thomas Henry Huxley (1893–94), vol. 5, 185
He recommended to Bridges: *Letters to Bridges,* 40
"pebble stones . . .": Alban Butler, vol. 11, 68
He quoted: Alban Butler, vol. 11, 70

p. 111 "The sight of the water . . .": *Journals,* 261
"alleged cure of a case . . .": *Further Letters,* 132
"mythological center . . .": *Letters to Bridges,* 40
"Henceforth . . .": *Poems,* 190
"As long as men are mortal . . .": *Poems,* 192

Herbert Lucas provided: Herbert Lucas (1893), 437
p. 112 "the number of cures . . .": Maher (1895), 153
"cures": Maher (1895), 154
"The paths to the Well . . .": Maher (1895), 155
"fine reddish moss . . .": Hammond, 49
p. 113 "man is descended . . .": *Further Letters,* 128
"similar position . . .": Mivart (1871), 217
p. 114 there were really two ways: Mivart (1871), 252–53
"in a very remote . . .": Mivart (1871), 266
"an act of philosophical faith . . .": Huxley (1870), 404
"as yet undiscovered": Mivart (1871), 5
the reviewer wrote: Bennett, 270–73
p. 115 "have a most potent influence": J. W. Gruber, 77
"enter into the realms of miracle . . .": J. W. Gruber, 75
"profound analytic . . .": Tyndall (1897), 178
"manlike Artificer": Tyndall (1897), 177
"Grant in the honey bee . . .": *Letters to Bridges,* 281
p. 116 "Repeat that, repeat . . .": *Poems,* 183
"The laps of running . . .": *Journals,* 252
"All the world . . .": *Journals,* 230
p. 117 "in Matter more . . .": *Correspondence . . . Dixon,* 139
pattern set by the Jesuits: Walsh, 202–16
His accomplishments in scientific prose: Cortie (1889), 546

5. The Spectacular Sunsets of the 1880s

p. 118 "As far as I have myself . . .": Ruskin (1903–12), vol. 37, 384–85
turned green: Smith, 28
blue sunlight: Bishop (May 1884), 107
a blaze of color: *Correspondence . . . Dixon,* 163
"the evening sky . . .": Jung, 15
p. 119 W. Clement Ley . . . and Annie Ley: W. Clement Ley (December 1883), 175–76; Annie Ley, 130
green sun: See various letters in *Nature* throughout November 1883.
"rather than from a supposed . . .": Smyth, 150
"the various accounts . . .": Symons (1884), 355
Knowledge . . . ran a letter: Noble, 418
p. 120 Lockyer began: Lockyer (1883), 10. See the modern analysis by Toon and Pollack, which confirms most of Lockyer's points.

Michael Faraday had completed: Judd, 88
Tyndall had carried: Judd, 88
And a German scientist: Kiessling, 33–34. See also Cortie (1889), 541.
"the body of evidence . . .": *Correspondence . . . Dixon,* 162

p. 121 "the green is between . . .": *Correspondence . . . Dixon,* 164
"in the nature of the glow . . .": *Correspondence . . . Dixon,* 163
six pastel drawings: See Symons (1888) and Simkin and Fiske for all six drawings; see Zaniello (1981) for the two that corroborate Hopkins' notes on greens and "inflamed flesh."
"On the 4th . . .": *Correspondence . . . Dixon,* 164

p. 122 "The two things together . . .": *Correspondence . . . Dixon,* 164
"It is to be earnestly hoped . . .": Smyth, 150
"bright weather": Ascroft, letter, July 12, 1886, Krakatoa Committee Files
"photographic experiments . . .": Dyason, manuscript letter, February 5, 1884, Miscellaneous Correspondence; manuscript letter, March 4, 1884, Krakatoa Committee Files

p. 123 "only as a poetic aspiration . . .": Constable, 69
Both Ascroft's and Dyason's drawings: See *Conversazioni Programmes 1872–1889,* Royal Society Library; Ascroft and Perry exhibited together on May 12, 1886.
"evidently science . . .": "Royal Society Conversazione," 10
"dry black veil . . .": Ruskin, vol. 28, 132–33. See "Mr. Ruskin's Weather Wisdom," 7, for a detailed report on Ruskin's style of lecturing.

p. 125 years of bad weather: Rosenberg, 214–15
"of a sunset in entirely pure weather . . .": Ruskin, vol. 34, 39
"blanched sun, blighted grass . . .": Ruskin, vol. 34, 40
"observation by instruments . . .": Ruskin, vol. 34, 39
he added a note: Ruskin, vol. 34, 78

p. 126 "blanches" the sun: Ruskin, vol. 34, 38
"in a hurry to see . . .": Ruskin, vol. 34, 40
Ascroft's drawings: See Zaniello (1981) for a print of one of Ascroft's drawings of Bishop's ring.
in Bishop's own words: Sereno E. Bishop (April 10, 1884), 549; Bishop (1887), 64
"A conspicuous object . . .": Sereno E. Bishop (1887), 64
His father, Charles R. Leslie: See Leslie (1896) for details about this fascinating boyhood.
"I have watched the sky . . .": Leslie (September 11, 1884), 463

p. 127 "the sun's going out": Ruskin, vol. 35, 579–80
"some increase of solar energy": Leslie (September 11, 1884), 463
"never been seen here . . .": Archibald, 560
"sometimes rose . . .": Ball, 148
"If there is going on . . .": Ball, 148–49

p. 128 "It is . . . right . . .": Ball, 149
green flash: *Observer's Handbook,* 160. See O'Connell (1958) for discussion and color photographs of the green flash; see O'Connell (1960) for discussion only.
"not due merely to contrast": Perry, manuscript essay, Krakatoa Committee Files
"It may be noticed . . .": Ball, 149–50

p. 129 "those who sympathize . . .": W. Clement Ley (1884), 353–54

Conclusion: A "Beautiful but Broken Arc"

p. 130 "I am a Greek philosopher . . .": Joseph Rickaby, Diary, April 17–24, 1895

p. 131 "Let us say . . .": Manuscript, D.IX.1, Campion Hall
heart of Goethe's: Wolff, 97

p. 132 "In those flowers . . .": Goethe (1863), 338–39
"The discovery . . .": Manuscript, D.IX.2, Campion Hall
"The advance of science . . .": Manuscript, D.IX.2, Campion Hall

p. 133 "If the virgin progeny . . .": Owen, 23–24
Such analysis was still controversial: A. J. Meadows (1972), 47–51
chemical constitution: Kirchhoff, 20
pangeometers: See Halsted, passim.

p. 134 that the sum of the angles: Cayley, 232
By the 1870s: See Helmholtz (1870) and Reimann.
"the weather cleared up": "Loss of H.M.S. Eurydice," 298

p. 135 "No Atlantic squall . . .": *Poems,* 72–73
"a heavy bank of clouds . . .": Weyand, 382 (London *Times,* March 26, 1878)

p. 136 "very fine weather . . .": W. Clement Ley (1878), 33
"an enormous black cloud . . .": W. Clement Ley (1878), 34
"resembling a white wall": W. Clement Ley (1878), 34
"as a bank . . .": W. Clement Ley (1878), 34
Years later, whenever scientists: Abercromby, 172
"meteorology, and not least of all . . .": W. Clement Ley (June 1883), 39

"natural sciences are definite . . .": Patmore (1890), 74
"The greatest . . .": Patmore (1890), 74
Hopkins applauded: *Further Letters,* 381
p. 137 "transformed into a mass . . .": Patmore (1890), 217
"infinity of possible strains . . .": *Sermons,* 151
"God sees whole . . .": *Sermons,* 151
"Of human nature . . .": *Sermons,* 171
"seedbed of being": Cotter, 45
"The pomegranate, burst open . . .": Audsley, 144
"the young pomegranate's . . .": Both the Byron and the Flaubert quotations are from the OED.
Although Hopkins' affinity: See Bump (1982).
"a rose-garden . . .": Christian, 37
p. 138 Rossetti had intended: Surtees, 131 n. 3
"cleave" of the "sphere . . .": *Sermons,* 171
"most startling . . .": *Sermons,* 114
ensarkōsis: Sermons, 171. See also Arnold and Addis, 437, for contemporary definitions of these terms.
"becoming man": Arnold and Addis, 39
"the Word . . .": Arnold and Addis, 751
"recognize" Mary: *Sermons,* 198
"the *kosmokratōr* . . .": *Sermons,* 198
p. 139 P. J. Treanor: *Sermons,* 307–8
"with a throne . . .": *Sermons,* 198
"coil or spiral . . .": *Sermons,* 198–99
"Now among the vertebrates . . .": *Sermons,* 199
"selves" or human "natures": *Sermons,* 146–47
"freedom of pitch . . .": *Sermons,* 149
p. 140 He allowed himself: Tierney, 32–33; Page, 53
Others recalled: Ruggles, 242–43; Page, 52–53
he walked out: Lahey, 142; Page, 55–56
"under the delusion . . .": Page, 47
"Not, I'll not . . .": *Poems,* 99
"beautiful but broken arc": Page, 47
"tragedy": Page, 52
p. 142 "the obvious he avoided . . .": Page, 53
"the balanced union . . .": Ruskin, vol. 28, 647
"We sat round him . . .": Fathers, 85
"If ever I came . . .": Fathers, 88
"It is very difficult . . .": Crofton, 768
p. 143 "There is a sort . . .": Crofton, 768 n. 1

"music and meter . . .": *Further Letters*, 377
"new words . . .": *Letters to Bridges*, 254
"popular account . . .": *Correspondence . . . Dixon*, 139
"Statistics and Free Will": *Letters to Bridges*, 292, 294
Egyptian etymology: See *Further Letters*, 257–73.
Chinese music: Barraud, 159
"his papers . . .": Manuscript letter from Everard Hopkins, n.d. (but June 1889), Bodleian
"I have only a few minutes . . .": Manuscript letter from Arthur Hopkins, June 11, 1889, Bodleian

p. 144 lived out his retirement: Denis Meadows, 160
He wrote but did not publish: Unpublished essays in Archives, English Province
"atrocious puns": Denis Meadows, 198
"brilliant, lively . . .": Hasting, 411

The British Association for the Advancement of Science

p. 13 Coleridge believed: Morrell and Thackray, 20
philosophers: Morrell and Thackray, 20
scientist: Morrell and Thackray, 20
Reverend Dingle spoke: *Report . . . BAAS* (1861), 76–77

An Oxford Circle of Family and Friends

p. 24 the sceptical and ultimately agnostic squire: Mrs. Humphrey Ward (1918), vol. 1, 148
Although Nettleship had planned: Nettleship (1901), xiv–xv; Parkin, vol. 1, 284

p. 25 "monastic form . . .": Holland, 30
"a lurking admiration . . .": Holland, 30
"new forms of religious society": Holland, 30

A Typical Oxford Examination Question

p. 28 Question number seven: *Oxford University Examination Papers*, no. 33 (1864), 53
Coincidentally: *Oxford University Calendar*, 1864, 31
Hopkins' practice reply: Manuscript, D.I.2, Campion Hall

The Lucretian Universe of Atoms

p. 40 The principles that form: See Munro, book 1, passim. In the Belfast Address, Tyndall actually outlines five propositions from *Democritus'* theory of atomism and adds the few ways in which Lucretius differs; their philosophies, however, are essentially the same.

Drawing Atoms

p. 42 When Dalton set out: Jones and Cohen, 139–40, or Dampier, 98–99

In Brodie's atomic calculus: See Brodie (1867).

p. 43 Charles Wright agreed: Private letter to Brodie, quoted in Brock, 141–42

Was Darwin an Atomist?

p. 50 "modes of subjective action": Howard E. Gruber, 397

"All organic units . . .": Darwin (1868), vol. 2, 402

Darwin himself: Darwin (1885), vol. 2, 375 n. 29

in L. C. Dunn's term: Dunn, 35–37

Darwin asserted: Darwin (1871), 502–3

Mr. Stockton: Mallock (1908), 20

p. 51 Mr. Storks: Mallock (1908), 16

S. J. Perry and the Stonyhurst Observatory

p. 61 Stonyhurst, he wrote: *Letters to Bridges,* 151

Stonyhurst was twice named: Cortie (1890), 32–33. For other detailed accounts of Stonyhurst Observatory, see Perry (1883) and "Stephen Joseph Perry, F.R.S."

"extraordinary darkness at midday . . .": Perry (May 1, 1884), 6. For his follow-up letters, see Perry (May 8, 1884), 32, and Perry (1886), 147.

Scales of Color

p. 66 "The Rectilinear Sides . . .": Newton, 126–28

"A Circle ADF . . .": Newton, 154–55

musical staff: Field (1820), 203

The Great Chain of Being and Evolutionary Theory

p. 70 "an analogy or likeness . . .": Joseph Butler (1736), xxvii
"all things are double . . .": Joseph Butler (1726), 97
McCosh argued that: McCosh and Dickie, 39–40
p. 71 "unity of design . . .": *Report . . . BAAS* (1853), 68
"a wonderful elm . . .": *Journals,* 153

Inscape and Wordsworth's "Spots of Time"

p. 73 "moments . . . scattered everywhere . . .": Wordsworth, *Prelude,* book 11
"Each scene in nature . . .": Manuscript, P.I.6, Campion Hall. Hopkins copied the passage from Shairp, 71.

Spectral Numbers

p. 75 "very fantastic and interesting": Manley Hopkins (1887), 20
"with 40–50 . . .": Galton (1883), 102 and fig. 64
who saw a single red tulip: Galton (1883), 116 and figs. 71–72
Hopkins described his own "patterns": Manley Hopkins (1887), 20–21
He added: "The Cardinal Numbers," 28

The Difference between Amateur and Professional Science

p. 80 "We walked along . . .": Tyndall, Diary A11, Royal Institution
"two great standing enigmas . . .": Tyndall (1871), 253, 256
It was this research: Judd, 88
"companion": Tyndall (1900), 211
p. 81 "employed to moisten the air . . .": Tyndall (1900), 217–18

T. H. Green on the Incarnation

p. 92 "most startling and original . . .": *Sermons,* 114
"the taking of flesh . . .": *Sermons,* 114
"an intellectual position . . .": Green (1883), vi

"the Word became Flesh . . .": Green (1885–88), vol. 3, 207
"the object of sense . . .": Green (1885–88), vol. 3, 207
"sensuous" seeing: Green (1885–88), vol. 3, 216, 219
"belief in a person . . .": Green (1885–88), vol. 3, 220

How "Liberal" Were the English Jesuits?

p. 104 "vital influence . . .": *Sermons by Fathers,* vol. 2, 345, 349–50
"rationalism" and "naturalism": *Sermons by Fathers,* vol. 3, 150
"emancipates the flesh . . .": *Sermons by Fathers,* vol. 3, 151
"wait with anxiety . . .": *Sermons by Fathers,* vol. 3, 149
p. 105 "O doubly predestined . . .": *Poems,* 338

Joseph Rickaby's Diary

p. 141 "the Scotist view . . .": Joseph Rickaby, Diary, June 16, 1877
"even antecedently . . .": Joseph Rickaby (1915), 29
"After a pietist boyhood . . .": Joseph Rickaby, Diary, June 1–8, 1887
"that old scholar-squire": Joseph Rickaby, Diary, March 16–23, 1901
"I don't find God . . .": Joseph Rickaby, Diary, April 26–May 4, 1898
"rather hides God . . .": Joseph Rickaby, Diary, April 26–May 4, 1898

Sources

Archival Materials

ASCROFT, WILLIAM

(1) Letters, Krakatoa Committee Files, Box 519, Library, Royal Society of London

(2) Drawings ("Sky Sketches"), Science Museum, South Kensington. See Ascroft under "Books and Articles" for *Catalogue.*

DYASON, JOHN SANFORD

(1) Letters, Krakatoa Committee Files, Box 519, and

(2) Miscellaneous Correspondence, MC.13.10 (1884), both sets in Library, Royal Society of London

(3) Drawings ("Chromatics of the Sky"), Science Museum, South Kensington

HOPKINS, GERARD MANLEY

(1) Oxford Essays, catalogued as "D" by Bischoff (see "Books and Articles"), Campion Hall, Oxford, with exception of those in (3) below

(2) Notebooks, with Bischoff catalogue numbers as follows: C.I., notes on trigonometry and mechanics; M.II., notes on *Nicomachean Ethics;* P.I.6, extract from Shairp's *Studies in Poetry and Philosophy,* q.v., alphabetical listing; Campion Hall, Oxford

(3) Oxford Essays, D.II.1 through D.II.6, Balliol College Library, Oxford

(4) Letters to and from Hopkins' family, MS. Eng. Misc. a.8, Modern Papers Room, Department of Western Manuscripts, Bodleian Library, Oxford

NOTE: Many of Hopkins' manuscripts are quoted in this book for the first time. I have silently expanded all of Hopkins' abbreviations (wd. for would, agst. for against, etc.) and have capitalized all the major words in the titles of his essays (although he capitalized the initial word only).

KRAKATOA COMMITTEE (SEE ALSO ASCROFT, DYASON, AND PERRY)

Press Clippings, Krakatoa Committee Files, Box 518, Library, Royal Society of London

MARCHANT, HENRY

Essays: "Life and Energy," "Radium and Life: A Dialogue between X and Y," "James Clerk Maxwell . . . His Life and Character," in Archives, English Province of the Society of Jesus, Farm Street, London

PERRY, STEPHEN JOSEPH

(1) Letters to Norman Lockyer, 1869–86, Norman Lockyer Archives, Norman Lockyer Observatory, Sidmouth (administered by the Department of Physics, University of Exeter)

(2) "The Upper Glow Preceding Sun-rise and Following Sunset Observed from Nov. 1883 to March 1884," essay in Krakatoa Committee Files, Box 516-2, GB Envelope 1, Library, Royal Society of London

RICKABY, JOSEPH

(1) Diary, 1877–1926, 47/8/7, and

(2) Responses to "Questions as to the Course of Theology," January 19, 1903, Y/1; both in Archives, English Province of the Society of Jesus, Mount Street, London

TYNDALL, JOHN

(1) Diary A11 (1883–84), and

(2) Journal, bound volume III (1855–72); both at Library, Royal Institution of London

Books and Articles

Abercromby, Ralph. "On the Origin and Course of the Squall Which Capsized H.M.S. 'Eurydice,' March 24th, 1878." *Quarterly Journal of the Meteorological Society* 10 (July 1884): 172–83.

Addis, William. "Supernatural Religion." *Dublin Review,* April 1875 : 357–411.

Airy, Sir George. *Autobiography of Sir George Biddell Airy.* Ed. Wilfred Airy. Cambridge: Cambridge University Press, 1896.

Alexander, Edward. "Ruskin and Science." *Modern Language Review* 64 (1969) : 508–21.

Allsopp, Michael. "Hopkins at Oxford, 1863–1867: His Formal Studies." *Hopkins Quarterly* 4 (Fall–Winter 1977–78): 161–76.

Altick, Richard D. "Four Victorian Poets and an Exploding Island." *Victorian Studies* 3 (March 1960): 249–60.

Archibald, E. Douglass. "The Solar (Dust?) Halo." *Nature*, October 9, 1884: 559–60.

Aristotle. *The Nicomachean Ethics of Aristotle.* Trans. Robert Williams. London: Longmans, Green, 1869.

———. *The Nicomachean Ethics.* Trans. H. Rackham. London: William Heinemann, 1926.

———. *The Nicomachean Ethics.* Trans. J. A. K. Thomson; rev. Hugh Tredenick. Harmondsworth: Penguin, 1976.

Arnold, Matthew. *Letters.* Ed. George W. E. Russell. 2 vols. New York and London: Macmillan, 1896.

Arnold, Thomas. *A Manual of English Literature.* 5th and rev. ed. London: Longmans, Green, 1885.

———. *Passages in a Wandering Life.* London: Edward Arnold, 1900.

Arnold, Thomas, and William Addis. *A Catholic Dictionary* (1884). 6th ed. New York: Catholic Publication Society, 1889.

Ascroft, William. *Catalogue of Sky Sketches from September 1883 to September 1886 (Illustrating Optical Phenomena Attributed to the Eruption at Krakatoa, in the Java Straits, August 27th, 1883).* London: South Kensington Museum, 1888.

"The Atomic Controversy." *Nature*, November 11, 1869: 44–45.

Audsley, W. and G. *Handbook of Christian Symbolism.* London: Day and Son, 1865.

Bacon, Francis. *Of the Advancement of Learning* (1605). Ed. G. W. Kitchin. London: J. M. Dent and Sons, n.d.

———. *The Complete Essays of Francis Bacon.* Ed. Henry Leroy Finch. New York: Washington Square Press, 1963.

Ball, Patricia M. *The Science of Aspects: The Changing Role of Fact in the Work of Coleridge, Ruskin, and Hopkins.* London: Athlone Press, 1971.

Barker, George Frederick. *Memoir of John William Draper, 1811–1882.* Washington, D.C.: National Academy of Arts and Sciences, 1886.

Barraud, Clement. "Reminiscences of Father Gerard Hopkins." *The Month* (July 1919): 158–59.

Barrett W. F. "Note on the Correlation of Color and Music." *Nature*, January 13, 1870: 286–87.

Bastian, H. Carleton. "Facts and Reasonings Concerning the Heterogeneous

Evolution of Living Things." *Nature,* June 30, 1870 : 170–77; July 7, 1870 : 193–201; July 14, 1870 : 219–28.
———. "Reply to Professor Huxley's Inaugural Address at Liverpool on the Question of the Origin of Life." *Nature,* September 22, 1870 : 410–12; September 29, 1870 : 431–34.
———. "The Evolution of Life: Professor Huxley's Address at Liverpool." *Nature,* October 20, 1870 : 492.
Bennett, Alfred W. "The Genesis of Species." *Nature,* February 2, 1870 : 220–73.
Benson, A. C. *Walter Pater.* London: Macmillan, 1906.
Bergonzi, Bernard. *Gerard Manley Hopkins.* New York: Macmillan, 1977.
Birkenhead, Sheila. *Illustrious Friends: The Story of Joseph Severn and His Son Arthur.* New York: William Morrow, 1965.
Bischoff, D. Anthony. "The Manuscripts of Gerard Manley Hopkins." *Thought* 26 (Winter 1951–52): 551–80.
———. "Gerard Manley Hopkins and Stratford, Essex." *Thought* 48 (Summer 1973): 266–73.
Bishop, George D. "Stephen Joseph Perry (1833–1889): Priest, Scientist, Educator." M.A. thesis, University of Manchester Institute of Science and Technology, 1977.
Bishop, Sereno E. "The Remarkable Sunsets." *Nature,* April 10, 1884, 549.
———. "The Equatorial Smoke-Screen from Krakatoa." *Hawaiian Monthly,* May 1884 : 106–10.
———. "The Origin of the Red Glows." *History and Work of the Warner Observatory, Rochester, N.Y., 1883–1886.* Vol. 1 (1887): 63–70. (Originally published in the *American Meteorological Journal,* July–August 1886.)
Bonnycastle, John. *An Introduction to Astronomy in a Series of Letters from a Preceptor to His Pupil.* 5th ed. London: J. Johnson, 1807.
"Books: John Clare." *Spectator,* June 17, 1865 : 668–70.
Bottrall, Margaret. *Gerard Manley Hopkins, Poems: A Casebook.* London: Macmillan, 1975.
Boyer, Carl B. "The Tertiary Rainbow: An Historical Account." *Isis* 49 (1958) : 141–54.
Bridges, J. M. "Evolution and Positivism." *Fortnightly Review,* June 1877 : 853–74; July 1877 : 89–114.
"British Association." *The Athenaeum,* June 30, 1860 : 886–92; July 7, 1860 : 18–32; July 14, 1860 : 58–69.
Brock, W. H. *The Atomic Debates: Brodie and the Rejection of the Atomic Theory.* Leicester: Leicester University Press, 1967.
Brodie, Benjamin. "On the Calculus of Chemical Operations." *Philosophical Transactions of the Royal Society,* part 2 (May 1866): 781–859.

———. "On the Mode of Representation Afforded by the Chemical Calculus, as Contrasted with the Atomic Theory." In "Chemistry of the Future," *Chemical News*, June 14, 1867:295–305.

Brown, Alexander Crum. "Remarks on Sir Benjamin Brodie's 'System of Chemical Notation.'" *Philosophical Magazine* 34 (August 1867): 129–36.

Bullard, Fred M. *Volcanoes of the Earth*. Rev. ed. Austin: University of Texas Press, 1976.

Bump, Jerome. "Manual Photography: Hopkins, Ruskin, and Victorian Drawing." *Texas Quarterly* 16 (Summer 1973): 90–116.

———. "Hopkins at Stonyhurst: A Letter to His Father." *Library Chronicle of the University of Texas*, n.s. 8 (1974): 47–51.

———. *Gerard Manley Hopkins*. Boston: Twayne, 1982.

Butler, Alban. *The Lives of the Fathers, Martyrs, and Other Principal Saints*. 12 vols. Dublin: James Duffy, 1866.

Butler, Cuthbert. *The Vatican Council: The Story Told from Inside in Bishop Ullathorne's Letters*. 2 vols. London: Longmans, Green, 1930. Revised as *The Vatican Council, 1869–1870, Based on Bishop Ullathorne's Letters*, ed. Christopher Butler. London: Collins and Harvill Press, 1962.

Butler, Bishop Joseph. *Fifteen Sermons Preached at the Rolls Chapel (1726)*. Ed. W. R. Matthews. London: George Bell and Sons, 1914.

———. *The Analogy of Religion, Natural and Revealed, to the Constitution and Course of Nature* (1736). Ed. Ronald Bayne. London: J. M. Dent and Sons, 1906.

Cage, John. *Color in Turner: Poetry and Truth*. New York: Praeger, 1969.

Cajori, Florian. *A History of Mathematics*. New York: MacMillan, 1893; 2d ed., rpt. New York: Chelsea House, 1980.

Capron, J. Rand. *Aurorae: Their Characters and Spectra*. London: E. and F. N. Spon, 1879.

"The Cardinal Numbers." *Nature*, May 10, 1888:27–28.

Cayley, Arthur. "Note on Lobatschewsky's *Imaginary Geometry*." *Philosophical Magazine* 29 (March 1865):231–33.

Charles-Edwards, T. *Saint Winefride and Her Well*. London: Catholic Truth Society, 1971.

"Chemistry of the Future." *Chemical News*, June 14, 1877, 295–305.

Christ, Carol T. *The Finer Optic: The Aesthetic of Particularity in Victorian Poetry*. New Haven: Yale University Press, 1975.

Christian, John. *The Pre-Raphaelites in Oxford*. Oxford: Ashmolean Museum, 1974.

Clarke, Richard F. "On Analogy." *The Month* 20 (February 1874): 178–92.

———. "A Serious Theological Difficulty." *The Month* 46 (September 1882): 1–20.

———. "Some Personal Recollections of Bishop Wilberforce." *The Month* 47 (1883): 200–209.

———. "Catholics at the English Universities." *The Month* 54 (July and August 1885): 345–58, 457–73; 55 (September and October 1885): 1–17, 153–69.

———. *Logic.* London: Longmans, Green, 1889.

———. "Recollections of Henry James Coleridge." *The Month* 78 (1893): 167–81.

———. "Father John Morris." *The Month* 79 (November 1893): 457–66.

———. "The Training of a Jesuit." *The Nineteenth Century* 40 (August 1896): 211–25.

Coleridge, Henry James. "Personal Recollections of an Old Oxonian." *The Month* 3 (December 1865): 508–20, 606–14; 4 (January 1866): 50–59.

———. "Oxford Studies—Mr. Pattison and Mr. Gillow." *The Month* 11 (July 1869): 100–108.

Coleridge, Henry James, and Richard F. Clarke. "Catholics and the Oxford Examinations." *The Month* 11 (August 1869): 213–16 (unsigned, but authors identified by Joseph Rickaby, "In Memoriam: Richard Frederick Clarke," q.v., above).

Collins, James. "Philosophical Themes in G. M. Hopkins." *Thought* 22 (March 1947): 67–106.

Constable, John. *The Correspondence with C. R. Leslie.* Vol. 3 of *John Constable's Correspondence.* Ed. R. B. Beckett. Ipswich: Suffolk Records Society, 1965.

Conversazioni Programmes 1872–1889. London: Royal Society, 1872–89.

Cornford, F. M. *Before and After Socrates.* Cambridge: Cambridge University Press, 1932.

———. *Plato's Theory of Knowledge: The* Theaetetus *and the* Sophist *of Plato.* 1st ed., 1935. London: Routledge and Kegan Paul, 1960.

Cortie, A. L. "The Eruption of Krakatoa." *The Month* 65 (March 1889): 367–79; 65 (April 1889): 534–48.

———. *Father Perry, the Jesuit Astronomer.* London: Catholic Truth Society, 1890.

———. "The Attitude of the Church toward Natural Science." *The Month* 94 (September 1899): 282–91.

Cotter, James Finn. *Inscape.* Pittsburgh: University of Pittsburgh Press, 1972.

Cox, G. V. *Recollections of Oxford.* 2d ed. London: Macmillan, 1870.

Crehan, J. H. "More Light on Gerard Hopkins." *The Month* 196 (October 1953): 205–14.

Crofton, M. W. "Probability." In *Encyclopedia Britannica,* 9th ed. (1885): 768–88.

Crombie, A. C. *Robert Grosseteste and the Origins of Experimental Science, 1100–1700.* Oxford: Clarendon Press, 1953.

Crosland, M. P., ed. *The Science of Matter: A Historical Survey.* Harmondsworth: Penguin, 1971.

Dampier, William C. and Margaret, eds. *Readings in the Literature of Science.* New York: Harper, 1959.

Darwin, Charles. *The Origin of Species: A Variorum Edition.* Ed. Morse Peckham. Philadelphia: University of Pennsylvania Press, 1959.

———. *The Variation of Animals and Plants under Domestication.* 2 vols. London: John Murray, 1868; 2d rev. ed., 1885.

———. "Pangenesis." *Nature,* April 27, 1871 : 502–3.

———. *The Life and Letters of Charles Darwin.* Ed. Francis Darwin. 3 vols. London: Macmillan, 1888.

———. *Darwin and Henslow: The Growth of an Idea—Letters, 1831–1860.* Ed. Nora Barlow. Berkeley and Los Angeles: University of California Press, 1967.

David, Christopher. *St. Winefride's Well: A History and Guide.* Slough: Kenion Press, 1971.

Dean, Francis. "Analogy of Color and Music." *Nature,* February 10, 1870: 385.

Dechevrens, Marc. "A Curious Halo." *Nature,* November 9, 1882 : 30–31.

Delphino, Federico. "On the Darwinian Theory of Pangenesis." *Scientific Opinion,* September 29, 1869 : 365–67; October 6, 1869 : 391–93; October 13, 1869 : 407–8.

"The Dodo Non-extinct." *Long Ago* 11 (January 1874): 21.

Draper, John William. *Human Physiology, Statical and Dynamic.* 2d ed. New York: Harper and Row, 1858.

———. *History of the Conflict between Religion and Science.* New York: Appleton, 1874; London: Henry S. King, 1875.

Dunn, L. C. *A Short History of Genetics: The Development of Some of the Main Lines of Thought: 1864–1939.* New York: McGraw-Hill, 1965.

Eisen, Stanley. "Huxley and the Positivists." *Victorian Studies* 7 (June 1964): 337–58.

Elliott, Ivo. *The Balliol College Register, 1833–1933.* Oxford: Oxford University Press, 1934.

Faber, Geoffrey. *Jowett: A Portrait with Background.* Cambridge: Cambridge University Press, 1957.

Fathers of the Society of Jesus, eds. *A Page of Irish History: Story of University College, Dublin, 1883–1909.* Dublin and Cork: Talbot Press, 1930.

Field, George. "Tritogenea, or, A Brief Outline of the Universal System." *The Pamphleteer* (London) 9, no. 17 (1816): 101–23.

———. *Chromatics, or, An Essay on the Analogy and Harmony of Colours.* London: Newman of Soho Square, 1817.

———. "Dianoia, the Third Organon Attempted; or Elements of Logic and Subjective Philosophy." *The Pamphleteer* 12, no. 34 (1818): 471–92.

———. "Aesthetics, or the Analogy of the Sensible Sciences Indicated." *The Pamphleteer* 17, no. 33 (1820): 195–227.

———. *Chromatography; or, A Treatise on Colors and Pigments and of Their Powers.* London: Charles Tilt, 1835.

———. *Rudiments of the Painter's Art, or a Grammar of Coloring, Applicable to Operative Painting, Decorative Architecture, and the Arts.* London: John Weale, 1850.

———. *Field's Chromatography: or, Treatise on Colours and Pigments as Used by Artists.* Revised by Thomas W. Salter. London: Winson and Newton, 1869.

———. *A Grammar of Coloring Applied to Decorative Painting and the Arts.* Revised by Ellis A. Davidson. London: Lockwood, 1875.

———. *Field's Chromatography.* Modernized by J. S. Taylor. London: Winson and Newton, 1885.

Fitch, Raymond. *The Poison Sky: Myth and Apocalypse of Ruskin.* Athens: Ohio University Press, 1982.

Fleming, Donald. *John William Draper and the Religion of Science.* Philadelphia: University of Pennsylvania Press, 1950.

Forest, D. W. *Francis Galton.* New York: Taplinger, 1974.

Freeman, Edward A. "Oxford after Forty Years." *Contemporary Review* 51 (May and June 1887): 609–23, 814–30.

Freeman, Kathleen. *Ancilla to the Pre-Socratic Philosophers* [translation of Hermann Diels, *Fragmente der Vorsokratiker,* 5th ed.]. Cambridge, Mass.: Harvard University Press, 1957.

Fremantle, Anne. *The Papal Encyclicals in Their Historical Context.* New York: Mentor, 1956.

Furneaux, Rubert. *Krakatoa.* Englewood Cliffs, N.J.: Prentice-Hall, 1964.

Gallwey, Peter. *St. Joseph and the Vatican Council.* London: Burns and Oates, 1870.

Galton, Francis. "Experiments in Pangenesis, by Breeding from Rabbits of a Pure Variety, into Whose Circulation Blood Taken from Other Varieties Had Previously Been Largely Transfused." *Proceedings of the Royal Society* 19 (1871): 393–410.

———. "Pangenesis." *Nature,* May 4, 1871: 5–6.

———. "On Blood-Relationship." *Proceedings of the Royal Society* 20 (1872): 394–402.

———. "Statistical Inquiries into the Efficacy of Prayer." *Fortnightly Review* 18 (August 1, 1872): 125–35.

———. *Inquiries into Human Faculty and Its Development.* 1st ed., 1883. Rev. ed., 1907. Rpt. London: J. M. Dent, 1911.

Gardner, W. H. *Gerard Manley Hopkins.* 2d ed. 2 vols. London: Oxford University Press, 1948–49.

Geisen, Gerard L. "Darwin and Heredity: The Evolution of His Hypothesis of Pangenesis." *Journal of the History of Medicine and Allied Science* 24 (1964): 375–411.

Geldart, Martin [Nitram Tradleg]. *A Son of Belial: Autobiographical Sketches.* London: Trübner, 1882.

Goethe, J. W. von. *Goethe's Theory of Colours.* 1st German ed., 1810. Trans. Charles L. Eastlake. London: John Murray, 1840. Rpt. London: Frank Cass, 1967.

———. "Essay on the Metamorphosis of Plants." Trans. Emily M. Cox; ed. Maxwell T. Masters. *Journal of Botany, British and Foreign* 1 (November and December 1863): 327–45, 360–74.

———. *Goethe's Botanical Writings.* Trans. Berte Mueller. Honolulu: University of Hawaii Press, 1952.

Gosse, Phillip Henry. *A Naturalist's Rambles on the Devonshire Coast.* London: John Van Voorst, 1853.

———. *Omphalos: An Attempt to Untie the Geological Knot.* London: John Van Voorst, 1857.

———. *The Romance of Natural History.* London: James Nisbet, 1860.

Gosse, Phillip Henry, and Emily Gosse. *Sea-Side Pleasures.* London: Society for the Propagation of Christian Knowledge, 1853.

Gould, Stephen Jay. "Knight Takes Bishop." *Natural History* (May 1986): 18–22, 28–33.

Gray, R. D. "J. M. W. Turner and Goethe's Colour Theory." In *German Studies Presented to Walter Horace Bruford,* 112–16. London: George G. Harrap, 1962.

Green, Thomas Hill. *The Witness of God and Faith: Two Lay Sermons.* Eds. Arnold and C. M. Toynbee. London: Longmans, Green, 1883.

———. *Works.* Ed. Richard L. Nettleship. 3 vols. London: Longmans, Green, 1885–88.

Grigson, Geoffrey. *Poems and Poets.* London: Macmillan, 1969.

Grote, John. *Exploratio Philosophica* (part 1). Cambridge: Deighton Bell, 1865. *Exploratio Philosophica* (parts I and II). Cambridge: Cambridge University Press, 1900.

———. *An Examination of the Utilitarian Philosophy.* Ed. Joseph B. Mayor. Cambridge: Cambridge University Press, 1870.

———. "Robert Leslie Ellis: A Study of Character." *Contemporary Review* 20 (June 1872): 56–71.

———. "On Glossology." *Journal of Philology* 4 (1872): 55–66, 157–81; 5 (1874): 153–82.

———. *A Treatise of the Moral Ideas.* Ed. Joseph B. Mayor. Cambridge: Deighton Bell, 1876.

Gruber, Howard E. *Darwin on Man: A Psychological Study of Scientific Creativity.* (Together with *Darwin's Early and Unpublished Notebooks,* ed. Paul H. Barrett.) New York: E. P. Dutton, 1974.

Gruber, J. W. *A Conscience in Conflict: The Life of St. George Jackson Mivart.* New York: Columbia University Press, 1960.

Halsted, George Bruce. "Bibliography of Hyper-Space and Non-Euclidean Geometry." *American Journal of Mathematics* 1 (1878): 261–76.

Hamlyn, D. W. *Sensation and Perception: A History of the Philosophy of Perception.* London: Routledge and Kegan Paul, 1961.

Hammond, Reginald J. W. *The Complete Wales.* London: Ward Lock, 1966.

Harper, Thomas Norton. *Peace through Truth or Essays on Subjects Connected with Dr. Pusey's Eirenicon.* 1st ser.: London: Longmans, Green, Reader and Dyer, 1866. 2d ser.: London: Burns and Oates, 1874.

———. "The Word." *Mind* 8 (July 1883): 372–401.

———. *The Immaculate Conception.* London: Burns and Oates, 1919.

Harre, Rom, ed. *Some Nineteenth Century British Scientists.* Oxford: Pergamon Press, 1969.

———. *The Philosophies of Science: An Introductory Review.* Oxford: Oxford University Press, 1972.

Hartner, Willy. "Goethe and the Natural Sciences." In *Goethe: A Collection of Critical Essays,* ed. Victor Lange, 145–60. Englewood Cliffs, N.J.: Prentice-Hall, 1968.

Hasting, McDonald. *Jesuit Child.* New York: St. Martin's, 1971.

Hawkes, Jacquetta. "Gowland Hopkins and Scientific Imagination." *The Listener,* February 2, 1950: 191–92.

Helmholtz, Hermann Ludwig Ferdinand von. "The Axioms of Geometry." *The Academy,* February 12, 1870: 128–31.

———. *On the Sensations of Tone as the Physiological Basis for the Theory of Music.* 4th German ed., 1877. 2d English ed., trans. Alexander J. Ellis. Rpt. New York: Dover, 1954.

Heuser, Alan. *The Shaping Vision of Gerard Manley Hopkins.* London: Oxford University Press, 1958.

Himmelfarb, Gertrude. *Darwin and the Darwinian Revolution.* New York: Norton, 1968.

Holland, Henry Scott. *Memoir and Letters.* Ed. Stephen Paget. London: John Murray, 1921.

Holmes, J. Derek. "Newman's Reputation and *The Lives of the English Saints.*" *Catholic Historical Review* 51 (January 1966): 528–38.

———. *More Roman than Rome: English Catholicism in the Nineteenth Century.* London: Burns and Oates, 1978.

Hooker, Joseph Dalton. *Life and Letters of Sir Joseph Dalton Hooker.* Ed. Leonard Huxley. 2 vols. London: John Murray, 1918.

Hopkins, Gerard Manley. *The Letters of Gerard Manley Hopkins to Robert Bridges.* Ed. Claude Colleer Abbott. 2d ed. London: Oxford University Press, 1955.

———. *The Correspondence of Gerard Manley Hopkins and Richard Watson Dixon.* Ed. Claude Colleer Abbott. 2d ed. London: Oxford University Press, 1955.

———. *Further Letters of Gerard Manley Hopkins Including His Correspondence with Coventry Patmore.* Ed. Claude Colleer Abbott. 2d ed. London: Oxford University Press, 1956.

———. *The Journals and Papers of Gerard Manley Hopkins.* Eds. Humphrey House and Graham Storey. London: Oxford University Press, 1959.

———. *The Sermons and Devotional Writings of Gerard Manley Hopkins.* Ed. Christopher Devlin. London: Oxford University Press, 1959.

———. *Poems and Prose of Gerard Manley Hopkins.* Ed. W. H. Gardner. Harmondsworth: Penguin, 1967.

———. *Poems.* Eds. W. H. Gardner and N. H. Mackenzie. 4th ed. London: Oxford University Press, 1967.

———. *Journals and Papers.* Ed. Giuseppe Gaetano Castorina. Bari: Adriatica Editrice (Italian Library of English Texts), 1975.

Hopkins, Manley. *Hawaii: The Past, Present, and Future of Its Island Kingdom. An Historical Account of the Sandwich Islands Polynesia.* 2d ed. London: Longmans, Green, 1866.

———. *The Cardinal Numbers.* London: Sampson Low, 1887.

House, Humphrey, and Madeline House. "Books Belonging to Hopkins and His Family." *Hopkins Research Bulletin,* no. 5 (1974): 26–41.

———. "Books Hopkins Had Access To." *Hopkins Research Bulletin,* no. 6 (1975): 17–21.

Hughes, F. J. "Tones and Colours." *The Athenaeum,* December 26, 1874: 887.

———. "Notes, Tones, and Colors." *The Athenaeum,* February 24, 1877: 265.

———. *Harmonies of Tones and Colors Developed by Evolution.* London: Marcus Ward, 1883.

Hutton, Arthur Wollaston, ed. *The Lives of the English Saints Written by Various*

Hands at the Suggestion of John Henry Newman. 6 vols. London: S. T. Freemantle, 1901.

Hutton, R. H. "The Metaphysical Society." *Nineteenth Century* 18 (August 1885): 177–96.

Huxley, Leonard. *The Life and Letters of Thomas Henry Huxley.* 2 vols. London: Macmillan, 1900.

Huxley, Thomas Henry. "On the Physical Basis of Life." *Fortnightly Review,* February 1, 1869: 129–45.

———. "The Scientific Aspects of Positivism." *Fortnightly Review,* June 1869: 653–90.

———. "Address of Thomas Henry Huxley." *Nature,* September 15, 1870: 400–406.

———. "Dr. Bastian and Spontaneous Generation." *Nature,* October 13, 1870, 473.

———. *Critiques and Addresses.* London: Macmillan, 1873.

———. "On the Hypothesis That Animals Are Automata, and Its History." *Fortnightly Review,* November 1, 1874: 554–80.

———. *A Manual of the Anatomy of the Invertebrated Animals.* New York: D. Appleton, 1878.

———. *Hume.* New York: Harper Brothers, 1879.

———. *Collected Essays.* 9 vols. London: Macmillan, 1893–94.

Jackson, William. *The Philosophy of Natural Theology: An Essay in Confutation of the Scepticism of the Present Day.* London: Hodder and Stoughton, 1874.

Janus [Lord Acton]. *The Pope and the Council.* London: Rivingtons, 1869; 2d ed., 1873.

Jebb, R. C. "On Mr. Tennyson's 'Lucretius.'" *Macmillan's Magazine* 18 (June 1868): 97–103.

Jenkin, Fleeming. "The Atomic Theory of Lucretius." *North British Review* 48 (1868): 211–42.

———. *Papers Literary, Scientific, Etc.* Eds. Sidney Colvin and J. A. Ewing. 2 vols. London: Longmans, Green, 1887.

Jevons, W. Stanley. *Elementary Lessons in Logic.* 2d ed. London: Macmillan, 1880.

Jones, H. M., and I. Bernard Cohen. *Science before Darwin: A Nineteenth-Century Anthology.* London: Andre Deutsch, 1963.

Jowett, Benjamin. *Select Passages from the Introductions to Plato.* Ed. Lewis Campbell. London: John Murray, 1902.

Judd, J. W. "Krakatoa." *Proceedings of the Royal Institution* 11 (May 1884): 85–88.

Jung, C. G. *Memories, Dreams, Reflections.* New York: Pantheon Books, 1961.

Keating, Joseph. "Impressions of Father Hopkins." *The Month* 114 (July, August, and September 1909): 59–68, 151–60, and 246–58.

Kelvin, Lord [William Thomson]. "On Vortex Motion." *Transactions of the Royal Society of Edinburgh* (1867): 217–60.

———. "The Size of Atoms." *Nature*, March 31, 1870: 551–53.

———. "Inaugural Address." *Nature*, August 3, 1871: 262–70.

———. *Popular Lectures and Addresses*. 3 vols. London: Macmillan, 1889.

Kiessling, K. I. "On the Cause of the Remarkable Optical Atmospheric Effects in 1883 and 1884." In *History and Work of the Warner Observatory, Rochester, N.Y., 1883–1886*. Vol. 1 (1887): 31–37.

Kirchhoff, G. "On the Relation between the Radiating and Absorbing Powers of Different Bodies for Light and Heat." Trans. F. Guthrie. *Philosophical Magazine* 20 (July 1860): 1–21.

Kitchen, Paddy. *Gerard Manley Hopkins: A Biography*. New York: Athenaeum, 1978.

Klein, Adrian Bernard. *Colour-Music: The Art of Light*. 2d ed. London: Crosby Lockwood and Son, 1930.

Knapp, John Leonard. *The Journal of a Naturalist*. 2d ed. London: John Murray, 1829.

Knight, David M. *Atoms and Elements: A Study of Theories in the Nineteenth Century*. London: Hutchinson, 1967; rev. ed., 1970.

Lahey, G. F. *Gerard Manley Hopkins*. London: Oxford University Press, 1930.

Lamb, H. H. *The Changing Climate: Selected Papers*. London: Methuen, 1966.

Landow, George P. "The Rainbow: A Problematic Image." In *Nature and the Victorian Imagination*, eds. U. C. Knoepflmacher and G. B. Tennyson, 341–69. Berkeley: University of California Press, 1977.

———. "Iconography and Point of View in Painting and Literature: The Example of the Shipwreck." *Studies in Iconography* 3 (1977): 89–104.

Lange, F. A. *History of Materialism and Criticism of Its Present Importance*. (1866; 2d German ed., 1873–75). 3 vols. Trans. Ernest Chester Thomas. London: Trübner, 1877–81.

Lechmere, W. L. "Oxford: 1863–1867." *Oxford and Cambridge Review*, May 1912: 73–113.

Leslie, G. D., and Fred A. Eaton. "Charles Robert Leslie, R. A." *Art Journal* (London) (1902): 144–48.

Leslie, Robert C. "Sun-Glows." *Nature*, September 11, 1884: 463.

———. "Sun-Glows." *Nature*, September 25, 1884: 512.

———. "The Sky-Glows." *Nature*, October 16, 1884: 583.

———. "Rosy Glow about the Moon." *Nature*, December 4, 1884: 102.

———. *A Sea-Painter's Log.* London: Chapman and Hall, 1886.

———. *Old Sea Wings, Ways, and Words.* 1st ed., 1890. Rpt. London: Chapman and Hall, 1930.

———. "With Charles Robert Leslie, R.A." *Temple Bar* 107 (March 1896): 353–69.

Levy, William Turner. *William Barnes: The Man and the Poems.* Dorchester: Longmans, 1960.

Lewes, George Henry. "Goethe as a Man of Science." *Westminster Review* (October 1852): 479–506.

———. *Comte's Philosophy of the Sciences.* London: Henry G. Bohn, 1853.

———. *The Life and Works of Goethe* (1855). 2d rev. ed., *The Life of Goethe* (1864); rpt. New York: Frederick Ungar, 1965.

Ley, Annie. "The Remarkable Sunsets." *Nature,* December 6, 1883 : 130.

Ley, W. Clement. "The Eurydice Squall." *Symons's Monthly Meteorological Magazine,* April 1878 : 32–39. Rpt. in Zaniello (1980), q.v., below.

———. "Squalls." *Nature,* June 7, 1883 : 132–33.

———. "Notes." *Nature,* December 20, 1883 : 175–76.

———. "Mr. Ruskin's Bogies." *Nature,* February 14, 1884 : 353–54.

Liddell, A. G. C. *Notes from the Life of an Ordinary Mortal.* London: John Murray, 1911.

Lindsay, Jack. *J. M. W. Turner: His Life and Work.* New York: New York Graphic Society, 1966.

Lockyer, Norman. "Coggia's Comet." *Nature,* July 16, 1874 : 212; July 23, 1874 : 226–27.

———. "The Recent Sunrises and Sunsets." London *Times,* December 8, 1883 : 10.

Lockyer, Norman, and Winifred L. Lockyer. *Tennyson as a Student and Poet of Nature.* London: Macmillan, 1910.

Lockyer, T. Mary, and Winifred L. Lockyer. *Life and Work of Sir Norman Lockyer.* London: Macmillan, 1928.

"Loss of H. M. S. Eurydice, with Three Hundred Seamen." *Illustrated London News,* March 30, 1878 : 298.

Lubbock, John. "On the Study of Science." *Contemporary Review* 50 (August 1886): 209–20.

Lucas, Herbert. "Dr. Bain and Free Will." *The Month* 21 (July 1874): 275–88.

———. "Climate and Time." *The Month* 30 (August 1877): 448–62.

———. "Free Will and Modern Psychology." *The Month* 32 (February and April, 1878): 241–56 and 490–504.

———. "Free Will and Modern Science." *The Month* 33 (June 1878): 243–56.

———. "The Bollandists and St. Winefride." *The Month* 79 (November 1893): 421–37.

———. "The Council of the Vatican: After Fifty Years." *Dublin Review* 167 (October–December 1920): 161–82.

Lucas, J. R. "Wilberforce and Huxley: A Legendary Encounter." *Historical Journal* 22 (1979): 313–30.

"A Luckless Poet" [John Clare]. *Spectator,* May 28, 1864: 615–17.

Lucretius. *De Rerum Natura Libri Sex.* Ed. and trans. H. A. J. Munro. 2 vols. Cambridge: Deighton Bell, 1864.

———. *De Rerum Natura.* Trans. W. H. D. Rouse. London: William Heinemann, 1924.

———. *On the Nature of the Universe.* Trans. R. E. Lathan. Harmondsworth: Penguin, 1951.

McChesney, Donald. *A Hopkins Commentary: An Explanatory Commentary on the Main Poems, 1876–1889.* New York: New York University Press, 1968.

McCosh, James, and George Dickie. *Typical Forms and Special Ends in Creation.* Edinburgh: T. Constable, 1856.

MacDonald, Lauchlin D. *John Grote: A Critical Estimate of His Writings.* The Hague: Martinus Nijhoff, 1966.

MacGregor, Geddes. *The Vatican Revolution.* London: Macmillan, 1958.

Macleod, Roy M., ed. *Nature* (centenary issue), November 4, 1969.

Madge, Charles. "What Is All This Juice?" *New Verse,* no. 14 (April 1935): 17–21.

Maher, Michael. "Holywell in 1894." *The Month* 83 (February 1895): 153–82.

———. *Psychology: Empirical and Rational.* 6th ed. London: Longmans, Green, 1908.

Mallock, W. H. *The New Republic, or Culture, Faith and Philosophy in an English Country House.* 1st ed., 1877. London: Chatto and Windus, 1908.

———. *Memoirs.* New York and London: Harper and Brothers, 1920.

Manier, Edward. *The Young Darwin and His Cultural Circle.* Dordrecht, Holland: D. Reidel, 1978.

Manning, Cardinal Henry Edward. *The Vatican Council and Its Definitions: A Pastoral Letter to the Clergy.* London: Longmans, Green, 1870.

Mansel, Henry Longueville. *Artis Logicae Rudimenta, from the Text of Aldrich.* Oxford: Henry Hammans, 1862.

Marchant, Henry. "Weather Forecasting." *The Month* 48 (1883): 64–69.

———. "A Contribution on Hypnotism." *The Month* 72 (1891): 349–61.

Masson, David. *Recent British Philosophy.* London: Macmillan, 1865. 2d ed., 1867; 3d ed., 1877.

Matthews, Gwynneth, ed. *Plato's Epistemology and Related Logical Problems.* London: Faber and Faber, 1972.

Maxwell, Clerk. "Atom." In *Encyclopedia Britannica,* 9th ed., vol. 3 (1878): 36–49.

Mayor, Joseph B. *A Sketch of Ancient Philosophy from Thales to Cicero.* Cambridge: Cambridge University Press, 1881.

Meadows, A. J. *The High Firmament: A Survey of Astronomy in English Literature.* Leicester: Leicester University Press, 1967.

———. *Science and Controversy: A Biography of Sir Norman Lockyer.* Cambridge, Mass.: MIT Press, 1972.

Meadows, Denis. *Obedient Men.* London: Longmans, 1955.

Mill, John Stuart. *A System of Logic, Ratiocinative and Inductive, Being a Connected View of the Principles and Evidence of the Methods of Scientific Investigation.* 1st ed., 1843. 7th ed. London: Longmans, Green, Reader, and Dyer, 1868.

———. "Bain's Psychology." *Edinburgh Review* 110 (October 1859): 187–321.

———. *Auguste Comte and Positivism.* London: Trübner, 1865.

Milroy, James. *The Language of Gerard Manley Hopkins.* London: Andre Deutsch, 1977.

Minchin, Edward A. "Living Crystals." *Proceedings of the Royal Institution,* May 21, 1898:723–31.

Minnaert, M. *The Nature of Light and Color in the Open Air* (1940). Trans. H. M. Kremer-Priest and K. E. Brian Jay. New York: Dover, 1954.

"Mr. Ruskin's Weather Wisdom." *Times* (London), February 5, 1884:7.

Mivart, St. George Jackson. "Difficulties of the Theory of Natural Selection." *The Month* 11 (July, August, and September 1869): 35–53, 134–53, and 275–89.

———. *On the Genesis of Species.* London: Macmillan, 1871.

———. "Catholic Positivism." *The Month* (February 1883): 170–81.

———. "Some Reminiscences of Thomas Henry Huxley." *Nineteenth Century* 42 (December 1897): 985–98.

Monro, C. J. "Correlation of Color and Music." *Nature,* February 3, 1870: 362–63.

Morley, Henry. *Jerome Cardan: The Life of Girolamo Gardano, of Milan, Physician.* 2 vols. London: Chapman and Hall, 1854.

Morrell, Jack, and Arnold Thackray. *Gentlemen of Science: Early Years of the British Association for the Advancement of Science.* Oxford: Clarendon Press, 1981.

Morris, Jan. *Oxford.* Oxford: Oxford University Press, 1978.

Morris, John. *Sermon Preached at St. Beuno's College, July 30, 1876, on Occasion of Silver Jubilee of Lord Bishop of Shrewsbury.* London: Burns and Oates, 1876.

Morris, John Brande. *Jesus the Son of Mary, or the Doctrine of the Catholic Church upon the Incarnation of God the Son.* 2 vols. London: James Toovey, 1851.

Müller, Max. *Chips from a German Workshop.* London: Longmans, Green, 1867.

———. *My Autobiography: A Fragment.* New York: Charles Scribner's Sons, 1901.

Mussner, Franz. *The Historical Jesus in the Gospel of St. John.* Trans. W. J. O'Hara. London: Burns and Oates, 1967.

Nettleship, Richard Lewis. "Prof. T. H. Green: In Memoriam." *Contemporary Review* 41 (May 1882): 857–81.

———. *Philosophical Remains.* 2d ed. Ed. A. C. Bradley. London: Macmillan, 1901.

"New Books" [Review of *Clouds* by Walton, q.v., below]. *Daily News* (London), September 3, 1868 : 2.

"The New Spectrum Discoveries." *London Review,* May 4, 1861 : 521–24; June 1, 1861 : 649–50.

Newman, Cardinal John Henry. *Characteristics from the Writings of John Henry Newman.* Ed. William Samuel Lilly. 5th ed. London: C. Kegan Paul, 1880.

Newton, Isaac. *Opticks, or a Treatise of the Reflections, Refractions, Infections and Colors of Light.* 4th ed., 1730. Ed. Edmund Whittiker. New York: Dover, 1952.

Nicolson, Marjorie Hope. *Newton Demands the Muse: Newton's "Opticks" and the Eighteenth Century Poets.* Princeton: Princeton University Press, 1946.

Noble, William. "The Recent Extraordinary Sunrises and Sunsets." *Knowledge,* June 6, 1884 : 418.

North, John, ed. *Mid–Nineteenth Century Scientists.* Oxford: Pergamon, 1969.

Observer's Handbook. 3d ed., 1969. Rpt. London: Her Majesty's Stationery Office, 1975.

O'Connell, D. J. K. *The Green Flash and Other Low Sun Phenomena.* New York: Interscience, 1958.

———. "The Green Flash." In *Light from the Sky.* San Francisco: W. H. Freeman, n.d. (Originally published in *Scientific American,* January 1960.)

Ogden, C. K. "Editorial" [Hopkins' Sprung Rhythm]. *Psyche* (London) 16 (1937): 5–50.

O'Reilly, J. P. "A Curious 'Halo.'" *Nature,* July 20, 1882 : 268.

Owen, Richard. *On Parthenogenesis, or the Successive Production of Procreating Individuals from a Single Ovum.* London: John Van Voorst, 1849.

Oxford University Calendar. Oxford: James Parker, 1863–67.

Oxford University Examination Papers. No. 14 (Responsions, Trinity Term, 1863); no. 33 (First Public Examination, Michaelmas Term, 1864); no. 69 (Second

Public Examination, Easter Term, 1867). Oxford: John Henry and James Parker, 1863–67.

Page, Frederick, et al. "Father Gerard Hopkins." *Dublin Review* 167 (July–September 1920): 40–66.

Paradis, James. *Thomas Henry Huxley.* Lincoln: University of Nebraska Press, 1978.

Parkin, George R. *Edward Thring, Headmaster of Uppingham School: Life, Diary, and Letters.* 2 vols. London: Macmillan, 1898.

Pater, Walter. *The Works of Walter Pater.* 9 vols. London: Macmillan, 1900–1901.

Patmore, Coventry. *Principle in Art, Etc.* 2d ed. London: George Bell, 1890.

———. *Courage in Politics and Other Essays, 1885–1896.* Ed. Frederick Page. London: Oxford University Press, 1921.

Patterson, Colin. *Evolution.* London: Routledge and Kegan Paul, 1978.

Pattison, Mark. *Suggestions on Academical Organization, with Special Reference to Oxford.* Edinburgh: Edmonston and Douglas, 1868.

———. "Philosophy at Oxford." *Mind* 1 (January 1876): 82–97.

———. "A Note on 'Evolution and Positivism.'" *Fortnightly Review,* o.s. 27 (August 1877): 285–86.

———. *Memoirs.* London: Macmillan, 1885.

———. *Essays.* 2 vols. Ed. Henry Nettleship. Oxford: Clarendon Press, 1889.

Perry, S. J. "The Planet Vulcan." *Monthly Notices of the Royal Astronomical Society* 37 (April 1877): 347–48.

———. "The Observatory at Stonyhurst College." *British Journal of Photography,* October 12, 1883: 604–5.

———. "Extraordinary Darkness at Midday." *Nature,* May 1, 1884: 6.

———. "Black Rain." *Nature,* May 8, 1884: 32.

———. "Celestial Photography." *The Month* 55 (December 1885): 472–81.

———. "Black Rain." *Nature,* June 17, 1886: 147.

"Father Perry" [Obituary]. *Letters and Notices* 20, nos. 98–102 (1889–90): 131–46.

Peterson, William S. *Victorian Heretic: Mrs. Humphrey Ward's* Robert Elsmere. Leicester: Leicester University Press, 1976.

Plato. Theaetetus and Sophist. Trans. Harold North Fowler. Cambridge, Mass.: Harvard University Press, 1921.

Poole, J. B., and Kay Andrews, eds. *The Government of Science in Britain.* London: Weidenfeld and Nicolson, 1972.

Prince, C. Leeson. *Observations upon the Topography and Climate of Crowborough Hill, Sussex.* 2d ed. Lewes: Farncombe, 1900.

Proctor, Richard Anthony. "Comet's Tails." *Cornhill Magazine* 30 (September 1874): 309–18.
Purbrick, Edward Ignatius. "'*Peace through the Truth.*'" *The Month* 5 (July 1866): 44–65.
———. "The Logic of [Huxley's] Lay Sermons." *The Month* 10 (May 1869): 409–21.
———. "Modern Ethics." *The Month* 11 (1869): 259–70.

Quirinus [J. J. I. Döllinger]. *Letters from Rome on the Council.* London: Rivingtons, 1870.

Radcliffe Observatory. *Results of Meteorological Observations Made at the Radcliffe Observatory, 1883–1884.* Oxford: James Parker, 1886.
Redgrave, Richard and Samuel. *A Century of British Painters.* 1st ed., 1866. 2d ed., 1890. Rpt. New York: Oxford University Press, 1947.
Reimann, Bernard. "On the Hypotheses Which Lie at the Bases of Geometry." Trans. W. K. Clifford. *Nature,* May 1, 1873: 14–17; May 8, 1873: 36–37.
Renan, Ernest. *The Life of Jesus.* 1st ed., 1863. New York: Modern Library, 1955.
Reports of the British Association for the Advancement of Science. For 1831–32, 2d ed., London: John Murray, 1835. For 1852, London: John Murray, 1853. For 1860, London: John Murray, 1861. For 1887, London: John Murray, 1888.
"Reports on Three Aurorae by Various Hands at Royal Observatory, Greenwich." *Proceedings of the Royal Meteorological Society* 5 (November 1870): 221–36.
Rickaby, John. "St. Augustine and Scientific Unbelief." *The Month* 28 (October 1876): 195–204.
———. "The Reign of Mist." *The Month* 28 (November 1876): 281–96.
———. "The Explanation of Miracles by Unknown Natural Forces." *The Month* 29 (January 1877): 68–85.
———. "Evolution and Involution." *The Month* 29 (March 1877): 269–85.
———. "Some Remarks on the Argument from Design." *The Month* 32 (April 1878): 404–19; 33 (May 1878): 28–46.
———. "Three Causes of Scepticism." *The Month* 35 (March 1879): 368–81; 36 (May 1879): 38–47.
———. "The Life and Times of Thomas Henry Huxley." *The Month* 97 (January 1901): 17–28.
Rickaby, Joseph. "'Man the Measure of All Things': Protagoras and the Positivists." *The Month* 12 (February 1870): 129–41.
———. "Auguste Comte and His Philosophy." *The Month* 12 (March and April 1870): 290–307 and 385–98.

———. "A Plea for Plato, with Remarks on His Last Translator" [Jowett]. *The Month* 14 (May–June 1871): 369–87.

———. "Modern Academics." *The Month* 20 (February 1874): 150–62.

———. "Professor Tyndall's Inaugural Address." *The Month* 22 (October 1874): 212–23.

———. "Mr. Mill's Essay on Nature." *The Month* 23 (January 1875): 50–65.

———. "Mr. Mill on Miracles." *The Month* 27 (1876): 351–67.

———. "Last Years of Dr. Pusey." *The Month* 90 (1897): 561–69.

———. "In Memoriam: Richard Frederick Clarke." *The Month* 96 (October 1900): 337–44.

———. *Free Will and Four English Philosophers.* London: Burns and Oates, 1906.

———. *The Lord My Light.* 1st ed., 1915. London: Burns and Oates, 1952.

———. *The Spiritual Exercises of St. Ignatius Loyola, Spanish and English, with a Continuous Commentary.* 1st ed., 1915. 2d ed. London: Burns and Oates and Washbourne, 1936.

Roach, J. P. C. "Victorian Universities and the National Intelligentsia." *Victorian Studies* 3 (December 1959): 131–50.

Roberts, Gerald. "The Jaded Muse: Hopkins at Stonyhurst." *Hopkins Quarterly* 6 (Spring 1979): 35–47.

Rogers, James E. Thorold. *Education at Oxford: Its Methods, Its Aids, and Its Rewards.* London: Smith, Elder, 1861.

Roos, David A. "Matthew Arnold and Thomas Henry Huxley: Two Speeches at the Royal Academy, 1881 and 1883." *Modern Philology* 74 (February 1977): 316–24.

Roscoe, H. E. "Opening Address to Section B." *Nature,* September 15, 1870: 406–8.

Roscoe, H. E., and A. Harden. *A New View of the Origin of Dalton's Atomic Theory.* London: Macmillan, 1896.

Rosenberg, John D. *The Darkening Glass: A Portrait of Ruskin's Genius.* New York: Columbia University Press, 1961.

Rosenstock, Gershon George. *F. A. Trendelenberg: Forerunner to John Dewey.* Carbondale: Southern Illinois University Press, 1964.

"The Royal Academy Exhibition." *Times* (London), May 11, 1843: 8.

"Royal Society Conversazione." *Times* (London), June 9, 1887: 10.

Ruggles, Eleanor. *Gerard Manley Hopkins: A Life.* New York: Norton, 1944.

Ruskin, John. "Remarks on the Present State of Meteorological Science." *Transactions of the Meteorological Society* 1 (1839). Rpt. *Symons's Monthly Meteorological Magazine* 5 (April 1870): 36–39. Also rpt. in Ruskin, *Works,* q.v., below, vol. 1, *Early Prose Writings,* 206–10.

———. *The Works of John Ruskin.* Eds. E. T. Cook and A. Wedderburn. 39 vols. London: George Allen, 1903–12.

Russell, C. A., and D. C. Goodman, eds. *Science and the Rise of Technology since 1800.* Bristol: John Wright and Sons, 1972.

Russell, F. A. Rollo. "The Sunsets and Sunrises of November and December, 1883, and January, 1884." *Meteorological Society Quarterly Journal* 10 (1884): 139–54.

Sagan, Carl. *The Dragons of Eden: Speculations on the Evolution of Human Intelligence.* New York: Ballantine, 1978.

Sapir, Edward. "Gerard Hopkins." *Poetry* 18 (September 1921): 330–36.

Schneider, Elizabeth W. *The Dragon in the Gate: Studies in the Poetry of G. M. Hopkins.* Berkeley: University of California Press, 1968.

Scholes, Percy A. *The Oxford Companion to Music.* 10th rev. ed. Ed. John Owen Ward. London: Oxford University Press, 1970.

Schonland, Basil. *The Atomists (1805–1933).* Oxford: Clarendon Press, 1968.

Scott, R. H. "Notes on a Double Rainbow Observed at Kirkwall." *Quarterly Journal of the Royal Meteorological Society* 1 (1837): 237.

Selsam, Howard. *T. H. Green: Critic of Empiricism.* New York: Columbia University Press, 1930.

Sermons by Fathers of the Society of Jesus. 3 vols. London: Burns and Oates, 1870–75.

Shairp, J. C. *Studies in Poetry and Philosophy.* Edinburgh: Edmonston and Douglas, 1868.

Sidgwick, Isabel. "A Grandmother's Tales." *Macmillan's Magazine* 78 (October 1898): 425–35.

Simkin, Tom, and Richard S. Fiske. *Krakatau 1883: The Volcanic Eruption and Its Effects.* Washington, D.C.: Smithsonian Institution Press, 1983.

Smith, C. Michie. "The Green Sun." *Nature,* November 8, 1883: 28.

Smyth, C. Piazzi. "The Remarkable Sunsets." *Nature,* December 13, 1883: 149–50.

"The Song of Chaucer's Clerk at Oxenford: 'Angelus ad Virginem.'" *The Month* 45 (January 1882): 100–111.

Sorley, W. R. *A History of English Philosophy.* Cambridge: Cambridge University Press, 1920.

Spencer, Herbert. *The Principles of Biology.* 2 vols. London: Williams and Norgat, 1864–67.

Stanley, W. F. "On Certain Effects Which May Have Been Produced in the Atmosphere by Floating Particles of Volcanic Matter from the Eruption of

Krakatoa and Mount St. Augustin." *Meteorological Society Quarterly Journal* 10 (1884): 187–95.

Stedman, Algernon M. M. *Oxford: Its Social and Intellectual Life.* London: Trübner, 1878. 2d rev. ed., retitled *Oxford: Its Life and Schools.* London: George Bell, 1887.

"Stephen Joseph Perry, F.R.S." *Nature,* January 23, 1890: 279–80.

Stewart, Balfour, and P. G. Tait. *The Unseen Universe.* New York: Macmillan, 1875.

Stonyhurst Observatory Meteorological Report. January 1870–December 1888.

"Stonyhurst Series of Philosophical Manuals." *Stonyhurst Magazine* 3 (November 1888): 243.

Strachey, Edward. *Miracles and Science.* London: Longmans, Brown, Green, and Longmans, 1854.

Sulloway, Alison. *Gerard Manley Hopkins and the Victorian Temper.* New York: Columbia University Press, 1972.

Surtees, Virginia. *The Paintings and Drawings of Dante Gabriel Rossetti (1828–1880): A Catalogue Raisonné.* Oxford: Clarendon Press, 1971.

Sutcliffe, Edmund F. *Bibliography of the English Province of the Society of Jesus, 1773–1953.* Roehampton: Manresa Press, 1957.

Sutherland, James A. *The Oxford Book of Literary Anecdotes.* New York: Pocket Books, 1976.

Symons, G. J. "On a White Rain or Fog-Bow." *Quarterly Journal of the Royal Meteorological Society* 2 (1875): 438–39.

———. "The Krakatoa Eruption." *Nature,* February 14, 1884: 355.

———, ed. *The Eruption of Krakatoa and Subsequent Phenomena: Report of the Krakatoa Committee of the Royal Society.* London: Trübner, 1888.

Tait, P. G. *Light.* 2d rev. ed. Edinburgh: Adam and Charles Black, 1889.

Thomas, Alfred. *Hopkins the Jesuit: The Years of Training.* London: Oxford University Press, 1969.

Thompson, Silvanus P. "'Halo': Pink Rainbow." *Nature,* July 27, 1882: 293.

———. *Life of Lord Kelvin.* 2 vols. London: Macmillan, 1910.

Thornton, R. K. R., ed. *All My Eyes See: The Visual World of Gerard Manley Hopkins.* Sunderland: Coelfrith Press, 1975.

Tierney, Michael, ed. *Struggle with Fortune: A Miscellany for the Centenary of the Catholic University of Ireland, 1854–1954.* Dublin: Brone and Nolan, 1954.

Toon, Owen B., and James B. Pollack. "Volcanoes and the Climate." *Natural History,* January 1977: 8–26, 101.

Tradleg, Nitram [Martin Geldart]. *Son of Belial: Autobiographical Sketches.* London: Trübner, 1882.

Tromhold, Sophus. *Under the Rays of the Aurora Borealis: In the Land of the Lapps and Kvaens.* Ed. and trans. Carl Siewers. 2 vols. Boston: Houghton, Mifflin, 1885.

Tyndall, John. *Address Delivered before the British Association at Belfast.* London: Longmans, Green, 1874.

———. *Fragments of Science for Unscientific People: A Series of Detached Essays, Lectures, and Reviews.* London: Longmans, Green, 1871.

———. "A Rare Solar Phenomenon." *Times* (London), January 12, 1888 : 6.

———. *Hours of Exercise in the Alps.* New York and London: D. Appleton, 1896.

———. *Fragments of Science: A Series of Detached Essays, Addresses and Reviews.* 2 vols. London and New York: D. Appleton, 1897.

———. *New Fragments.* 3d. ed. New York and London: D. Appleton, 1900.

Tyndall, John, and Henry Thompson. "The 'Prayer for the Sick': Hints towards a Serious Attempt to Estimate Its Value." *Contemporary Review* 20 (July 1872): 205–10.

Vaughan, (Cardinal) H. *The Year of Preparation for the Vatican Council.* 2 vols. London: Burns and Oates, 1869–70.

Verney, Captain Edmund H. *The Last Four Days of the "Eurydice."* Portsmouth: Griffin, 1878.

Vernon, H. M., and K. Dorothy Vernon. *A History of the Oxford Museum.* Oxford: Clarendon Press, 1909.

Von Erdhardt-Siebold, Erika. "Harmony of the Senses in English, German, and French Romanticism." *PMLA* 47 (June 1932): 577–92.

Wallace, William. *Epicureanism.* London: Society for the Propagation of Christian Knowledge, 1880.

———. *Lectures and Essays on Natural Theology and Ethics.* Ed. Edward Caird. Oxford: Clarendon Press, 1898.

Walsh, James Joseph. *Catholic Churchmen in Science.* 2d ser. 1909. Rpt. Freeport: Books for Libraries, 1969.

Walton, Elijah. *Clouds: Their Forms and Combinations.* London: Longmans, Green, 1868.

Ward, F. O. "Chemistry of the Future." *Chemical News,* June 14, 1867 : 38–40.

Ward, Mrs. Humphrey. "Marius the Epicurean." *Macmillan's Magazine* 52 (June 1885): 132–39.

———. *Robert Elsmere.* London: Macmillan, 1888.

———. *A Writer's Recollections.* 2 vols. London: Harper and Brothers, 1918.

Weekly Weather Report. The Meteorological Office, London, 1878. London: Her Majesty's Stationery Office, 1878.

Weyand, Norman, ed. *Immortal Diamond: Studies in Gerard Manley Hopkins.* New York: Sheed and Ward, 1949.

Wheelwright, Philip, ed. *The Presocratics.* New York: Odyssey, 1966.

Whewell, William. *The History of the Inductive Sciences, from the Earliest to the Present Time.* 1st ed., 1837. 3d ed., with additions. 3 vols. London: John W. Parker and Son, 1857.

———. *The Philosophy of the Inductive Sciences.* 2d ed., 1847. Rpt. 2 vols. New York: Frank Cass, 1967.

White, Gilbert. *The Natural History of Selborne.* Ed. Richard Mabley. Harmondsworth: Penguin, 1977.

Wilberforce, Bishop Samuel. "Darwin's *Origin of Species.*" *Quarterly Review* 108 (July 1860): 225–64.

Williams, L. Pearce. "The Historiography of Victorian Science." *Victorian Studies* 9 (March 1966): 197–204.

Williamson, Alexander W. "Inaugural Address." *Nature,* September 18, 1873: 406–15.

Wilson, Arnold. *A Dictionary of British Marine Painters.* Leigh-on-Sea: F. Lewis, 1967.

Wolff, Erwin B. "On Goethe's Reputation as a Scientist in Nineteenth Century England." *German Life and Letters* 6 (1952–53): 92–101.

Woolf, Robert Lee. *Gains and Losses: Novels of Faith and Doubt in Victorian England.* New York: Garland, 1977.

Woodhall, Ralph. *The Theology of the Incarnation.* Cork: Mercier, 1968.

Zaniello, Thomas A. "A Note on the Catalogue of the Manuscripts of Hopkins' 'Oxford Essays.'" *Papers of the Bibliographical Society of America* 69 (1975): 409–11.

———. "An Early Example of the Musical Analogy in Hopkins." *Hopkins Research Bulletin,* no. 7 (1976): 15–16.

———. "The Sources of Hopkins' Inscape: Epistemology at Oxford, 1864–1868." *Victorian Newsletter,* no. 52 (Fall 1977): 17–23.

———. "The Tonic of Platonism: The Origins and Use of Hopkins' 'Scape'." *Hopkins Quarterly* 5 (Spring 1978): 5–16.

———. "Hopkins' 'Eurydice' and a Victorian Meteorological Report." *American Notes and Queries* 17 (February 1979): 89–90.

———. "The Scientific Background of Hopkins' 'Eurydice': Two Documents." *Hopkins Quarterly* 7 (Spring 1980): 15–28.

———. "The Spectacular English Sunsets of the 1880's." In James Paradis and Tom Postelwait, eds. *Victorian Science and Victorian Values: Literary Perspectives,* vol. 360 (1981) of *Annals of the New York Academy of Sciences,* 247–67. Rpt. New Brunswick: Rutgers University Press, 1985.

———. "The Stonyhurst Philosophers." *Hopkins Quarterly* 9 (Winter 1983): 133–59.

Zeller, E. *The Stoics, Epicureans, and Sceptics.* Trans. Oswald J. Reichel. London: Longmans, Green, 1870.

Index